HISTORY AND PRINCIPLES OF LITERARY CRITICISM

Edited by Lisa Roy

HISTORY AND PRINCIPLES OF LITERARY CRITICISM

Edited by Lisa Roy

[Edited with Introduction, Author's Information, Complete Text, Summary and Analysis and Study Questions]

Lisa Roy
M.A. English, B.Ed.
Calcutta University

ANMOL PUBLICATIONS PVT. LTD.
NEW DELHI - 110 002 (INDIA)

ANMOL PUBLICATIONS PVT. LTD.

H.O.: 4374/4B, Ansari Road, Darya Ganj,
New Delhi-110 002 (India)
Ph.: 23278000, 23261597

B.O.: No. 1015, Ist Main Road, BSK IIIrd Stage
IIIrd Phase, IIIrd Block
Bangalore - 560 085 (India)
Visit us at: www.anmolpublications.com

History and Principles of Literary Criticism

First Published, 2009

PRINTED IN INDIA

Printed at Balaji Offset Press, Delhi.

Contents

Preface

Over the course of the past three or four decades literary theory and criticism have come to play a central role in the academic study of the humanities and social sciences. The diverse, often apparently competing or incompatible approaches, perspectives, and modes of inquiry that continue to flourish today under the generic label " theory " have brought most scholars to a welcome awareness of the importance of attending at least to methodological concerns in critical practice. Moreover, criticism as it is currently understood (we are writing in the early months of 2004) no longer confines itself to the study of literature: its discourses now extend well beyond literature to intersect with anthropology, philosophy, psychology, linguistics, political science, and much else besides, even as the objects of critical analysis by " literary " scholars encompass all forms of cultural production, literary and nonliterary.

Criticism still embraces exegesis, interpretation, and evaluation, as it has traditionally done, but today it often encroaches upon the territory of " theory, " whether we characterize theory as discussion and debates about basic definitions, as the search for necessary and sufficient foundations for evaluating critical practice, or as the self-reflexive process of making explicit underlying social, historical, or ideological interests and presuppositions. The semantic boundaries between " theory " and " criticism " blur. We see the terms often used interchangeably. Frequently, however, they occur together to signal at once their overlapping as well as their divergent possible meanings, and this is the reason both appear in the title of this book.

Author

Preface

Chapter 1

Inature and Office of Criticism

- Purpose of Literary Study. The study or reading of literature ordinarily has a threefold purpose, knowledge, pleasure, and culture.
  This purpose shows us both the character of the literature which should be read and the manner in which it should be read. As a rule we should read only books of recognized excellence, and read them with sympathetic intelligence. Trashy books, whatever pleasure they may give, add but little to knowledge or culture; and immoral books often leave an ineradicable stain upon the soul. Fortunately there are good books enough to satisfy every taste and supply every need.
- Necessity of Comprehending. A literary work cannot be of much use till it is understood. It is useless to read books entirely beyond our grasp. In the perusal of an author we should endeavor to enter as fully as possible into his thoughts and feelings. Our primary aim should be not to criticise but to comprehend. This is sometimes, especially for the young student, a difficult task. It requires patient, painstaking labour; but in the end it brings a rich reward in profit, enjoyment, and power.
  In the study of a literary classic we should aim at more than a mere intellectual apprehension of its technique and other external features. The soul should rise into sympathy with it, and feel its spiritual beauty. All literary study that falls short of

this high end, however scholarly or laborious it may be, is essentially defective. The externalities of a piece of literature are comprehended in vain, unless they lead to a fuller understanding and appreciation of its spirit and life. Unfortunately, at the present time, philology and literary analysis frequently stop short of the realization of the supreme end of literary study. What should be only a means is sometimes exalted to an end.

- Definition of Criticism. Criticism, as its etymology indicates, is the act of judging. Literary criticism endeavors to form a correct estimate of literary productions. Its endeavor is to see a piece of writing as it is. It brings literary productions into comparison with recognized principles and ideal standards; it investigates them in their matter, form, and spirit; and, as a result of this process, it determines their merits and their defects.

  The end of literary criticism is not fault-finding but truth. The critic should be more than a censor or caviler. He should discover and make known whatever is commendable or excellent. At its best, criticism is not a mere record of general impressions but the statement of an intelligent judgment. It is not biased or vitiated by prejudice, ignorance, or self-interest; but, proceeding according to well-defined principles, it is able to trace the steps by which it reaches its ultimate conclusions.

- History of Criticism. Criticism is a natural attendant of all forms of art. Literary criticism is almost as old as literature itself. No sooner had a writer produced a literary work, even in the most ancient times, than his contemporaries proceeded to express their judgments concerning it. Among the ancient Greeks Plato and Aristotle were both critics; and the latter's work on "Poetics" is still valuable for its discussion of fundamental principles. Quintilian, Cicero, and Horace were distinguished Roman critics; and the poet's Ars Poetica, read in every college course, is an admirable presentation of many critical principles. But it is in modern times, and particularly during the nineteenth century, that criticism received its highest development. In England not a few of its leading literary menDryden, Pope, Addison, Johnson, Coleridge, Jeffrey, Macaulay, Carlyle, Matthew Arnoldhave been critics; and in America we meet with such honored names as Poe, Emerson, Whipple, Lowell, Stedman, and many others. In recent years criticism has greatly gained in breadth and geniality.

- Standard of Criticism. All criticism involves comparison. For every species of literature there is an ideal of form, content, and spirit, which serves the intelligent critic as a standard of judgment. This ideal is based on a realization of the recognized principles of literary art. These principles pertain to diction, structure, matter, and spirit or purpose. No one will deny that the diction should be well chosen; that the structure of the sentences should be correct and clear; and that, in the case of poetry, the laws of versification should be observed. These elements contribute to excellence of form. In addition to these external elements there should be unity of thought, symmetry of presentation, truth of statement, and sincerity and self-restraint in sentiment. These elements give substantial worth to the matter or content of literature. Besides all this there is a grace or elegance or force, proceeding from the personality of the writer and transcending all rules of art, that gives a peculiar charm to the best literature.

  Sometimes the personal element or spirit of a work is so pleasing that it more than counterbalances defects of form, and wins its way to the popular heart.
- Classic Writers. Our classic writers are those who have most nearly approached the ideal. The writings of Addison, Goldsmith, Irving, Lowell, and others,

embody in a high degree excellence of matter and form; and in addition to this there is a pervading spirit that imparts an irresistible charm to their works. While the works of no one writer, whether ancient or modern, can be taken as an absolute standard of judgment, the perusal of classic works is exceedingly helpful.

These works familiarize us with what is excellent in thought, expression, and spirit. They cultivate the taste; and at length it becomes impossible for the student to be satisfied with what is incorrect, slovenly,tawdry, or untruthful.

- Requisites of Criticism. Many things are required for the best criticism. First of all, the critic ought to be a person of sound judgment. It is in a measure true that critics, like poets, "are born, not made." The critic should have the power to divest himself of prejudice; and, like a judge upon the bench, should decide every question by the law and the evidence. He should be a man of broad sympathies and wide culture; nothing that is human should be foreign to him. He should be able to enter into the feelings of every class and to appreciate the principles of every school. He should have a strong imagination to enable him to realise the conditions of other ages or of other social arrangements. Without these natural gifts of a sound judgment, broad sympathy, and vigorous imagination, the critic is apt to be limited, narrow, or unjust in his criticism. The history of literature reveals numberless critical blunders; indeed, almost every attempt to introduce new literary forms, as in the case of Wordsworth, Coleridge, and Keats, has met with bitter opposition from uncatholic critics.
- Criticism an Acquired Art. Criticism is an art that may in large measure be acquired. The requisite faculties may be developed by a course of study. The principles that are to guide the critical judgment are

provided in grammar, rhetoric, logic, aesthetics, and moral science. Wide reading in various departments will banish narrowness and provincialism. Study and experience will bring a cosmopolitan culture. Though few are capable of attaining to eminence as critics, it is possible for every one to acquire some degree of literary taste and to form an intelligent judgment of a literary work.

- Diversity in Criticism. Diversity of judgment is a notable feature in the history of criticism. It tends to shake one's confidence in the critical art. It often happens that what one critic praises another condemns. This fact has been presented by Irving, with delightful humour. "Even the critics," he says in the conclusion of the "Sketch Book," "whatever may be said of them by others, the author has found to be a singularly gentle and good-natured race; it is true that each has in turn objected to some one or two articles, and that these individual exceptions, taken in the aggregate, would amount almost to a total condemnation of his work; but then he has been consoled by observing, that what one has particularly censured, another has as particularly praised; and thus, the encomiums being set off against the objections, he finds his work, upon the whole, commended far beyond its deserts."
- Sources of Diversity. This diversity of literary criticism, which at first sight tempts us to question the value of the art, is easily traced to its causes. These are found not in the nature of the art but in the manner of its application. Many reviewers nowadays do not take the pains to read the works they pass judgment upon. Their estimate is based on little more than a rapid survey of the preface and table of contents. This fact renders a considerable part of current newspaper criticism comparatively worthless. It is still worse when to this superficiality is added a flippant manner that seems intent on

nothing but a display of the critic's smartness. Other critics write from the standpoint of a particular sect or school of thought, and undervalue or overvalue a work through a partisan spirit. Defective or erroneous principles are used as standards of judgment. Still others are impressionists; and instead of testing a work by recognized critical canons, they simply record how "it strikes them." Differences of taste and character naturally produce some diversity of view, but in general the painstaking and impartial application of critical principles to a literary work will yield pretty uniform results. The merits and defects of the work will be brought to light, and conscientious and broad-minded critics will be found in the main to agree in their praise or their censure.

- Utility of Criticism. Criticism is not, as has sometimes been supposed, a parasitic growth on literature. It is a handmaid of literature; it belongs to the household of literature. Though it does not deserve to rank with the great creative forms of literature, such as the epic, the drama, or the novel, it is capable of a high degree of excellence. Some of the greatest English writers, as we have seen, have been critics. Not a few of the critical essays of De Quincey, Macaulay, Carlyle, Arnold, Lowell, and others, have an honorable place in the literature of the English-speaking world. Literary criticism has a distinct value for three classes of persons. To the young student it gives a clear insight into literary form, and cultivates his taste for literary excellence. To the author it is at once a stimulant and wholesome restraint; it rewards him for what is good and chastises him for what is bad. To the public it is useful in pointing out what books are worth reading and in showing the principles by which a work is to be judged. It elevates the popular taste and intelligence.
- Materials of Criticism. All literature is, in some sense, material for criticism. It may be examined, tested by

critical laws, and its worth estimated in the class to which it belongs. But as a rule literary criticism is confined to literature in the narrower sense; that is to say, to literature that aims at artistic excellence. This includes the various forms of poetry and the principal kinds of prose,history, oratory, essays, and fiction. These various kinds of literature, in their higher forms, aim at presenting their subject-matter in such a way as to minister to the pleasure of the reader.

- Molding Influences. In criticising it is important to recognize certain general molding influences in literature. Among the most potent of these influences are race, epoch, and surroundings. We cannot fully understand any work of literature, nor justly estimate its relative excellence, without an acquaintance with the national traits of the writer, the general character of the age in which he lived, and the physical and social conditions by which he was surrounded. These considerations,independently of specific critical canons that determine intrinsic excellence, must be taken into account when the critic wishes to decide upon the relative value of a work. It is evidently unjust to demand in writers of an uncultivated period the same delicacy of thought, feeling, and expression that is required in the writers of an age of refinement and intelligence. The indecencies in Chaucer and Shakespeare are to be attributed to the grossness of their times.
- The Artistic Element. There is an artistic element in literature upon which the value of any work largely depends. There is art in the choice and marshaling of words. Furthermore, every department of literaturehistory, poetry, fictionhas a separate and definite purpose. In the successful realization of this purpose each species or form of literature must wisely choose its means. This conscious and intelligent adaptation of a means to an end is art.

Apart from the careful selection and arrangement of words in sentences, the historian chooses the incidents he will relate, the order in which they will appear, the relative prominence they will have, and the symmetry and completeness of his whole work. The novelist selects or invents his story, portrays from actual life or creates a number of characters, constructs or modifies his plot, and unfolds the movement toward a predestined end. In all this there is a constant exercise of the creative faculty; and the complete product is as much a work of art as is a painting or statue, which requires the same sort of intellectual effort.

- Matter and Form. In any literary production we may distinguish between the thoughts that are presented and the manner in which they are presented. We may say, for example, "The joys of heaven are infinite"; or, ascending to a higher plane of thought and feeling, we may present the same thought in the language of Moore in his "Paradise and the Peri":

"Go, wing thy flight from star to star,
From world to luminous world, as far
As the universe spreads its flaming wall;
Take all the pleasures of all the spheres,
And multiply each through endless years,
One minute of Heaven is worth them all."

It is thus evident that the interest and worth of literature depend largely on the manner in which the thought and emotion are expressed. In general the matter of discourse, which aims at the communication of ideas, is of more importance than the form.

Words without thought, no matter how skillfully and musically they may be arranged, are nonsense. But in the lighter sorts of prose, which aim at entertainment, and in poetry, which is dependent on meter and harmony, form is of preeminent importance. The story of "Rip Van Winkle," for instance, owes its perennial charm to the inimitable grace and humour with which Irving has told it.

There is a natural and intimate relation between matter and form; one is the soul, the other is the body. Form is not to be unduly magnified by itself; it is excellent only when it is a fitting embodiment of the thought and feeling expressed. Form should be molded by the thought and emotion, as the rose or oak is shaped by the potency of its inner life. When, in any way, the form is out of keeping with the subject, the effect upon a cultivated taste is a disagreeable incongruity. In the language of Horace,

"Sad words befit the brow with grief o'erhung;
Anger, that fires the eyeball, bids the tongue
Breathe proud defiance; sportive jest and jeer
Become the gay; grave maxims the severe."

Review Questions

- What is the threefold object of literary study? What kind of literature should be read? Why?
- What should be our primary aim in studying an author? What does this often require? What should be aimed at besides outward form? What mistake is frequently made?
- What is criticism? What is the purpose of literary criticism? How is this purpose accomplished? What sources of error are mentioned?
- What is said of the history of criticism? Name two Greek critics. Who were the great Roman critics? Mention some distinguished English and American critics. What is said of recent criticism?
- What serves as a standard of criticism? On what is this ideal based? Mention some elements of excellent form; some elements of excellent content. What is said of the personal element or spirit?
- Who are our classic writers? Why study classic works?
- What natural gifts should a critic have? Why should he have broad sympathies? What is said of critical blunders?
- How is criticism an acquired art? What is the

advantage of wide reading? What may every one hope to acquire?

- What is said of diversity in criticism? Illustrate.
- What are the sources of diversity? What is said of much newspaper criticism? What is meant by impressionists? What is said of painstaking and impartial criticism?
- What is said of the relation of criticism to literature? What of its rank? For what three classes has it a special value? How?
- What are the materials of literary criticism? To what class of literature is it chiefly devoted?
- Name three great molding influences. Why should they be considered? Illustrate.
- What is meant by the artistic element? In what does the historian's art consist? the novelist's?
- What may be distinguished in any literary production? Illustrate. On what does the worth of literature largely depend? Which is the more important, matter or form? Where is form specially important? Illustrate. What is the relation of matter to form? When the form is out of keeping with the matter, what is the result?

Illustrative and Practical Exercises

The following critiques should be studied with the view of answering such questions as these:

Does the critic seek the truth? Is he prejudiced? Is he chiefly concerned with matter or form? Is his judgment sound? Is he broad or narrow in his sympathies? Does he judge by mere impressions? Is he superficial or thorough? Does he belong to a particular school? Is his criticism in any way helpful? Does he try to interpret the author? Is he chiefly concerned to show his own learning or brilliancy? Is he genial and tolerant? Is he dogmatic and intolerant? Is he courteous and kind? Is he ill-mannered and unkind? What points are criticised?

Headley's "Sacred Mountains"

The Reverend Mr. Headley (why will he not put his full title in his title-pages?) has in his "Sacred Mountains" been reversing the facts of the old fable about the mountains that brought forth the mouseparturiunt montes; nascitur ridiculus musfor in this instance it appears to be the mousethe little ridiculus musthat has been bringing forth the "mountains," and a great litter of them, too.POE.

Byron's "Hours of Idleness"

The poesy of this young Lord belongs to the class which neither gods nor men are said to permit. Indeed, we do not recollect to have seen a quantity of verse with so few deviations in either direction from that exact standard. His effusions are spread over a dead flat, and can no more get above or below the level, than if they were so much stagnant water. As an extenuation of this offence, the noble author is peculiarly forward in pleading minority. We have it in the title-page, and on the very back of the volume; it follows his name like a favourite part of his style. Much stress is laid upon it in the preface, and the poems are connected with this general statement of his case, by particular dates, substantiating the age at which each was written.LORD BROUGHAM in Edinburgh Review.

Keats's "Endymion"

The author is a copyist of Mr. Hunt, but ten times more tiresome than his prototype; his nonsense is gratuitous, he writes it for its own sake, and more than rivals the insanity of his master. He writes at random the suggestions of his rhyme without having hardly a complete couplet to endorse a complete idea in the book. If any one should be bold enough to purchase it, and patient enough to get beyond the first book and find any meaning, we entreat him to make us acquainted with his success; we shall then return to the task which we now abandon in despair.Quarterly Review.

Wordsworth

The simple Wordsworth, framer of a lay

As soft as evening in his favourite May;
Who warns his friend "to shake off toil and trouble,
And quit his books, for fear of growing double";
Who, both by precept and example, shows
That prose is verse, and verse is merely prose;
Convincing all, by demonstration plain,
Poetic souls delight in prose insane,
And Christmas stories, tortured into rhyme,
Contain the essence of the true sublime;
Thus, when he tells the tale of Betty Foy,
The idiot mother of "an idiot boy,"
A moon-struck silly lad who lost his way,
And, like his bard, confounded night with day;
So close on each pathetic part he dwells,
And each adventure so sublimely tells,
That all who view the "idiot in his glory,"
Conceive the bard the hero of the story.
BYRON in "English Bards and Scotch Reviewers."

Croker's Edition of Boswell's Life of Johnson

This work has greatly disappointed us. Whatever faults we mayhave been prepared to find in it, we fullyexpected that it would be a valuable addition to English literature; that itwould contain many curious facts, and many judicious remarks; that the style of the notes would be neat, clear, and precise; and that the typographical execution would be, as in new editions of classical works it ought to be, almost faultless. We are sorry to be obliged to say that the merits of Mr. Croker's performance are on a par with those of a certain leg of mutton on which Dr. Johnson dined, while travelling from London to Oxford, and which he, with characteristic energy, pronounced to be "as bad as bad could be, ill fed, ill killed,ill kept, and ill dressed." This edition is ill compiled, illarranged, ill written, and ill printed.MACAULAY inEdinburgh Review.

Carlyle

There is in Carlyle's fiercer and more serious passages a fiery glow of enthusiasm or indignation, in his lighter ones a quaint felicity of unexpected humour, in his expositions a vividness of presentment, in his arguments a sledge-hammer force, all of which are not to be found together anywhere else, and none of which is to be found anywhere in quite the same form. And despite the savagery, both of his indignation and his laughter, there is no greater master of tenderness. Wherever he is at home, and he seldom wanders far from it, the weapon of Carlyle is like none other,it is the very sword of Goliath.

SAINTSBURY

Gray

Against the right of Gray to be considered one of the leading English men of letters no more stringent argument has been produced than is founded upon the paucity of his published work. It has fairly been said that the springs of originality in the brain of a great inventive genius are bound to bubble up more continuously and in fuller volume than could be confined within the narrow bounds of the poetry of Gray.

But the sterility of the age, the east wind of discouragement steadily blowing across the poet's path, had much to do with this apparent want of fecundity, and it would be an error to insist too strongly on a general feature of the century in this individual case. When we turn to what Gray actually wrote, although the bulk of it is small, we are amazed at the originality and variety, the freshness and vigour of the mind that worked thus tardily and in miniature.GOSSE.

Shakespeare

Shakespeare has no peculiarity, no importunate topic; but all is duly given; no views, no curiosities; no cow-painter, no bird-fancier, no mannerist is he: he has no discoverable egotism; the great he tells greatly; the small, subordinately. He is wise without emphasis or assertion; he is strong, as nature is strong, who lifts the land into mountain slopes without effort, and by the same rule as she floats a bubble in the air, and likes as well to do the one as the other. This makes that equality of power in farce, tragedy, narrative, and love-songs; a merit so incessant, that each reader is incredulous of the perception of other readers.EMERSON.

Dowden's "Life of Shelley"

This Shelley biography is a literary cake-walk. The ordinary forms of speech are absent from it. All the pages, all the paragraphs, walk by sedately, elegantly, not to say mincingly, in their Sunday-best, shiny and sleek, perfumed, and with boutonnieres in their button-holes; it is rare to find even a chance sentence that has forgotten to dress. If the book wishes to tell us that Mary Godwin, child of sixteen, had known afflictions, the fact saunters forth in this nobby outfit: "Mary herself was not unlearned in the lore of pain."MARK TWAIN.

Milton's "Lycidas"

One of the poems on which much praise has been bestowed, is "Lycidas"; of which the diction is harsh, the rhymes uncertain, and the numbers unpleasing. What beauty there is we must therefore seek in the sentiments and images. It is not to be considered as the effusion of real passion; for passion runs not after remote allusions and obscure opinions. Passion plucks no berries from the myrtle and ivy, nor calls upon Arthur and Mincius, nor tells of rough satyrs and "fauns with cloven heel." Where there is leisure for fiction, there is little grief.

SAMUEL JOHNSON

Emerson

And, in truth, one of the legitimate poets Emerson, in my opinion, is not. His poetry is interesting, it makes one think; but it is not the poetry of one of the born poets. I say it of him with reluctance, although I am sure that he would have said it of himself; but I say it with reluctance, because I dislike giving pain to his admirers, and because all my own wish, too, is to say of him what is favorable. But I regard myself, not as speaking to please Emerson's admirers, not as speaking to please myself; but rather, I repeat, as communing with Time and Nature concerning the productions of this beautiful and rare spirit, and as resigning what of him is by their unalterable decree touched with caducity, in order the better to mark and secure that in him which is immortal.

MATTHEW ARNOLD

George Eliot

What peculiarities of George Eliot's are likely to leave a strong impress after her? I answer, she, of all novelists, has attacked the profound problems of our existence. She has taught that the mystery worthy of a great artist is not the shallow mystery device, but the infinite perspective of the great, dark enigmas of human nature; that there is a deeper interest in human life seen in the modern, scientific daylight, than in life viewed through a mist of ancient and dying superstitions; that the interest of human character transcends the interest of invented circumstances; that the epic story of a hero and a heroine is not so grand as the natural history of a community. She, first of all, has made cross sections of modern life, and shown us the busy human hive in the light of a great artistic and philosophic intellect.

EDWARD EGGLESTON

Wordsworth

He has won for himself a secure immortality by a depth of intuition which makes only the best minds at their best hours worthy, or indeed capable, of his companionship, and by a homely sincerity of human sympathy which reaches the humblest heart. Our language owes him gratitude for the habitual purity and abstinence of his style, and we who speak it, for having emboldened us to take delight in simple things, and to trust ourselves to our own instincts.LOWELL.

Paradise Lost

It is requisite that the language of an heroic poem should be both perspicuous and sublime. In proportion as either of these two qualities is wanting, the language is imperfect. Perspicuity is the first and most necessary qualification;

insomuch that a good-natured reader sometimes overlooks a little slip even in the grammar or syntax, where it is impossible for him to mistake the poet's sense. Of this kind is that passage in Milton, wherein he speaks of Satan,

"God and his Son except,
Created thing nought valued he nor shunned,"
and that in which he describes Adam and Eve,
"Adam the goodliest man of men since born,
His sons, the fairest of her daughters Eve."
ADDISON.

Friedrich Nietzsche

From the first to the last page of Nietzsche's writings the careful reader seems to hear a madman, with flashing eyes, wild gestures, and foaming mouth, spouting forth deafening bombast; and through it all, now breaking out into frenzied laughter, now sputtering expressions of filthy abuse and invective, now skipping about in a giddy agile dance, and now bursting upon the auditors with threatening mien and clenched fists. So far as any meaning at all can be extracted from the endless stream of phrases, it shows, as its fundamental elements, a series of constantly reiterated delirious ideas, having their source in illusions of sense and diseased organic processes. Here and there emerges a distinct idea, which, as is always the case with the insane, assumes the form of an imperious assertion, a sort of despotic command.

MAX NORDAU

Chapter 2

The Author and His Work

- Personality of the Author. Every literary work reveals, to a greater or less degree, the personality of the author. Every literary production may be regarded as the fruitage of the writer's spirit; and there is good authority for saying that "men do not gather grapes of thorns or figs from thistles." A book exhibits not only the attainments, culture, and literary art of the writer but also his intellectual force, emotional nature, and moral character. Wide attainments are revealed in breadth of view and in mastery of large resources. Culture is exhibited in a general delicacy of thought, feeling, and expression. Literary art is shown in the choice of words and in their arrangement in sentences and paragraphs. The artistic sense, without which a finished excellence is not attainable, reveals itself in the proportion, symmetry, and completeness of a work.
- Thought and Feeling. The intellectual and the emotional nature o a writer is clearly reflected in his works. Intellectual force, for example, is recognized in the firm grasp of a subject, in the marshaling of details toward a predetermined end, and in the vigour of utterance. The Essays of Macaulay, however much they may lack in delicate refinement of thought and feeling, display a virile force of intellect; and many a page of Carlyle fairly throbs with energy of spirit. A large, sensitive soul manifests itself in sympathy with nature and human life. The

"wee, modest, crimson-tipped" daisy, and the limping wounded hare touched the tender sympathies of Burns; and it was Wordsworth who said, "To me the meanest flower that blows can give Thoughts that do often lie too deep for tears." There is no class of society, from kings to beggars, from queens to hags, with which Shakespeare has not entered into sympathy, thinking their thoughts and speaking their words.

- Moral Character. The moral character of an author appears in his general attitude toward truth and life. A strong moral sense appears in a firm adherence to right and an unblinded condemnation of wrong. A genial, charitable spirit is shown in a kindly disposition to overlook the weaknesses of men and to magnify their virtues. Life may be looked upon as something earnest, exalted, divine; or it may be regarded as insignificant, wretched, and ending at death. It is character that gives fundamental tone to literature; and, as Matthew Arnold has said, the best results are not attainable without "high seriousness." The difference between the flippant and the earnest writer is easily and instinctively recognized. No one can read Ruskin, for instance, without feeling his sincerity and integrity, even in his most impracticable vagaries. In Addison, Goldsmith, and Irving we find a genial, uplifting amiability; and Whittier, in his deep love of human freedom and justice, appears as a resolute iconoclast and reformer.
- Authorship and Character. It is sometimes supposed that the art of authorship can be divorced from the personality of the writer. In serious authorship this supposition is a mistake. The best writing is more than grace of rhetoric and refinement of intellectual culture. Back of all outward graces there is need of a right-thinking and truth-loving soul. One of the essential things in the training of a great writer is the development of an upright, noble character.

Milton was right in maintaining that the great poet should make his life a noble poem. As a rule the writers of the world's greatest classics have been men of sincerity, truth, and honour. Such was the character of Plato, Vergil, Dante, Chaucer, Shakespeare, Milton, Wordsworth, Tennyson, Browning, and many others. Our best American writers, almost without exception, have been distinguished for moral worth. In men like Burns, Byron, and Heine, the absence of a high moral purpose has detracted, in spite of their unquestioned intellectual power, from the excellence of a large part of their writings.

- Autobiographic Elements. Our knowledge is of two kinds: the first comes from our own experience; the other, from the experience and testimony of our fellow-men. Personal experience carries with it a conviction and power that do not usually belong to the knowledge received from the testimony of others. What we have experienced has become a part of our lives. The writers of vitality and power are those who draw largely on their individual resources,the treasures of their own experience. They write, not from the memory, but from the heart. If they borrow from others, they assimilate the information, and thus vitalize it before giving it out again. The best part of our knowledge is that which comes to us through experience and assimilation. It is a permanent possession. When an author's experience, either in an ideal or a realistic form, is introduced in his work, it becomes an interesting biographical element. It presents a part of his life, and often it exhibits the transforming and glorifying power of his genius. In the drama "She Stoops to Conquer," for example, Goldsmith has turned to excellent account a humiliating incident of his youth. His "Deserted Village" is full of childhood reminiscences. Scott's poems and novels are in large measure only an expansion of the mediaeval and other lore that he enthusiastically collected in his youth and early manhood. George Eliot's earlier novels are filled with the scenes and characters of her early life; and Dickens's best novel, "David Copperfield," is largely autobiographical. An author's best workthat which possesses the greatest degree of interest and vitalityis generally that which springs from the treasure of his deepest experience, and is the fullest expression of his individual thought and feeling.

- View of Life. Every writer of originality and power takes a fundamental view of life. He has settled convictions of some sort in regard to the world in which he lives. Sometimes this view comes from religion and sometimes from philosophy or science, though in any case it is apt to be influenced by the writer's physical condition. German philosophy has influenced many able writers,Coleridge, Carlyle, Emerson, and others in England and America; and at the present time the theory of evolution is leaving a deep impress on literature. Whence came this magnificent universe? What is the origin and destiny of man? Is the general drift of human affairs upward or downward? These are great fundamental questions, and the answers we give them lie at the bottom of our thinking and give tone to our writing. The world is not the same to the Christian theist and to the agnostic. Human life has a deeper significance to the man who believes in the loving providence of God than to the man who believes only in the existence of matter and natural law. The man who believes in the presence and sovereignty of God in all things looks hopefully to the future. He is optimistic rather than pessimistic. The presence of an exuberant vitality reveals itself in a cheerful, buoyant tone. Scott's exuberant spirit forms a pleasing contrast with Carlyle's dyspeptic cynicism. It is often highly important to understand the fundamental beliefs of a writer. His works may be in a measure unintelligible till his standpoint is fully understood. Sometimes his various writings are only an expansion and application of one or two great fundamental principles. The works of Herbert Spencer, for example, are in the main an elaboration of the theory of evolution. Byron represented a skeptical reaction against the conventional manners and beliefs of his day. The essential feature of Emerson's work is found in a single sentence in "Nature." "We learn," he says, "that the Highest is present to the soul of man, that the dread universal Essence, which is not wisdom, or love, or beauty, or power, but all in one, and each entirely, is that for which all things exist, and that by which they are; that spirit creates; that behind nature, throughout nature, spirit is present; that spirit is one, and not compound; that spirit does not act upon us from without, that is, in space and time, but spiritually, or through ourselves."

- Literary School. In like manner it is interesting and sometimes illumining to know the literary school or tendency to which a writer belongs. Every author has his limitations and idiosyncrasies. First of all, he may be a writer of prose alone or of poetry alone. In prose he may confine himself to a single department, as fiction or history; or in poetry he may be chiefly lyric, didactic, or dramatic. Within these narrower spheres he may identify himself with a single tendency or group of writers. In history he may be philosophic or narrative; in fiction he may be a romanticist or a realist; in poetry he may be subjective or objective in his treatment of themes. Scott's romanticism, for instance, which delights in mediaeval scenes and incidents, is very unlike Dickens's realism, which depicts the scenes and incidents of actual contemporary life. George Eliot's psychologic novels are different from those of either Scott or Dickens.

Bryant's clear descriptions of nature stand in striking contrast with Poe's mystical melodies.

- Mood and Purpose. It is important to understand the mood and purpose of an author. We are not in a position fairly to judge a work until we know its spirit and object. Until we know whether the writer is playful or earnest, joyous or sad, satirical or serious, we cannot give his words the right tone and value; and until we see clearly what he is driving at, we cannot properly estimate the successive steps in his production nor judge of its worth as a whole.

The moods expressed in literature are exceedingly various. Since literature is the expression of the intellectual life of man, it embodies the various moods and passions to which human nature is subject. Sometimes, for example, there is laughing humour, as in Holmes's "The Deacon's Masterpiece." Sometimes there is violent anger, as in Byron's "English Bards and Scotch Reviewers." We feel his unrestrained wrath, as he exclaims,

"Prepare for rhymeI'll publish right or wrong;
Fools are my theme, let satire be my song."
Sometimes the mood is one of pensive meditation,
as when Gray sits alone
in the country churchyard amid deepening twilight:
"The curfew tolls the knell of parting day,
The lowing herd winds slowly o'er the lea,
The plowman homeward plods his weary way,
And leaves the world to darkness and to me."

Sometimes it is a righteous indignation that blazes and burns, as when Carlyle exclaims, in the presence of selfishness and wrong: "Foolish men imagine that because judgment for an evil thing is delayed, there is no justice but an accidental one, here below. Judgment for an evil thing is many times delayed some day or two, some century or two, but it is sure as life, it is as sure as death! In the centre of the world-whirlwind, verily now as in the oldest days, dwells and speaks a God. The great soul of the world is just."

Often the mood or spirit of gifted writers is something

too intangible to be firmly grasped, yet its presence is felt as a pervasive and delightful atmosphere. A work is sometimes suffused with the divine touch of genius, as the delicate and indescribable hues of autumn glorify the valleys and mountains. While hovering near the earth for a time, the spirit of genius, as in Shakespeare and Ruskin, sometimes suddenly and spontaneously soars to regions of supernal splendor,altitudes of beauty absolutely inaccessible to ordinary and unaided mortals.

The purpose of a literary work, like its mood or spirit, may be various. In a measure it varies with the department of literature to which the work belongs. The purpose of history, which brings before us the achievements of the past, is chiefly instruction. The oratory of the pulpit and the forum aims at persuasion. Fiction aims primarily at entertainment, though it may also be made the vehicle for religious, sociological, or moral teachings. Poetry aims at pleasure by means of melody, felicity of expression, the picturing of moods and scenes, and the narration of interesting incidents or important events. When the purpose of a production is clearly apprehended we are prepared to judge of the wisdom of the author in his choice and adaptation of means.

- Study of an Author's Life. The foregoing considerations show us the value of an acquaintance with an author's life. Without this acquaintance we are not prepared, in many cases, to understand or judge his productions. A good biography will acquaint us with the circumstances in which his talents were developed, and disclose to us the autobiographic materials which have been embodied in his works. It will reveal to us his views of life and his principles of art. It will show us, in short, the man behind the work, and thus help us to grasp the full significance of his utterance.

No one is absolutely independent of his surroundings. Men are frequently led, and sometimes driven by them, into the lines of work which they pursue. Hawthorne's stories, for the most part, grew out of his New England life. Had he been brought up south of the Potomac, they would have been different. Had Irving never gone to England, he would not have written "Bracebridge Hail"; and had he not sojourned in Spain, he would not have written "Alhambra" and the "Life of Columbus." Byron's "Childe Harold" is but a poetic record of his travels. Thus it is seen that an author's work, in large measure, grows out of his surroundings and experience, and cannot be thoroughly understood without an acquaintance with his life. It sometimes happens, as Shelley has sung in his interesting "Julian and Maddalo," that

"Most wretched men
Are cradled into poetry by wrong;
They learn in suffering what they teach in song."

Review Questions

- How is a book related to its author? What does it exhibit? What is said of the artistic sense?
- How is intellectual force revealed? How does a sensitive nature show itself? Illustrate.
- In what does the moral nature appear? What gives fundamental tone to literature? Illustrate.
- What must be back of the best writing? What was Milton's opinion of the poet? What is said of the world's great classics?
- Whence does our knowledge come? What gives power and vitality to a piece of literature? What is meant by autobiographic elements? Illustrate from Goldsmith and Dickens.
- What is said of a writer's fundamental views? Whence do they come? Illustrate. What questions lie at the basis of our thinking? Illustrate. What has physical vitality to do with literature? What thought dominates Spencer's works? What is the dominant belief of Emerson?
- Mention some of a writer's limitations. Explain the difference between Scott and Dickens; between Bryant and Poe.
- Why is it important to know the mood and purpose

of an author? Why are the moods different? Give examples of different moods. Explain the general purpose of history, oratory, fiction, and poetry. Why should we know the purpose of an author?

- Why study the biography of an author? What will it reveal to us? What have surroundings to do with an author? Give illustrations. What is the quotation from Shelley?

Illustrative and Practical Exercises

The following selections should be studied with reference to such questions as these:

What light does the selection throw on the author? Is he a man of large attainments? Does it show refinement of thought and feeling? Does it display literary art? Has it virile force? Does it show a true sense of right? Is there a large, noble nature back of it? Does it grow out of the author's personal experience? Has it the force of conviction? How does the author conceive of the world? What does he think of God? How does he regard human life? Is he hopeful or pessimistic? Is he a writer of prose, poetry, or both? To what school of writing does he belong? What is the mood or spirit,humorous, buoyant, serious, sad, ironical, angry, genial, urbane? What is its purpose,to instruct, please, persuade?

The love of dirt is among the earliest of passions, as it isthe latest. Mud-pies gratify one of our first and bestinstincts. So long as we are dirty, we are pure. Fondness for the ground comes back to a man after he has seen the round of pleasure and business, eaten dirt, and sown wild-oats, drifted about the world, and taken the wind of all its moods. The love of digging in the ground (or of looking on while he pays another to dig) is as sure to come back to him as he is sure, at last, to go under the ground and stay there.CHARLES DUDLEY WARNER.

The end of learning is to repair the ruins of our first parents by regaining to know God aright, and out of that knowledge to love him, to imitate him, to be like him, as we may the nearest by possessing our souls of true virtue, which being united to the heavenly grace of faith makes up the highest perfection.

MILTON

We are like lambs in a field, disporting themselves under the eye of the butcher, who chooses out first one and then another for his prey. So it is that in our good days we are all unconscious of the evil Fate may have presently in store for ussickness, poverty, mutilation, loss of sight or reason.

SCHOPENHAUER.

Alas! 'tis true I have gone here and there,
And made myself a motley to the view;
Gor'd mine own thoughts, sold cheap what is most dear,
Made old offences of affections new;
Most times it is that I have looked on truth
Askance and strangely.SHAKESPEARE.

In order to secure my credit and character as a tradesman, I took care not only to be in reality industrious and frugal, but to avoid the appearances to the contrary. I dressed plain, and was seen at no places of idle diversion. I never went out a fishing or shooting; a book, indeed, sometimes debauched me from my work, but that was seldom, was private, and gave no scandal; and to show that I was not above my business, I sometimes brought home the paper I purchased at the stores through the streets on a wheelbarrow.FRANKLIN.

Given, a man with moderate intellect, a moral standard not higher than the average, some rhetorical affluence and great glibness of speech, what is the career in which, without the aid of birth or money, he may most easily attain power and reputation in English society? Where is the Goshen of mediocrity in which a smattering of science and learning will pass for profound instruction, where platitudes will be accepted as wisdom, bigoted narrowness as holy zeal, unctuous egoism as God-given piety? Let such a man become an evangelical preacher; he will then find it possible to reconcile small ability with great ambition, superficial knowledge with the prestige of erudition, a middling morale with a high reputation for sanctity.GEORGE ELIOT. Careless seems the great Avenger; history's pages but record One death-grapple in the darkness 'twixt old systems and the Word; Truth forever on the scaffold, Wrong forever on the throne, Yet that scaffold sways the future, and, behind the dim unknown, Standeth God within the shadow, keeping watch above his own. LOWELL. Thus I live in the world rather as a spectator of mankind than as one of the species, by which means I have made myself a speculative statesman, soldier, merchant, and artisan, without ever meddling with any practical part in life.

I am very well versed in the theory of a husband or a father, and can discern the errors in the economy, business, and diversions of others better than those who are engaged in them; as standers-by discover blots, which are apt to escape those who are in the game. I never espoused any party with violence, and am resolved to observe an exact neutrality between the Whigs and Tories, unless I shall be forced to declare myself by the hostilities of either side.

ADDISON.

Outout are the lightsout all!
And over each quivering form,
The curtain, a funeral pall,
Comes down with the rush of a storm;
And the angels, all pallid and wan,
Uprising, unveiling, affirm
That the play is the tragedy "Man,"
And its hero the Conqueror Worm.POE.

The essays professedly serious, if I have been able to execute my own intentions, will be found exactly conformable to the precepts of Christianity, without any accommodation to the licentiousness and levity of the present age. I therefore look back on this part of my work with pleasure, which no praise or blame of man can diminish or augment. I shall never envy the honors which wit and learning obtain in any other cause, if I can be numbered among the writers who have given ardor to virtue and confidence to truth.SAMUEL JOHNSON.

What tho' on hamely fare we dine,
Wear hodden gray, and a' that;
Gie fools their silks, and knaves their wine

A man's a man for a' that.
For a' that, and a' that,
Their tinsel show, and a' that;
The honest man, though e'er sae poor,
Is king of men for a' that.BURNS.

I said to myself that my hero should work his way through life as I had seen real living men work theirs; that he should never get a shilling he had not earned; that no sudden turn should lift him in a moment to wealth and high station; that whatever small competency he might gain, should be won by the sweat of his brow; that before he could find so much as an arbor to sit down in, he should master, at least, half the ascent of the "Hill of Difficulty"; that he should not even marry a beautiful girl or a lady of rank. As Adam's son he should share Adam's doom, and drain, throughout life, a mixed and moderate cup of enjoyment.CHARLOTTE BRONTE.

Day set on Norham's castled steep,
And Tweed's fair river, broad and deep,
And Cheviot's mountains lone:
The battled towers, the donjon keep,
The loophole grates, where captives weep,
The flanking walls that round it sweep,
In yellow lustre shone.
The warriors on the turrets high,
Moving athwart the evening sky,
Seemed forms of giant height;
Their armor, as it caught the rays,
Flashed back again the western blaze,
In lines of dazzling light.SCOTT.

It is a restful chapter in any book of Cooper's when somebody doesn't step on a dry twig and alarm all the reds and whites for two hundred yards around. Every time a Cooper person is in peril, and absolute silence is worth four dollars a minute, he is sure to step on a dry twig. There may be a hundred handier things to step on, but that wouldn't satisfy Cooper. Cooper requires him to turn out and find a dry twig; and if he can't do it, go and borrow one. In fact the Leather Stocking Series ought to have been called the Broken

Twig Series

MARK TWAIN.

Live and love,
Doing both nobly, because lowlily;
Live and work, strongly, because patiently!
And, for the deed of Death, trust to God
That it be well done, unrepented of,
And not to loss. And thence with constant prayers
Fasten your souls so high, that constantly
The smile of your heroic cheer may float
Above all floods of earthly agonies,
Purification being the joy of pain.

MRS. BROWNING.

Chapter 3

Some Aesthetic Principles

- AEsthetics. The science of beauty in general is called AEsthetics, to which we have to look for some of the principles that are to guide our critical judgment. Unfortunately for us, the science of beauty has not yet been fully and satisfactorily wrought out, and the ablest writers, from Aristotle to Herbert Spencer, exhibit great diversity of view. There are two main theories of beauty: the one makes beauty subjective, or an emotion of the mind; the other makes it objective, or a quality in the external object. Without entering into the intricacies and difficulties of the discussion, beauty will here be regarded as that quality in literature which awakens in the cultivated reader a sense of the beautiful. This sense of the beautiful is a refined and pleasurable feeling; and, as we shall see, it is traceable to a variety of sources.
- Literary Taste. Literary taste is that power or faculty of the mind which apprehends and appreciates what is beautiful and artistic in literature. It embraces two elements: first, the apprehension of the aesthetic quality; and secondly, an appreciation or emotional response to its appeal. These two elements are not always equally developed in the critic; and it frequently happens that an artistic literary production affords exquisite pleasure without a clear apprehension of the aesthetic elements from which the pleasure springs. In literary criticism, as has already been shown, the standard of taste is the ideal,

developed by an application of necessary and recognized principles, which the intelligent critic is able to form in every department of literature. The capacity of taste is a natural gift; but, like other powers of the mind, it is capable of great development. It is cultivated by a study of the principles of beauty and by a contemplation of beautiful objects in nature and art. Bad taste exhibits itself in a failure to apprehend and appreciate what is genuinely beautiful; it often mistakes defects for excellences. A refined taste responds to what is delicate in beauty, and a catholic taste recognizes and responds to beauty of every kind. The critic who would do honour to his office must have a taste both refined and catholic.

- AEsthetic Elements. Literary beauty may pertain either to the form or to the content. Deferring to subsequent chapters the elements of external beauty, we here consider the elements of internal beauty. Though beauty of form and beauty of content may thus be distinguished, they are always combined in works of the highest excellence. Both alike have their source in the cultivated, creative spirit of the writer. They cannot be effectually learned by rule; and the best training for successful authorship is the development of the intellectual and moral faculties. Vividness of description is a frequent source of literary beauty. Scenes, objects, and events are sometimes so presented as to become visible to the inner eye. Thus Tennyson describes the flinging of Arthur's sword:

  "The great brand
  Made lightnings in the splendor of the moon."

Carlyle was a master of graphic description, and in a few touches he thus brings De Quincey before us: "One of the smallest man figures I ever saw; shaped like a pair of tongs, and hardly above five feet in all. When he sate, you would have taken him by candlelight for the beautifullest little child;

blue-eyed, sparkling face, had there not been something, too, which said, 'Eccovithis child has been in hell!'"

Meditative reflection, when aptly associated with circumstance or occasion, may become a pleasing source of beauty. When employed by way of introduction, it may, as frequently in Irving and Hawthorne, strike the keynote of what follows. Sometimes it gives natural expression to the vague thought or feeling that had been produced in the reader by the preceding narrative and that would otherwise have remained unsatisfied. In the darkness and silence of night the poet hears the striking of a deep-toned bell. Naturally he thinks of the flight of time.

"The bell strikes one. We take no note of time
But from its loss: to give it then a tongue
Is wise in man. As if an angel spoke,
I feel the solemn sound. If heard aright,
It is the knell of my departed hours."

A meditation may, as a conclusion, impart a satisfying completeness to a piece. Nothing could be finer, for example, than Addison's reflections at the close of his essay on the tombs of Westminster Abbey: "When I look upon the tombs of the great, every emotion of envy dies in me; when I read the epitaphs of the beautiful, every inordinate desire goes out; when I meet with the grief of parents upon a tombstone, my heart melts with compassion; when I see the tomb of the parents themselves, I consider the vanity of grieving for those whom we must quickly follow. When I see kings lying by those who deposed them, when I consider rival wits placed side by side, or the holy men that divided the world with their contests and disputes, I reflect with sorrow and astonishment on the little competitions, factions, and debates of mankind. When I read the several dates of the tombs, of some that died yesterday, and some six hundred years ago, I consider that great day when we shall all of us be contemporaries, and make our appearance together."

Harmony of thought and expression is another source of excellence. The thought should be clothed in a perfect body, so that nothing can be added or subtracted without marring the beauty. The following stanza from Holmes's "The Last Leaf" will serve for illustration:

"The mossy marbles rest
On the lips that he has prest
In their bloom;
And the names he loved to hear
Have been carved for many a year
On the tomb."

When, in addition to perfect harmony between spirit and form, the sound reenforces the sense, there is an added element of beauty. The intellect is thus assisted in imaging or realizing the scene. As the heroine returns to her palace in Tennyson's "Godiva,"

"All at once
With twelve great shocks of sound, the shameless noon
Was clashed and hammered from a hundred towers."

A well-known illustration is furnished in Pope's "Essay on Criticism":

"Soft is the strain when Zephyr gently blows,
And the smooth stream in smoother numbers flows;
But when loud surges lash the sounding shore,
The hoarse, rough verse should like the torrent roar."

The felicitous expression of some well-known truth or experience is always pleasing. In its happiest form such an expression is received as the final embodiment of its truth. It is henceforth taken up by the multitude and quoted as having the authority of a sacred text. Pope tells us, for example, that

"To err is human; to forgive, divine";

and also that

"Fools rush in where angels fear to tread."

But no other English writer has equaled Shakespeare in the number of felicitous expressions that have passed into current use. His works are a veritable mine of jeweled phrases. We often feel, for example, that somehow there is a mysterious power controlling our lives; and this experience he voices in the well-known lines,

"There's a divinity that shapes our ends,
Rough-hew them how we will."

Yet at the same time, recognizing the truth of human freedom, he declares,

"Our remedies oft in ourselves do lie,
Which we ascribe to heaven; the fated sky
Gives us free scope, only doth backward push
Our slow designs when we ourselves are dull."

High spiritual truth, in fitting expression, is a source of great beauty. There are three great provinces of thought,man, nature, and God. The last is the greatest of all; and the highest achievement of literature is to lead us to a new or fuller appreciation of his character. As we look upon the irrepressible and unending conflict between good and evil in this world, we are sometimes tempted to doubt a favorable issue; but Lowell tells us, in self-evidencing words, that "Behind the dim unknown Standeth God within the shadow, keeping watch above his own." To Ruskin the various phenomena of nature brought a sweet message: "All those passings to and fro of fruitful shower and grateful shade, and all those visions of silver palaces built about the horizon, and voices of moaning winds and threatening thunders, and glories of colored robe and cloven ray, are but to deepen in our hearts the acceptance, and distinctness, and dearness of the simple words, 'Our Father, which art in heaven.'"

Another principal source of literary beauty is found in a worthy expression of noble thought and sentiment. This may be regarded as the soul of enduring literature, and it is as exhaustless as the human mind itself. The dauntless love of liberty that breathes through Patrick Henry's famous speech is thrilling in its eloquence: "What is it that gentlemen wish? What would they have? Is life so dear, or peace so sweet, as to be purchased at the price of chains and slavery? Forbid it, Almighty God! I know not what course others may take, but, as for me, give me liberty, or give me death!" Carlyle conceived of nature as the vesture of God; and, as he speaks of the universe, this thought lifts his style to great majesty: "Oh, could I transport thee direct from the beginnings to the endings, how were thy eyesight unsealed, and thy heart set flaming in the Light-sea of celestial wonder! Then sawest thou that this fair

Universe, were it in the meanest province thereof, is in very deed the star-domed City of God; that through every star, through every grass-blade, and most, through every Living Soul, the glory of a present God still beams. But Nature, which is the Time-vesture of God, and reveals Him to the wise, hides Him from the foolish."

Love is a perennial inspiration both in prose and poetry. It partakes of the divine, for "God is love." Its highest manifestations, whether in the family, among relatives and friends, or between lovers, are always beautiful; and perhaps Browning was not far wrong when he sang,

"There is no good in life but lovebut love!
What else looks good, is some shade flung from love;
Love yields it, gives it worth."

The portrayal of noble character is always inspiring. It appeals to the better side of our nature, and strengthens our confidence in humanity.

No literary art can confer immortality on what is ignoble. The fiction that is devoted to obscene realism, whatever may be the prestige of its authors or its current vogue, is surely doomed. Only that which is morally good is destined to live through the ages. The genial Dickens will always be more popular than the satirical Thackeray. Boswell's "Life of Johnson" owes its principal charm not to any trick of style, but to the honest, rugged piece of manhood it brings before us. Only a man of Luther's heroic spirit could have inspired this magnificent tribute in Carlyle's "Heroes and Hero-Worship": "I will call this Luther a true great man; great in intellect, in courage, affection, and integrity; one of our most lovable and precious men.

Great, not as a hewn obelisk, but as an Alpine mountain,so simple, honest, spontaneous, not setting up to be great at all; there for quite another purpose than being great! Ah yes, unsubduable granite, piercing far and wide into the heavens; yet in the clefts of it fountains, green, beautiful valleys with flowers! A right spiritual hero and prophet; once more, a true son of nature and fact, for whom these centuries, and many that are to come yet, will be thankful to Heaven."

Heroic self-sacrifice strongly appeals to us. Whenever a man or woman gives up self for the good of others, we intuitively admire and honour the deed. The story of Thermopylae, the leap of Curtius into the yawning chasm, the charge of the Light Brigade, "... though the soldier knew Some one had blundered," are instances of heroic self-sacrifice which the world is unwilling to forget. There is a charm in Tennyson's "Godiva" or his "Enoch Arden" beyond the reach of mere art; it is found in the noble spirit of the heroine who replies to the taunt of her husband, "But I would die"; and in the deep self-renunciation of the hero who, in heartbreaking anguish, prayed, "Help me not to break in upon her peace." The beauty of a life of simplicity and benevolence is seen in the immortal Vicar of Wakefield. His unaffected goodness has made him dear to successive generations. In like manner we pay a spontaneous tribute to Chaucer's "poure parson of a toune," and to the preacher of the

"Deserted Village":

"A man he was to all the country dear,
And passing rich with forty pounds a year;
Remote from towns he ran his godly race,
Nor e'er had changed, nor wished to change, his place.
Unskilful he to fawn, or seek for power,
By doctrines fashioned to the varying hour;
Far other aims his heart had learned to prize,
More bent to raise the wretched than to rise."

The fitting description of scenes and incidents of grandeur imparts dignity and charm to a production. Grandeur is of two kinds: first, the grandeur or sublimity of natural objects, such as the ocean, a storm, an earthquake, or other exhibitions of tremendous power; and secondly, the moral sublime, in which the heroic soul rises superior to dangers and death. Milton's "Paradise Lost" abounds in grave and sublime passages. Byron reaches the sublime in many of the descriptions of "Childe Harold," of which the following will serve for illustration:

"Far along
From peak to peak, the rattling crags among,
Leaps the live thunder! Not from one lone cloud,

But every mountain now hath found a tongue,
And Jura answers, through her misty shroud,
Back to the joyous Alps, who call to her aloud."

Perhaps no finer instance of the moral sublime is to be found than in the bearing of Luther before the Imperial Diet in the city of Worms. He was confronted by the chief dignitaries of Church and Empire. The emperor himself, Charles V, was present. "Will you, or will you not, retract?" solemnly demanded the speaker of the Diet. "Unless," replied the intrepid reformer, "unless I am convinced by the testimony of Holy Scripture or by clear and indisputable reasoning, I cannot, and will not, retract anything; for it is unsafe for a Christian to do anything against his conscience. Here I stand, I cannot do otherwise, God help me. Amen!"

Another source of beauty is found in tenderness and pathos. These feelings appeal to the gentler side of our nature. The pathos may arise from various causes,from bereaved affection, from fond memories, from sore disappointments, or from helpless suffering. Every one is familiar with Dickens's description of the death of little Nell in "Old Curiosity Shop." Irving's story of "The Broken Heart" is deeply pathetic.

The deathbed scene of Colonel Newcome in Thackeray's great novel is notable for its simple pathos: "At the usual evening hour the chapel bell began to toll, and Thomas Newcome's hands outside the bed feebly beat time. And just as the last bell struck, a peculiar sweet smile shone over his face, and he lifted up his head a little, and quickly said 'Adsum!' and fell back. It was the word used at school, when names were called; and lo, he, whose heart was that of a little child, had answered to his name, and stood in the presence of his Master." There is a tender regret in Hood's little poem, "I Remember":

"I remember, I remember,
The fir-trees dark and high;
I used to think their slender tops
Were close against the sky;
It was a childish ignorance,
But now 'tis little joy

To know I'm further off from heaven
Than when I was a boy."

The ludicrous often adds charm to literature. It is divided into two species,wit and humour. Wit consists in the discovery of remote analogies or relations, and produces an amusing surprise. It has various forms. In the pun, which is a rather low order of wit, there is a play on the meaning of words. Punning is an art easily acquired; but a pun is usually an impertinence to be excused only by its felicity. Hood was one of the most ingenious of punsters; and in his ballad, "Faithless Nelly *Gray," the wit of each stanza is found in a pun.*

"Ben Battle was a soldier bold,
And used to war's alarms;
But a cannon-ball took off his legs,
So he laid down his arms."

Satire ridicules the follies and vices of men, and is frequent in both ancient and modern literature. Sometimes it is good-natured, but oftener it is bitter. Swift's "Tale of a Tub" is a fierce attack upon ecclesiastical divisions, while Pope's "Dunciad," which impales many of his contemporary writers, almost ruined the reputations it touched. Addison in the Spectator is genial in his satire. Byron is a master of powerful satire, and in the "English Bards and Scotch Reviewers" he indiscriminately lampoons his contemporaries. For example:

"Shall gentle Coleridge pass unnoticed here,
To turgid ode and tumid stanza dear?
Though themes of innocence amuse him best,
Yet still obscurity's a welcome guest.
If inspiration should her aid refuse
To him who takes a Pixy for a muse,
Yet none in lofty numbers can surpass
The bard who soars to elegize an ass.
How well the subject suits his noble mind!
'A fellow-feeling makes us wondrous kind!'"

A parody is a burlesque imitation and degradation of something serious. In his song, "Those Evening Bells," Moore wrote in pensive mood,

"And so 'twill be when I am gone;

That tuneful peal will still ring on,
While other bards shall walk these dells,
And sing your praise, sweet evening bells."

But in Hood's parody of the same title, this stanza is travestied as follows:

"And so 'twill be when she is gone;
That tuneful peal will still ring on,
And other maids with timely yells
Forget to stay those evening bells."

The other principal form of the ludicrous is humour. It is wit modified by a genial or sympathetic feeling. It has its origin in the disposition or character, while wit springs alone from the intellect. It often pervades an entire production. While wit generally breaks out in brief and sudden flashes, humour is frequently diffused through an entire work like a delicious fragrance. Addison's Sir Roger de Coverley papers in the Spectator are delightful examples of delicate humour. Hood's "Up the Rhine" is a rich commingling of wit and humour. Dickens's "Pickwick Papers" and Mark Twain's "Innocents Abroad" are humorous works of a broader type. Irving's minor writings are suffused with a delightful humour.

And no one who has read the humorous beginning of the "Vicar of Wakefield" is likely to forget it: "I was ever of opinion, that the honest man who married and brought up a large family, did more service than he who continued single and only talked of a population. From this motive, I had scarcely taken orders a year, before I began to think seriously of matrimony, and chose my wife, as she did her wedding-gown, not for a fine glossy surface, but for such qualities as would wear well."

Review Questions

- What is meant by aesthetics? What are the two theories of beauty? How is beauty considered in this book?
- What is meant by taste? What are its two elements? What is said of their development? How may taste be cultivated? How is bad taste exhibited? What is

the distinction between a refined and a catholic taste?

- To what may literary beauty pertain? What elements are considered in this chapter? Where do we find beauty of form and of content united? Why is vivid description an element of beauty? Give an illustration. How may meditative reflection become an element of beauty? Illustrate. What is meant by harmony of thought and expression? Give an example. How may sound reenforce the sense? Illustrate. What is said about felicitous expression? What writers excel in felicity of expression?

Illustrate. What is said of high spiritual truth? Name the three great provinces of thought. What does Lowell think of the evils in the world? What does Ruskin say of the phenomena of nature? What is said of noble thought and sentiment? What makes Patrick Henry's speech thrilling? How did Carlyle conceive of nature? What is said of love in literature? What is Browning's idea? What is the effect of portraying noble character? What is said of obscene realism? To what does Boswell's "Life of Johnson" owe its principal charm? What does Carlyle say of Luther? What is said of heroic self-sacrifice? Illustrate. Where do we see the beauty of simple goodness portrayed? What is the effect of the fitting portrayal of grandeur? What two kinds of grandeur are distinguished? Mention some objects of natural grandeur. Illustrate from Byron. Give an illustration of the moral sublime. To what does pathos appeal? Illustrate. Repeat the quotation from Hood. What two species of the ludicrous are distinguished? What is wit? What is a pun? Illustrate. What is satire? What are the two kinds of satire? Give an illustration. What is a parody? Illustrate. How does humour differ from wit? Give an example of humour.

Illustrative and Practical Exercises

The following extracts should be carefully studied for the

purpose of determining their elements of internal excellence or beauty. They should be tested by such questions as these:

Is the extract descriptive or meditative? What gives vividness to the description? What points are brought out in the meditation? What is the main thought or feeling presented? Does it pertain to man, nature, or God? What phases of nature are considered? What element of character is set forth? Is there dignity or felicity of expression? Is grandeur portrayed? Is it physical or moral? Is there tenderness or pathos? What gives it this element? Is there art or humour? What kind of wit? What is the chief source of beauty?

A man from Maine, who had never paid more than twenty-five cents for admission to an entertainment, went to a New York theatre where the play was "The Forty Thieves," and was charged a dollar and a half for a ticket. Handing the pasteboard back, he remarked, "Keep it, Mister; I don't want to see the other thirty-nine.

"ANON

Old Ironsides

O better that her shattered hulk
Should sink beneath the wave;
Her thunders shook the mighty deep,
And there should be her grave;
Nail to the mast her holy flag,
Set every threadbare sail,
And give her to the god of storms,
The lightning and the gale.HOLMES.

Though I speak with the tongues of men and of angels, and have not charity, I am become as sounding brass, or a tinkling cymbal. And though I have the gift of prophecy, and understand all mysteries, and all knowledge; and though I have all faith, so that I could remove mountains, and have not charity, I am nothing. And though I bestow all my goods to feed the poor, and though I give my body to be burned, and have not charity, it profiteth me nothing.PAUL.

Forth goes the woodman, leaving unconcerned

The cheerful haunts of man, to wield the axe
And drive the wedge in yonder forest drear,
From morn to eve his solitary task.
Shaggy, and lean, and shrewd, with pointed ears
And tail cropped short, half lurcher and half cur,
His dog attends him! Close behind his heel
Now creeps he slow; and now, with many a frisk
Wide-scampering, snatches up the drifted snow
With ivory teeth, or ploughs it with his snout;
Then shakes his powdered coat, and barks for joy.
Heedless of all his pranks, the sturdy churl
Moves right toward the mark; nor stops for aught,
But now and then with pressure of his thumb,
To adjust the fragrant charge of a short tube,
That fumes beneath his nose; the trailing cloud
Streams far behind him, scenting all the air.COWPER.

Oh, the grave! the grave! It buries every error, covers every defect, extinguishes every resentment. From its peaceful bosom spring none but fond regrets and tender recollections. Who can look down upon the grave even of an enemy, and not feel a compunctious throb that he should ever have warred with the poor handful of earth that lies moldering before him? But the grave of those we loved,what a place for meditation! There it is we call up, in long review, the whole history of virtue and gentleness, and the thousand endearments lavished upon us, almost unheeded, in the daily intercourse of intimacy; there it is that we dwell upon the tenderness, the solemn, awful tenderness of the parting scene.

IRVING

Joan of Arc

The executioner had been directed to apply his torch from below. He did so. The fiery smoke rose up in billowy columns. A Dominican monk was then standing almost at her side. Wrapped up in his sublime office, he saw not the danger, but still persisted in his prayers. Even then when the last enemy was racing up the fiery stairs to seize her, even at that moment did this noblest of girls think only for him, the one friend that would not forsake her, and not herself; bidding him with her last breath to care for his own preservation, but to leave her to God.

DE QUINCEY.

O, lay thy hand in mine, dear!
We're growing old;
But Time hath brought no sign, dear,
That hearts grow cold.
Tis long, long since our new love
Made life divine;
But age enricheth true love,
Like noble wine.MASSEY.

The noon-day sun came slanting down the rocky slopes of La Ricca, and its masses of entangled and tall foliage, whose autumnal tints were mixed with the wet verdure of a thousand evergreens, were penetrated with it as with rain. I cannot call it colour, it was conflagration. Purple, and crimson, and scarlet, like the curtains of God's tabernacle, the rejoicing trees sank into the valley in showers of light, every separate leaf quivering with buoyant and burning life; each, as it turned to reflect or to transmit the sunbeam, first a torch and then an emerald. Far up into the recesses of the valley, the green vistas, arched like the hollows of mighty waves of some crystalline sea, with the arbutus flowers dashed along their flanks for foam, and silver flakes of orange spray tossed into the air around them, breaking over the gray walls of rock into a thousand separate stars, fading and kindling alternately as the weak wind lifted and let them fall.RUSKIN.

Gineral C. is a dreffle smart man;
He's ben on all sides that give places or pelf,
But consistency still wuz a part of his plan,
He's been true to one party,and thet is himself;
So John P.
Robinson he
Sez he shall vote for Gineral C.
Gineral C. he goes in fer the war;
He don't vally principle more 'n an old cud;
Wut did God make us raytional creeturs fer,

But glory an' gunpowder, plunder an' blood?
So John P.
Robinson he
Sez he shall vote for Gineral C.LOWELL.

Woman

Not she with traitorous kiss her Saviour stung,
Not she denied him with unholy tongue;
She, while apostles shrank, could dangers brave,
Last at the cross and earliest at the grave.BARRETT.
Tears, idle tears, I know not what they mean,
Tears from the depths of some divine despair
Rise in the heart, and gather to the eyes,
In looking on the happy Autumn-fields,
And thinking of the days that are no more.
Fresh as the first beam glittering on a sail
That brings our friends up from the underworld,
Sad as the last which reddens over one
That sinks with all we love below the verge;
So sad, so fresh, the days that are no more.TENNYSON.

No nation which did not contemplate this wonderful universe with an awe-stricken and reverential belief that there was a great unknown, omnipotent, and all-wise and all-just Being, superintending all men in it, and all interests in itno nation ever came to very much, nor did any man either, who forgot that. If a man did forget that, he forgot the most important part of his mission in this world. CARLYLE.

Goldsmith

Think of him reckless, thriftless, vain if you likebut merciful, gentle, generous, full of love and pity. He passes out of our life and goes to render his account beyond it.

Think of the poor pensioners weeping at his grave; think of the noble spirits that admired and deplored him; think of the righteous pen that wrote his epitaphand the wonderful and unanimous response of affection with which the world has paid the love he gave it. His humour delighting us still; his song fresh and beautiful as when he first charmed with it; his words in all our mouths; his very weaknesses beloved and familiarhis benevolent spirit seems still to smile upon us; to do gentle kindnesses; to succor with sweet charity; to caress, to soothe, and forgive; to plead with the fortunate for the unhappy and the poor

THACKERAY.

We watched her breathing through the night,
Her breathing soft and low,
As in her breast the wave of life
Kept heaving to and fro.
Our very hopes belied our fears,
Our fears our hopes belied,
We thought her dying when she slept,
And sleeping when she died.
For when the morn came, dim and sad,
And chill with early showers,
Her quiet eyelids closed,she had
Another morn than ours.

HOOD.

Chapter 4

Words, Sentences, Paragraphs

- English Composite. The English language is composite, its words being drawn from various sources. The original and principal element is Anglo-Saxon, which prevailed in England for about five hundred years. By the conquest of William of Normandy, French was introduced into England, and was spoken by the ruling classes for about three hundred years. The amalgamation of the Anglo-Saxon and the Norman Frencha process that was fairly completed in the fourteenth centuryresulted in modern English. But numerous words came in from other sources. The early introduction of Roman Christianity into England, and the revival of learning at the close of the Middle Ages, introduced a large Latin element. The Celtic population of the British Isles contributed a few words, such as pibroch, clan, bard. A considerable Greek element has been introduced by theology and science, and English conquests and commerce have introduced words from almost every portion of the globe, of which pagoda, bazaar, veda, bamboo, taboo, and raccoon will serve as examples. The composite character of our language has made it very copious and very interesting. No other language has so many words, our largest dictionaries defining more than a hundred thousand. Every word has its history, and often a very interesting one. Raccoon, for instance, takes us back to the adventures of the redoubtable John Smith in Virginia. The word bishop carries us back to the introduction of Christianity among the Anglo-Saxons at the close of the sixth century, and then through the Latin to the primitive days of the Church, when an episkopos, or overseer, presided over the newly founded congregations in the leading cities of Greece. Taboo reminds us of English explorations and conquests in the islands of the Pacific. Thus nearly every word may be traced to its source and, rightly understood, is freighted with tales of conquest, battle, exploration, commerce, science, and invention. It carries with it its meaning and atmosphere of association, which the intelligent and skillful writer knows how to use to advantage.

- Anglo-Saxon and Latin Elements. The Anglo-Saxon or Teutonic element of our language embraces about sixty per cent of the words in common use. It may be regarded as the trunk, on which the other elements have been grafted as branches. The Latin element embraces about thirty per cent of an ordinary vocabulary, nearly two thirds of which, or about twenty per cent, comes through the French. The question has been raised as to which element is preferable. Should a writer's style be Saxonized or Latinized? No absolute rule can be laid down. The two elements supplement each other. In general the Anglo-Saxon element comprises concrete terms, and the Latin element abstract terms. As Trench has pointed out, "The great features of nature, sun, moon, and stars, earth, water, and fire; the divisions of time; three out of the four seasons, spring, summer, and winter; the features of natural scenery, the words used in earliest childhood, the simpler emotions of the mind; all the prime social relations, father, mother, husband, wife, son, daughter, brother, sister,these are of native growth and unborrowed." It is thus seen that the Anglo-Saxon element is full of force in its presentation of definite concrete objects;

and it is a noteworthy fact that our best writers use a large proportion of native words. In ordinary discourse none of our best writers, perhaps, fall below seventy per cent of Anglo-Saxon. But in philosophy, which deals largely with abstract ideas, the Anglo-Saxon element, as in passages from Herbert Spencer, may fall as low as sixty per cent. It is interesting to estimate the percentage of Anglo-Saxon or Latin in an author. This may easily be done by counting the number of words in a given passage for the denominator, and the number of Anglo-Saxon or Latin words for the numerator of a common fraction, which may then be reduced to a decimal.

What Element to Choose. A writer's style should be determined by higher considerations than the deliberate purpose to use as far as possible any single element of our language. Such a purpose degenerates into affectation, and becomes a mannerism. The following extract from a sonnet by Addison Alexander shows what may be done by short Anglo-Saxon words; but, because of its lack of musical rhythm and fine poetic quality, it is not to be commended as a model:

"Think not that strength lies in the big round word,
Or that the brief and plain must needs be weak.
To whom can this be true who once has heard
The cry for help, the tongue that all men speak
When want, or woe, or fear, is in the throat,
So that each word gasped out is like a shriek
Pressed from the sore heart, or a strange wild note
Sung by some fay or fiend."

With this may be compared the following lines from a sonnet by Longfellow, in which the musical effect of the Latin element will be clearly recognized:

"I saw the long line of the vacant shore,
And the sea-weed and the shells upon the sand,
And the brown rocks left bare on every hand,
As if the ebbing tide would flow no more.

Then heard I, more distinctly than before,
The ocean breathe and its great breast expand,
And hurrying came on the defenceless land
The insurgent waters with tumultuous roar."

The use of Latin words often gives clearness and melody to style; and instead of a violent effort to Saxonize his writing, an author should clothe his thoughts in the diction that is most fitting and expressive.

- Diction. Aristotle truly said that "the beginning of style is correctness of diction." By diction is meant the choice and use of words. Good diction lies at the basis of good writing. Words are used to express ideas; and in view of this fundamental principle, it follows that they should be intelligible and correct. They should belong to our language; and hence the use of foreign words and phrases, except to supply a real want in English, is generally in bad taste. The use of provincial expressions, such as tote for carry, is to be avoided, except in the portrayal of provincial character. Archaic words, as well as those that have not yet established themselves, should not be employed. For these two classes of words Pope has laid down an excellent rule in his "Essay on Criticism":

  "In words, as fashions, the same rule will hold,
  Alike fantastic, if too new or old;
  Be not the first by whom the new are tried,
  Nor yet the last to lay the old aside."

There is sometimes an obvious effort among young or half-cultured writers to seek after unusual words. Unless the purpose of discourse is to be defeated, it is evident that the words used by a writer should have their accepted and exact meaning. The study of etymology, though sometimes misleading, is very helpful in learning the exact force of words. There are very few words in our language that are exactly synonymous; and while synonyms are often loosely used, the skillful writer is careful to distinguish their different shades of meaning. This nice use of words, impossible to the uncultivated mind, adds an exquisite charm to writing. A very common fault of diction results in what is called "fine writing." This fault consists in the choice of high-sounding words to express commonplace ideas. It is the besetting vice of half-educated writers.

In the hands of such persons a "fair lady" becomes a "female possessing considerable personal attractions," and "drinking liquor" turns into "ingurgitating spirituous stimulus." Except for purposes of wit or humour, this affectation is not to be tolerated.

- Sentences. In reading various authors, it is readily observed that they use different kinds of sentences. Some writers use short sentences, others long and complicated sentences. In comparing recent authors with those of two or three centuries ago, it will generally be found that shorter sentences are now more frequent. This brevity and simplicity of predication has resulted in greater clearness. But the constant use of short, simple sentences produces a disagreeable monotony.

Sentences are rhetorically distinguished as loose, periodic, and balanced. A loose sentence is one in which the meaning is complete at one or more points before the end. Thus, at the beginning of "Pilgrim's Progress," we read: "As I walked through the wilderness of this world, I lighted on a certain place where was a den, and laid me down in that place to sleep; and as I slept, I dreamed a dream." A periodic sentence holds the meaning in suspense till the close. For example, Macaulay writes: "If any man could have succeeded in this attempt, a man of talents so rare, of judgments so prematurely ripe, of temper so calm, and of manners so plausible, might have been expected to succeed."

A balanced sentence consists of two parts, the one corresponding to the other. In Johnson's famous parallel we read: "The style of Dryden is capricious and varied, that of Pope is cautious and uniform; Dryden obeys the motions of his own mind, Pope constrains his mind to his own rules of composition. Dryden is sometimes vehement and rapid; Pope is always smooth, uniform, and gentle." A good style is apt to make use of all three kinds of sentences, which give an agreeable diversity to composition. The exclusive use of any one form produces monotony. In studying a writer's style, it is important to determine the prevailing type, as well as the average length, of his sentences.

This investigation will give us some insight into a source of his weakness or power, and furnish a basis of interesting comparison with others. Every sentence should have clearness, unity, harmony, and strength. Of these four qualities, clearness is the most important; for without it the purpose of discourse is defeated. Apart from the right choice and position of words, clearness is secured by unity of thought.

This requires that the main subject retain a dominant place throughout the sentence. The writer should not allow himself to be switched off from the main proposition. Harmony is attained by the choice of euphonious words, and by their arrangement in an agreeable or rhythmical order. Strength is secured, in large measure, by the omission of unnecessary words. The error of repeating the same thought in different words is called tautology, while the use of more words than are necessary is known as pleonasm or redundancy. The fault of redundancy is most likely to be found in the use of adjectives; and a chaste or classic style appears particularly in a severe self-restraint in the use of qualifying expressions.

- *Paragraph*. A paragraph consists of a group of sentences related in thought. It contains the discussion of a single phase of the subject. The nature of the paragraph determines its laws. The paragraph, like each sentence, should be characterized by unity. The opening sentence should contain the subject, or phase of the subject, to be discussed. The succeeding treatment should be cumulative in character, so that the reader is led on by a sense of the unfolding of the point under consideration. There are various ways of expanding or building up the paragraph. It may be expanded by a process of definition. Frequently one specification after another is given till all sides of the subject have been presented. Sometimes a general statement is followed by concrete and individual instances. Again, the development of the paragraph takes the form of proof or illustration. But whatever may be the form of development, it should grow in importance till the conclusion. The importance of paragraphing is often lost sight of by even experienced writers. Sometimes there is an absence of clear, definite thought. Hence it happens that we frequently find whole pages without any break to indicate the transitions of thought. Such writing is apt to leave a confused or obscure impression.

Words, Sentences, Paragraphs

- Why is the English language called composite? Which is the principal element? How was French introduced? What was the origin of our present English? Whence came the Latin element? Name some other elements and their sources. What is said of the copiousness of our language? of the history of words? Give illustrations.
- What per cent in daily use is Anglo-Saxon? What per cent is Latin? What proportion of the Latin element comes through the French? Which element is preferable? What classes of words are Anglo-Saxon? What per cent of Anglo-Saxon words is used by our best writers? How do you estimate the percentage?
- How is the purpose to use a single element of our language characterized? Contrast the sonnets of Alexander and Longfellow. What should determine the writer's choice of words?
- What did Aristotle say of diction? What is meant by diction? What qualities should diction have? What is said of the use of foreign words and phrases? What is a provincialism? Define archaism and neologism. What is Pope's rule in regard to them? What is said of the study of etymology? of synonyms? of the nice

use of words? What is meant by fine writing? Give an illustration.

- What is the difference in the sentences of recent and older writers? What is the gain in short predication? What is the rhetorical classification of sentences? Define loose, periodic, and balanced sentences. Illustrate. What is said of a good style? What four characteristics should a sentence have?
  Which is the most important? Why? What is meant by unity? How is harmony attained? How is strength or energy secured? Explain tautology and redundancy. By what is a classic style characterized?
  33. What is a paragraph? What should be its chief characteristic? What should the opening sentence do? How is the paragraph expanded or developed? What is the effect of bad paragraphing?

Illustrative and Practical Exercises

The following extracts should be tested by such questions as these:

- What percentage of the words is Anglo-Saxon? What percentage is Latin? From what sources are there other words? Is the diction pure, appropriate, and precise? Are there provincialisms, archaisms, neologisms? Are synonyms carefully discriminated? Is the diction high-flown? What proportion of sentences are simple? complex? compound? What proportion are loose? periodic? balanced? What is the average number of words? Are the sentences clear? Do they show unity of structure? Are they harmonious? Are they forcible? Can any words be omitted without loss? Is there tautology or redundancy? Are the paragraphs well built up? By what means are they developed?
- Yea, here they heard continually the singing of birds, and saw every day the flowers appear in the earth, and heard the voice of the turtle in the land. In this country the sun shineth night and day; wherefore this

was beyond the valley of the Shadow of Death, and also out of the reach of Giant Despair; neither could they from this place so much as see Doubting-Castle. Here they were within sight of the City they were going to: also here met them some of the inhabitants thereof; for in this land the shining ones commonly walked, because it was upon the borders of heaven.BUNYAN.

- God that made the world and all things therein, seeing that he is Lord of heaven and earth, dwelleth not in temples made with hands; neither is worshipped with men's hands, as though he needed any thing, seeing he giveth to all life, and breath, and all things; and hath made of one blood all nations of men for to dwell on all the face of the earth, and hath determined the times before appointed, and the bounds of their habitation; that they should seek the Lord, if haply they might feel after him, and find him, though he be not far from every one of us; for in him we live, and move, and have our being; as certain also of your own poets have said, for we are also his offspring.

PAUL.

Criticism, either didactic or defensive, occupies almost all his prose, except those pages which he has devoted to his patrons; but none of his prefaces were ever thought tedious.

They have not the formality of a settled style, in which the first half of the sentence betrays the other. The clauses are never balanced, nor the periods modeled; every word seems to drop by chance, though it falls into its proper place. Nothing is cold or languid; the whole is airy, animated, and vigorous; what is little, is gay; and what is great, is splendid. He may be thought to mention himself too frequently; but while he forces himself upon our esteem, we cannot refuse him to stand high in his own.

Everything is excused by the play of images and the spriteliness of expression. Though all is easy, nothing is feeble; though all seems careless, there is nothing harsh; and though, since his earlier works, more than a century has passed, they have nothing yet uncouth or obsolete.

SAMUEL JOHNSON.

The only accession which the Roman empire received, during the first century of the Christian era, was the province of Britain. In this single instance, the successors of Caesar and Augustus were persuaded to follow the example of the former, rather than the precept of the latter. The proximity of its situation to the coast of Gaul seemed to invite their arms; the pleasing though doubtful intelligence of a pearl fishery attracted their avarice; and as Britain was viewed in the light of a distinct and insulated world, the conquest scarcely formed any exception to the general system of continental measures. After a war of about forty years, undertaken by the most stupid, maintained by the most dissolute, and terminated by the most timid of all the emperors, the far greater part of the island submitted to the Roman yoke.

GIBBON.

A mob is a society of bodies voluntarily bereaving themselves of reason, and traversing its work. The mob is man voluntarily descending to the nature of the beast. Its fit hour of activity is night. Its actions are insane, like its whole constitution. It persecutes a principle; it would whip a right; it would tar and feather justice by inflicting fire and outrage upon the houses and persons of those who have these. It resembles the prank of boys who run with fire-engines to put out the ruddy aurora streaming to the stars. The inviolate spirit turns that spite against the wrong-doers.

The martyr cannot be dishonored. Every lash inflicted is a tongue of fame; every prison a more illustrious abode; every burned book or house enlightens the world; every suppressed or expunged word reverberates through the earth from side to side. Hours of sanity and consideration are always arriving to communities, as to individuals, when the truth is seen, and the martyrs are justified.

EMERSON.

I deny not but that it is of greatest concernment, in the Church and Commonwealth, to have a vigilant eye how books demean themselves, as well as men; and thereafter to confine, imprison, and do sharpest justice on them as malefactors. For books are not absolutely dead things, but do contain a potency of life in them to be as active as that soul was whose progeny they are; nay, they do preserve as in a vial the purest efficacy and extraction of that living intellect that bred them. I know they are as lively, and as vigorously productive, as those fabulous dragon's teeth; and, being sown up and down, may chance to spring up armed men. And yet, on the other hand, unless wariness be used, as good almost kill a man as kill a good book: who kills a man kills a reasonable creature, God's image; but he who destroys a good book kills reason itself, kills the image of God, as it were, in the eye. Many a man lives a burden to the earth; but a good book is the precious life-blood of a master-spirit, embalmed and treasured up on purpose to a life beyond life.

MILTON.

Thus the Puritan was made up of two different men, the one all self-abasement, penitence, gratitude, passion, the other proud, calm, inflexible, sagacious. He prostrated himself in the dust before his Maker; but he set his foot on the neck of his king. In his devotional retirement, he prayed with convulsions, and groans, and tears. He was half-maddened by glorious or terrible illusions. He heard the lyres of angels or the tempting whispers of fiends. He caught a gleam of the Beatific Vision, or woke screaming from dreams of everlasting fire. But when he took his seat in the council, or girt on his sword for war, these tempestuous workings of the soul had left no perceptible trace behind them. People who saw nothing of the godly but their uncouth visages, and who heard nothing from them but their groans and their whining hymns, might laugh at them. But those had little reason to laugh who encountered them in the hall of debate or in the field of battle.

MACAULAY.

More manifest still are the physiological benefits of emotional pleasures. Every power, bodily and mental, is increased by "good spirits," which is our name for a general emotional satisfaction. The truth that the fundamental vital actionsthose of nutritionare furthered by laughter-moving conversation, or rather by the pleasurable feeling causing laughter, is one of old standing; and every dyspeptic knows that in exhilarating company, a large and varied dinner, including not very digestible things, may be eaten with impunity, and, indeed, with benefit, while a small, carefully chosen dinner of simple things, eaten in solitude, will be followed by indigestion.

HERBERT SPENCER.

Chapter 5

Figures of Speech

- Definition. A figure of speech is a deviation from the plain and ordinary mode of speaking. Its object is greater effect. Figures originated, perhaps, in a limitation of vocabulary; and many words that are now regarded as plain were at first figurative. But the use of figures is natural, and at present they are used to embellish discourse and to give it greater vividness and force. To say with Thomson, for example, "But yonder comes the powerful King of day, Rejoicing in the east," is far more vivid and forceful than to say "the sun is rising." Nearly all great writers, especially poets, enrich their style by the use of figures.

  Kinds of Figures. There are various kinds of figures, which may be reduced, however, to three classes or groups. The figures based upon resemblance are simile, metaphor, personification, and allegory. Those founded on contiguity are metonymy, synecdoche, exclamation, hyperbole, apostrophe, and vision. Those resting upon contrast are antithesis, climax, epigram, and irony. Other forms of classification have been proposed. There are figures of diction and figures of thought; the former are found in the choice of words, the latter in the form of the sentence. To figures of diction has been given the name of figures of intuition, because they present a sensible image to the mind; to figures of thought has been given the name of figures of emphasis, because they emphasize the thought. We thus get the following division:

Figures of Speech

Simile
Metaphor
Personification
Allegory
Metonymy
Synecdoche
Apostrophe
Vision

Figures of Emphasis

Interrogation
Exclamation
Climax
Antithesis
Epigram
Irony
Hyperbole

- Figures of Resemblance.
  - Simile is a form of comparison in which one thing is likened to another. It is usually introduced by like or as, or some other word of comparison; as, "The twilight hours like birds flew by, As lightly and as free." It is obvious that the things compared in simile should have some sort of resemblance. When the points of resemblance are too remote the simile is said to be farfetched. This was a frequent mistake among the so-called "metaphysical poets" of the seventeenth century. Except in burlesque or mock-heroic styles, dignified subjects should not be likened to what is trifling or low. The effect of such a simile is ridiculous, as in the well-known lines from Butler's "Hudibras": "And, like a lobster boiled, the morn From black to red began to turn."
  - Metaphor is an abridged simile, the words expressing likeness being omitted. In the

sentence, "Roderick Dhu fought like a lion," we have a simile; but when we say, "He was a lion in the fight," we have a metaphor. The metaphor is briefer and more striking than the simile; it springs from greater emotion or mental energy, and often imparts great force or beauty to a passage. Thus, likening human life to a voyage at sea, Shakespeare says:

"There is a tide in the affairs of men,
Which, taken at the flood, leads on to fortune;
Omitted, all the voyage of their life
Is bound in shallows and in miseries."

There are several errors that are not infrequent in the use of metaphor. A metaphor should not be blended with plain language in the same sentence, nor should it be extended too far. The latter fault is called "straining the metaphor." Two incongruous metaphors should not be used in the same sentence. In the following lines from Addison his muse is first conceived of as a steed that needs to be restrained with a bridle, and then as a ship that is eager to be launched:

"I bridle in my struggling Muse with pain,
That longs to launch into a bolder strain."

— Personification is the attribution of life to inanimate things. When we speak of "the thirsty ground" or "the angry ocean," we endow these objects with the feelings of living creatures. Personification is a bold species of metaphor; it is the offspring of vivid feeling or conception, and often lifts discourse to a high plane. Thus, in "Romeo and Juliet," we read,

"Night's candles are burnt out, and jocund day
Stands tiptoe on the misty mountain tops";
and in Shelley's "Queen Mab,"
"How wonderful is Death,
Death and his brother Sleep!
One, pale as yonder waning moon,

With lips of lurid blue;
The other, rosy as the morn
When, throned on ocean's wave,
It blushes o'er the world:
Yet both so passing wonderful!"

— Allegory is the description of one object in terms of another. It is a sort of continued metaphor in which, however, the main subject of discourse is not mentioned. In the following beautiful allegory, the Jewish people are described in the character of a vine: "Thou hast brought a vine out of Egypt; thou hast cast out the heathen, and planted it. Thou preparedst room before it, and didst cause it to take deep root, and it filled the land. The hills were covered with the shadow of it, and the boughs thereof were like the goodly cedars. She sent out her boughs unto the sea, and her branches unto the river. Why hast thou then broken down her hedges, so that all they which pass by the way do pluck her? The boar out of the wood doth waste it, and the wild beast of the field doth devour it. Return, we beseech thee, O God of hosts; look down from heaven, and behold, and visit this vine; and the vineyard which thy right hand hath planted, and the branch that thou madest strong for thyself."

The parable and the fable are closely akin to allegory. A parable is a brief narrative of real or imaginary incidents for the purpose of inculcating some moral or religious truth. It has been described as "an earthly story with a heavenly meaning." A considerable part of Christ's teaching was in parables, many of which are as beautiful as they are profound. A fable is a fictitious story introducing animals or even inanimate things as rational speakers and actors, for the purpose of teaching or enforcing a moral. The fables of AEsop are almost universally known, and the fables of La Fontaine exhibit a high degree of artistic merit.

- Figures of Contiguity.
  - Metonymy consists in naming an object by one of its attributes or accompaniments. It is based, not on resemblance, but on relation, such as cause and effect, container and thing contained, material and thing made of it, etc. When we say, for example, that "gray hairs are venerable," we mean old age, putting an effect for the cause. In the sentence, "Socrates drank the fatal cup," the container is put for the thing contained, namely, the deadly hemlock. The general effect of metonymy is to bring before the mind a definite image, and thus to impart a graphic quality to the style. To say, "The pen is mightier than the sword," is more graphic and forcible than to say, "Literature is mightier than war."
  - Synecdoche puts a part for the whole, or a whole for the part; as, "The harbor was crowded with masts." Synecdoche is a species of metonymy, and has the same effect of giving vividness. This is apparent in a well-known quatrain from Goethe: "Who ne'er his bread in sorrow ate, Who ne'er the mournful midnight hours Weeping upon his bed has sate, He knows you not, ye heavenly Powers."
  - Exclamation is a figure of thought. It is the result of kindled emotion, and expresses in exclamatory form what would usually be stated in declarative form. Thus Hamlet, outraged at the conduct of his mother, bursts forth: "O that this too too solid flesh would melt, Thaw and resolve itself into a dew! Or that the Everlasting had not fixed His canon 'gainst self-slaughter! O God! God! How weary, stale, flat and unprofitable, Seem to me all the uses of this world!" Though chiefly confined to poetry, exclamation is frequent in fervid prose, and Carlyle's works fairly bristle with exclamation points.

— Apostrophe is a direct address to the absent as present, the inanimate as living, or the abstract as personal. It is closely allied to personification, with which it is often associated. This figure is expressive of intense emotion. The following passage from "King Lear" will serve for illustration: "Blow, winds, and crack your cheeks! rage! blow! You cataracts and hurricanoes, spout Till you have drench'd our steeples, drown'd the cocks! You sulphurous and thought-executing fires, Vaunt-couriers to oak-cleaving thunderbolts, Singe my white head! And thou, all-shaking thunder, Smite flat the thick rotundity o' the world!"

— Vision is a description of absent things as present. It is suited only to animated discourse in either prose or poetry. In the midst of the argument of Milton's "Areopagitica" we find this splendid outburst portraying the future of England: "Methinks I see in my mind a noble and puissant nation rousing herself like a strong man after sleep, and shaking her invincible locks; methinks I see her, as an eagle, mewing her mighty youth, and kindling her undazzled eyes at the full midday beam; purging and scaling her long abused sight at the fountain itself of heavenly radiance; while the whole noise of timorous and flocking birds, with those also that love the twilight, flutter about, amazed at what she means, and in their envious gabble would prognosticate a year of sects and schisms."

— Hyperbole is an exaggerated form of statement, and is used to magnify or diminish an object. It is quite natural, under the impulse of strong emotion or imagination, to use exaggerated statements, and frequently it serves to lend piquancy and force to style. But this tendency is dangerous, and should be kept under restraint. As a rule it is best to see and describe things as they are. The following from "Julius Caesar" will serve as an example of hyperbole: "Why, man, he doth bestride the narrow world Like a Colossus, and we petty men Walk under his huge legs and peep about To find ourselves dishonorable graves."

- Figures of Contrast.
  - Antithesis presents a strong contrast of words or sentiments, usually in the form of balanced sentences. It gives force to style by uniting opposite things in one conception. Its excessive use, however, becomes monotonous; and antithesis in construction, without a real contrast of thought, is confusing and disagreeable. Macaulay, perhaps, makes more frequent use of antithesis than any other of our great modern writers. Of the Puritans he says: "If they were unacquainted with the works of philosophers and poets, they were deeply read in the oracles of God; if their names were not found in the registers of heralds, they felt assured that they were recorded in the Book of Life; if their steps were not accompanied by a splendid train of menials, legions of ministering angels had charge over them."
  - Climax arranges its words, phrases, or clauses in an order of increasing impressiveness. Its proper use gives an accumulative force to the sentence. No better illustration of the climax can be given than the well-known one in Cicero's oration against Verres: "To bind a Roman citizen is an outrage; to scourge him is an atrocious crime; to put him to death is almost parricide; but to crucify himwhat shall I call it?" The arrangement of the words or clauses in a descending order is called anticlimax or bathos.

It is frequently used in wit and humour. The following sentence is a ridiculous anticlimax: "The enemy is now hovering upon our borders, preparing to press the knife to our throats, to devastate our fields, to quarter themselves in our houses, and to devour our poultry." The principle of the climax is of wide application. Not only in the sentence but also in the paragraph, chapter, and entire work, there should be, as far as possible, progress in the importance, intensity, or amplitude of the thought.

— Interrogation strengthens an affirmation or denial by throwing it into the form of a question. It is a figure frequent in poetry and emotional prose. The following example from Gray's "Elegy" will be sufficient for illustration: "Can storied urn or animated bust Back to its mansion call the fleeting breath? Can Honor's voice provoke the silent dust, Or Flattery soothe the dull cold ear of death?" These questions are not asked for information, but for rhetorical effect, and they forcibly suggest the truth of their negation.

— Epigram is the pungent phrasing of a shrewd observation. It may be recognized by two characteristics,it must be brief, and it must have an unexpected turn of thought. This turn of thought may spring from an apparent contradiction, from the solemn assertion of a truism, from a play on words, or from other sources. There is an apparent contradiction in Wordsworth's epigrammatic line, "The child is father of the man." There is a play on words in the following epigrammatic characterization of a loud and violent speaker: "He mistakes perspiration for inspiration."

— Irony expresses a thought contrary to the form

of words. Its seeming praise is really condemnation; its compliments are insults. Its advantage lies in the difficulty its victim experiences in making a reply. It is useful in chastising follies and vices; but as a rule ironic touches are to be preferred to continuous irony. The following is from Thackeray: "So was Helen of Greece innocent. She never ran away with Paris, the dangerous young Trojan. Menelaus, her husband, ill-used her; and there never was any siege of Troy at all. So was Bluebeard's wife innocent. She never peeped into the closet where the other wives were with their heads off. She never dropped the key, or stained it with blood; and her brothers were quite right in finishing Bluebeard, the cowardly brute! Yes, Madam Laffarge never poisoned her husband, and Mary of Scotland never blew up hers; and Eve never took the appleit was a cowardly fabrication of the serpent's."

Review Questions

- What is a figure? How did it originate? What is its object? In what two ways is it used? Illustrate. 35. To how many classes may figures be reduced? On what are these several groups based? Name the figures based on resemblance; those based on contiguity; on contrast. What name is given to figures of diction? to figures of thought? State the figures of intuition; of emphasis.
- What is a simile? How is it introduced? Give an illustration. What errors should be avoided in the use of simile? What is a metaphor? What is its effect as compared with a simile? What errors in the use of metaphor are to be avoided? What is mixed metaphor? Illustrate. What is personification? Give an example. What is allegory? Illustrate. What is a parable? Give an example. What is a fable?

- What is metonymy? On what is it based? Illustrate. What is its effect on style? What is synecdoche? Illustrate. What is exclamation? Illustrate. What is apostrophe? To what is it closely related? Illustrate. What is vision? Illustrate. What is hyperbole? Give an example. What is said of the use of hyperbole?
- What is antithesis? What is said of its use? Give an example. What is climax? Give an illustration. What is bathos? Illustrate. What is interrogation? Illustrate. What is epigram? How recognized? Illustrate. What is irony? What is said of its use? Illustrate.

Illustrative and Practical Exercises

The following passages should be studied in the light of such questions as these:

What figure or figures does the piece contain? Is it a figure of resemblance, contiguity, or contrast? Is it a figure of diction or of thought? What is its effect? Does it give force or beauty to the sentence? How would the thought be expressed in plain language? Is it used consistently? In what way does it strengthen or weaken the sentence? Is the figure trite or original? Is it farfetched or natural? What percentage of sentences is figurative? Are figures more common in prose or poetry? Why?

Do the minor or the major poets use more figures?

What stronger breast-plate than a heart untainted?
Thrice is he armed that hath his quarrel just;
And he but naked though locked up in steel
Whose conscience with injustice is corrupted.

SHAKESPEARE.

Hast thou left thy blue course in heaven, golden-haired son of the sky? The west hath opened its gates; the bed of thy repose is there. The waves gather to behold thy beauty; they lift their trembling heads; they see thee lovely in thy sleep; but they shrink away with fear. Rest in thy shadowy cave, O Sun! and let thy return be in joy.

MACPHERSON.

I see before me the Gladiator lie;

He leans upon his hand; his manly brow
Consents to death, but conquers agony,
And his drooped head sinks gradually low;
And through his side the last drops, ebbing slow
From the red gash, fall heavy, one by one,
Like the first of a thunder-shower; and now
The arena swims around him; he is gone,
Ere ceased the inhuman shout which hailed the wretch who won.

BYRON.

If a man indulges himself in murder, very soon he comes to think little of robbing; and from robbing he comes next to drinking and Sabbath-breaking, and from that to incivility and procrastination.

DE QUINCEY.

Assemble all the poor men of your sort;
Draw them to Tiber banks and weep your tears
Into the channel, till the lowest stream
Do kiss the most exalted shores of all.SHAKESPEARE.

No doubt but ye are the people, and wisdom shall die withyou.JOB.

The Assyrian came down like the wolf on the fold,
And his cohorts were gleaming in purple and gold;
And the sheen of their spears was like stars on the sea,
When the blue wave rolls nightly on deep Galilee.BYRON.

The best of men
That e'er wore earth about him was a sufferer,
The first true gentleman that ever breathed.DEKKER.

The glories of our birth and state
Are shadows, not substantial things;
There is no armor against fate;
Death lays his icy hand on kings.
Scepter and crown
Must tumble down,
And in the dust be equal made
With the poor crooked scythe and spade.SHIRLEY.

What a piece of work is man! how noble in reason!
how infinite in faculty! in form and moving how

express and admirable! in action how like an angel!
in apprehension how like a god! the
beauty of this world! the paragon of animals! And yet,
to me, what is this quintessence of dust?
man delights not me; no, nor woman neither,
though by your smiling you seem to say
so.SHAKESPEARE.

Great lords, wise men ne'er sit and wail their loss,
But cheerly seek how to redress their harms.
What though the mast be now thrown overboard,
The cable broke, the holding anchor lost,
And half our sailors swallowed in the flood?
Yet lives our pilot still. Is 't meet that he
Should leave the helm, and, like a fearful lad,
With tearful eyes, add water to the sea,
And give more strength to that which hath too much,
While in his moan the ship splits on the rock,
Which industry and courage might have saved?
Ah, what a shame! ah, what a fault were this!
SHAKESPEARE.

The unwonted lines which momentary passion had ruled in Mr. Pickwick's clear and open brow gradually melted away, as his young friend spoke, like the marks of a black lead pencil beneath the softening influence of India rubber.

DICKENS.

When thus, as I may say, before the use of the loadstone, or knowledge of the compass, I was sailing in a vast ocean, without other help than the pole-star of the ancients, and the rules of the French stage among the moderns.DRYDEN.

Once as I told in glee
Tales of the stormy sea,
Soft eyes did gaze on me,
Burning but tender;
And as the white stars shine
On the dark Norway pine,
On that dark heart of mine
Fell their soft splendor.
LONGFELLOW.

Since the vessel of thy unbounded ambition hath been wrecked in the gulf of thy self-love, it would be proper that thou shouldst take in the sails of thy temerity, and cast the anchor of repentance in the port of sincerity and justice, which is the port of safety; lest the tempest of our vengeance make thee perish in the sea of the punishment thou deservest.

ANON.

She never told her love,
But let concealment, like a worm in the bud,
Feed on her damask cheek; she pined in thought;
And, with a green and yellow melancholy,
She sat like Patience on a monument,
Smiling at grief.SHAKESPEARE.

England ne'er had a king until his time;
Virtue he had, deserving to command;
His brandished sword did blind men with its beams;
His arms spread wider than a dragon's wings;
His sparkling eyes, replete with awful fire,
More dazzled, and drove back his enemies,
Than midday sun fierce beat against their faces.
What should I say? his deeds exceed all speech;
He never lifted up his hand, but conquered.

SHAKESPEARE.

Earth proudly wears the Parthenon,
As the best gem upon her zone,
And Morning opes with haste her lids
To gaze upon the Pyramids;
O'er England's abbeys bends the sky,
As on its friends, with kindred eye;
For out of Thought's interior sphere
Those wonders rose to upper air;
And Nature gladly gave them place,
Adopted them into her race,
And granted them an equal date
With Andes and with Ararat.EMERSON.

NOTE

In addition to the extracts here given, the student might examine those connected with previous chapters, and discover the various figures they contain. Furthermore, it is recommended that he study the figures in a whole piece; as Milton's "L'Allegro" or "Il Penseroso," Goldsmith's "Deserted Village," Gray's "Elegy," Burns's "Cotter's Saturday Night," Wordsworth's "Ode on Intimations of Immortality," Coleridge's "Ancient Mariner," Moore's "Paradise and the Peri," Shelley's "Adonais," Tennyson's "Passing of Arthur," Longfellow's "Building of the Ship," Lowell's "Vision of Sir Launfal," and many others that will occur to the teacher. Let him determine the percentage of figurative sentences, and compare the results with those obtained from an examination of the prose of Macaulay, Ruskin, Carlyle, De Quincey, Lowell, and other standard writers. This comparison will throw light on the essential difference between poetry and prose.

Chapter 6

Style

- Definition. Style means an author's mode of expression. It is not, as is sometimes supposed, an artificial trick, but a genuine expression of the mind and character. Buffon had the right idea when he said, "The style is the man." It derives its leading characteristics from the intellect, culture, and character of the writer. A man of independent force and integrity gives natural expression to his personality. His style reveals his mental and moral qualities. Only weaklings, who are afraid to be natural and who are destitute of substantial worth, become conscious imitators or affect artificial peculiarities. We have already considered style as related to diction, different kinds of sentences, and figures of speech. It remains to consider it, first, in relation to the various kinds of discourse, and, secondly, to the generic types of mind.
- Kinds of Discourse. There are four generic kinds of discourse, namely, description, narration, exposition, and argument. Though frequently united in the same work, or even in the same paragraph, they are yet clearly distinguishable. Each has a well-defined purpose and method, to which the mode of expression is naturally bent or adapted. The result is what may be called a descriptive, narrative, expository, or argumentative style. These different kinds of discourse will now be considered and illustrated in greater detail.

— Description is the portrayal of an object by means of language. The object described may belong either to the material or the spiritual world. It may be a single flower, a landscape, or a stellar system. The purpose of description is to enable the reader to reproduce the scene, object, or experience in his own imagination. In general there are two kinds of description,the objective and the subjective; but the laws of both are the same. There must be a judicious selection and grouping of the details, and their number must be so restricted as not to produce confusion. Objective description portrays objects as they exist in the external world. It points out in succession their distinguishing features. Thus we read in Wordsworth's "A Night Piece,"

"The traveller looks upthe clouds are split
Asunderand above his head he sees
The clear moon, and the glory of the heavens.
There, in a black-blue vault she sails along,
Followed by multitudes of stars, that, small
And sharp, and bright, along the dark abyss
Drive as she drives; how fast they wheel away,
Yet vanish not!the wind is in the tree,
But they are silent;still they roll along
Immeasurably distant; and the vault

— Built round by those white clouds, enormous clouds." Subjective description notes the effects produced by an external object or scene on the mind and heart. The eye of the writer is turned inward rather than outward; he brings before us the thoughts, feelings, fancies that are started within his soul. Thus Browning speaks of music in his early poem, "Pauline": "For music (which is earnest of a heaven, Seeing we know emotions strange by it, Not else to be revealed) is as a voice, A low voice calling fancy, as a friend, To the green woods in the gay summer time; And she fills all the way with dancing shapes Which have made painters pale, and they go on, While stars look at them and winds call to them, As they leave life's path for the twilight world *Where the dead gather."*

— Narration is a recital of incidents or events in an orderly sequence. It is closely related to description, with which it is frequently joined in the same paragraph. The one is used to aid or supplement the other. Like description, narration has its place in nearly every form of composition; and in history, fiction, and epic poetry it constitutes, perhaps, the body of discourse. The incidents narrated should be selected according to their interest and importance; they should usually be presented in their chronological order, and there should be a perceptible and often a rapid movement toward a definite end. In all artistic narration we find unity, proportion, and completeness. The following extract from Addison's "Vision of Mirza" will serve for illustration: "On the fifth day of the moonwhich, according to the custom of my forefathers, I always keep holyafter having washed myself and offered up my morning devotions, I ascended the high hills of Bagdat, in order to pass the rest of the day in meditation and prayer. As I was here airing myself on the tops of the mountains, I fell into a profound contemplation on the vanity of human life; and, passing from one thought to another, 'Surely,' said I, 'man is but a shadow, and life a dream.'"

— Exposition explains the nature or meaning of things. The purpose of description is to form a picture; of narration, to portray an event; of exposition, to set forth the distinctive nature of an object or conception. The methods of exposition are various. In the first place, the distinguishing features of an object may be presented; and in this case exposition partakes of the nature of description. In the second place, an object or idea may be explained by pointing out its effects; and in this case exposition partakes of the character of narration. In the third place, we may explain or define an object or conception by indicating its resemblance or its unlikeness to something else that is known. But whatever method of exposition is adopted, it should be full and definite enough to impart a clear idea of the thing explained. Every text-book will furnish examples of exposition; the following is taken from Hitchcock's "Geology": "A volcano is an opening in the earth from whence matter has been ejected by heat, in the form of lava, scoria, or ashes. Usually the opening called the crater is an inverted cone; and around it there rises a mountain in the form of a cone, with its apex truncated, produced by the elevation of the earth's crust and the ejection of lava."

— Argumentation is the process of establishing the truth or falsity of a thing. The means it uses is called proof or evidence, and will be considered more fully in a subsequent chapter treating of oratory. This proof or evidence may be derived from principles originating in the mind, in which case it is called intuitive; or it may be found in external sources, in which case it is called empirical. The latter includes, among other forms of proof, a statement of facts, a consideration of the nature or circumstances of the case, the testimony of eyewitnesses, and an appeal to authority or generally accepted principles. When the argument is attended with an appeal to the feelings and will, it is known as persuasion. In the following extract, note the three facts adduced by Mark Antony to prove that Caesar was not ambitious. "He was my friend, faithful and just to me: But Brutus says he was ambitious; And Brutus is an honorable man. He hath brought many captives home to Rome, Whose ransoms did the general coffers fill: Did this in Caesar seem ambitious? When that the poor have cried, Caesar hath wept: Ambition should be made of sterner stuff.You all did see that on the Lupercal I thrice presented him a kingly crown, Which he did thrice refuse: was this ambition?"

- Generic Differences of Mind. As we have just seen, style is affected in a measure by the species of discourse. It is determined, further, by the mental constitution of the writer, and varies according to the dominance of particular faculties. We may distinguish four generic types of mind, which are reflected in four fundamental differences of style.
  - When the logical faculties of the mind predominate, the style will be simple, direct, and plain. It is apt to be dry. The following extract from Locke's "Thoughts on Education" will serve for illustration: "I say this, that, when you consider of the breeding of your son, and are looking out for a schoolmaster, or a tutor, you would not have (as is usual) Latin and logic only in your thoughts. Learning must be had, but in the second place, as subservient only to greater qualities. Seek out somebody that may know how discreetly to frame his manners; place him in hands, where you may, as much as possible, secure his innocence, cherish and nurse up the good, and gently correct and weed out any bad inclinations, and settle in him good habits. This is the main point; and, this being provided for, learning may be had into the bargain."

— Again, the imagination may predominate. In this case the writer is continually leaving the main thought to bring in additional and embellishing ideas, particularly if he is a man of wide experience or great learning. The result is apt to be an elaborate or stately style. Lowell's style is eminently characterized by a play of the imagination. His essay on Spenser begins as follows: "Chaucer had been in his grave one hundred and fifty years ere England had secreted choice material enough for the making of another great poet. The nature of men living together in societies, as of the individual man, seems to have its periodic ebbs and floods, its oscillations between the ideal and the matter-of-fact, so that the doubtful boundary line of shore between them is in one generation a hard sandy actuality strewn only with such remembrances of beauty as a dead sea-moss here and there, and in the next is whelmed with those lacelike curves of ever-gaining, ever-receding foam, and that dance of joyous spray which for a moment catches and holds the sunshine." When the imagination is ill-governed, and especially in the case of inexperienced writers, the resulting style is apt to be florid or bombastic. The following passage from Headley's "Sacred Mountains," connected with a description of the crucifixion, is imaginative extravagance,a vain, artificial effort at the sublime: "I know not but all the radiant ranks on high, and even Gabriel himself, turned with the deepest solicitude to the Father's face, to see if He was calm and untroubled amid it all. I know not but His composed brow and serene majesty were all that restrained Heaven from one universal shriek of horror when they heard groans on

Calvarydying groans. I know not but they thought God had given His glory to another, but one thing I do know, that when they saw through the vast design, comprehended the stupendous scene, the hills of God shook to a shout that never before rang over their bright tops, and the crystal sea trembled to a song that had never before stirred its bright depths, and the 'Glory to God in the Highest' was a sevenfold chorus of hallelujahs and harping symphonies." Thoughtful writers of refined taste are more reserved and reverent in speaking of occurrences in the celestial world.

— Again, the sensibilities may be in the ascendant. There is then a quick and full response to the beauties of nature and human life. The style becomes warm, graphic, glowing, pictorial. Unless held in check by intellectual culture, an excess of sensibility is likely to degenerate into sentimentalism. When combined with judgment and imagination, as in the case of Ruskin, an emotional temperament yields admirable results. Take the following splendid passage from "Modern Painters," descriptive of a sunrise in the Alps: "Wait for one hour, until the east again becomes purple, and the heaving mountains, rolling against the darkness, like waves of a wild sea, are drowned one by one in the glory of its burning; watch the white glaciers blaze in their winding paths about the mountains, like mighty serpents with scales of fire; watch the columnar peaks of solitary snow, kindling downwards, chasm by chasm, each in itself a new morning; their long avalanches cast down in keen streams brighter than the lightning, sending each its tribute of driven snow, like altar-smoke, up to the heaven; the rose-light of their silent domes flushing that heaven about them and above them, piercing with purer light through its purple lines of lifted cloud, casting a new glory on every wreath as it passes by, until the whole heavenone scarlet canopyis interwoven with a roof of waving flame, and tossing, vault beyond vault, as with the drifted wings of many companies of angels; and then, when you can look no more for gladness, and when you are bowed down with fear and love of the Maker and Doer of this, tell me who has best delivered this His message unto men!"

Once more, force of will, firmness of conviction, energy of character are conducive to strength. Where these exist there will be directness of aim, and the style will be clear, unwavering, and strong. There will be positiveness of statement, and sometimes intolerant dogmatism. Carlyle and Macaulay are among our strongest writers, the former being rugged, and the latter more polished in his strength. Macaulay's broad-shouldered, stout-limbed constitution is reflected in such passages as the following from his essay on Lord Bacon: "The moral qualities of Bacon were not of a high order. We do not say that he was a bad man. He was not inhuman or tyrannical. He bore with meekness his high civil honors, and the far higher honors gained by his intellect. He was very seldom, if ever, provoked into treating any person with malignity and insolence. No man more readily held up the left cheek to those who had smitten the right. No man was more expert at the soft answer which turneth away wrath. His faults werewe write it with paincoldness of heart and meanness of spirit. He seems to have been incapable of feeling strong affection, of facing great dangers, of making great sacrifices. His desires were set on things below. Wealth,

> precedence, titles, patronage, the mace, the seals, the coronet, large houses, fair gardens, rich manors, massive services of plate, gay hangings, curious cabinets, had as great attractions for him as for any of the courtiers who dropped on their knees in the dirt when Elizabeth passed, and then hastened home to write to the King of Scots that her Grace seemed to be breaking fast."

- Symmetrical Faculties. When the mental faculties are symmetrical and harmonious in their operation, no particular feature of style may stand out prominent. It will bend to suit the exigencies of the subject. It will rise and sink with the varying thought and feeling. It will be judicious, and at times commonplace. But if, at the same time, mental symmetry is united with fineness of fibre and with adequate culture and practice, the style will probably be, as in the case of Addison and Irving, full of grace and elegance. Note the easy grace with which Addison begins his first paper on the "Pleasures of the Imagination": "Our sight is the most perfect and most delightful of all our senses. It fills the mind with the largest variety of ideas, converses with its objects at the greatest distance, and continues longest in action without being tired or satiated with its proper enjoyments. The sense of feeling can indeed give us a notion of extension, shape, and all other ideas that enter at the eye, except colors; but at the same time it is very much strained, and confined in its operations, to the number, bulk, and distance of its particular objects. Our sight seems designed to supply all these defects, and may be considered as a more delicate and diffusive kind of touch, that spreads itself over an infinite multitude of bodies, comprehends the largest figures, and brings into our reach some of the most remote parts of the universe." Every passing mood and every peculiarity of mind or character are reflected in the style. It may be gay, humorous, serious, sad, melancholy, according to the state of the writer's feelings. It may be colloquial or stately, concise or diffuse, plain or florid, flowing or abrupt, feeble or energetic, natural or affected, commonplace or epigrammatic,as varied, in fact, as the character and mental constitution of the writers. But every writer has a prevailing style; and it is an interesting study to determine the nature of his mind and character from his works.

- Importance of Style. A good style is a matter of importance. The success or failure of a literary work depends largely upon the manner in which its statements are presented. The classic works of Greece and Rome owe their popularity and influence not so much to the facts which they contain as to the art with which their contents are given. Our most popular English writings, especially in fiction and poetry, owe their vogue, in no small degree, to some excellence or charm of style. It is chiefly in history, science, and philosophy that the weight of fact and thought may be in a measure independent of style. Darwin's "Origin of Species" would be a great book even if its style were far more uninteresting than is really the case.

Review Questions

- What is style? Whence does it derive its characteristics? What is Buffon's remark? Who become imitators? 40. What four general kinds of discourse are there? To what four kinds of style do they lead? What is description? What is its purpose? What two kinds of description are there? Illustrate. What is narration? How is it related to description? Where is it dominant?

  How should its facts be presented? What is necessary in artistic narration? Illustrate. What is exposition? How does it differ from description and narration? What three kinds of exposition are mentioned? What constitutes a good exposition? Illustrate. What is argumentation? What means does it use? What two kinds of proof are mentioned? What may constitute empirical proof? Illustrate.

- What further determines style? What four generic types of mind are there? What is the result when the logical faculties are dominant? What is the effect of a dominant imagination? What author is quoted in illustration? When the imagination is ill-regulated, what is the result? What illustration is given? What is the effect of strong sensibilities? Into what may sentiment degenerate? What is the result when combined with judgment and imagination? Who is quoted in illustration? What is the effect of will power? Who are mentioned as strong writers?
- What is said of symmetrical faculties? What will be the result when united with delicacy and culture? Who are mentioned in illustration? What may be reflected in style? What kinds of style thus result? Why has every writer a distinctive style?
- Why is a good style important? To what do many writings, ancient and modern, owe their popularity?

Illustrative And Practical Exercises

The following extracts should be carefully studied. The diction, forms of sentences, and figures, as presented in the two preceding chapters, may be investigated along with the further elements of style just considered. Such questions as the following may be applied to the selections:

What kind of discourse is it? Is it descriptive? Is it objective or subjective? What points are described? Is it narrative? Is it expository? By what means is the elucidation made? Is it argumentative? What kind of proof is used? Is the thought the chief concern of the writer? Is the piece imaginative? Does it abound in adjectives? Does it present pictures? Is it stately and in full dress? What faculty predominates? Does it glow with feeling? Does it reach the point of sentimentalism? Does it show a love of nature? of humanity? Do the emotions count for more than the thought? Is it energetic or vehement? Has the writer positive convictions? Is he hesitating or dogmatic? Is it graceful or elegant? Does it exhibit eccentricity or sanity? Is it smooth, abrupt, laconic, epigrammatic, humorous, colloquial? Are there other characteristics?

Long lines of cliff breaking have left a chasm;
And in the chasm are foam and yellow sands;
Beyond, red roofs about a narrow wharf
In cluster; then a mouldered church; and higher
A long street climbs to one tall-towered mill;
And high in heaven behind it a gray down
With Danish barrows; and a hazel-wood,
By autumn nutters haunted, flourishes
Green in a cuplike hollow of the down.

TENNYSON.

The Normans gave way. The English pressed forward. A cry went forth among the Norman troops that Duke William was killed. Duke William took off his helmet, in order that his face might be distinctly seen, and rode along the line before his men. This gave them courage. As they turned again to face the English, some of the Norman horse divided the pursuing body of the English from the rest, and thus all that foremost portion of the English army fell, fighting bravely.

DICKENS.

Poetry of late has been termed a force, or mode of force, very much as if it were the heat, or light, or motion known to physics. And, in truth, ages before our era of scientific reductions, the energiathe vital energyof the minstrel's song was undisputed. It seems to me, in spite of all we hear about materialism, that the sentiment imparting this energythe poetic impulse, at leasthas seldom been more forceful than at this moment.

STEDMAN.

How inexhaustibly the spirit grows!
One object, she seemed erewhile born to reach

With her whole energies and die content,
So like a wall at the world's edge it stood,
With nought beyond to live for,is that reached?
Already are new undreamed energies
Outgrowing under, and extending farther
To a new object; there's another world!BROWNING.

I have heard that nothing gives an author so great pleasure as to find his works respectfully quoted by other learned authors. This pleasure I have seldom enjoyed; for though I have been, if I may say it without vanity, an eminent author (of almanacs) annually, now a full quarter of a century, my brother authors in the same way (for what reason I know not) have ever been very sparing in their applauses; and no other author has taken the least notice of me: so that, did not my writings produce me some solid pudding, the great deficiency of praise would have quite discouraged me.

FRANKLIN.

Studies serve for delight, for ornament, and for ability. Their chief use for delight is in privateness and retiring; for ornament, is in discourse; and for ability, is in the judgment and disposition of business; for expert men can execute, and perhaps judge of particulars, one by one; but the general counsels, and the plots and marshalling of affairs, come best from those that are learned. To spend too much time in studies, is sloth; to use them too much for ornament, is affectation; to make judgment wholly by their rules, is the humour of a scholar: they perfect nature, and are perfected by experience; for natural abilities are like natural plants, that need pruning by study; and studies themselves do give forth directions too much at large except they be bounded in by experience. BACON.

We want the same glorious privileges which we enjoy to go down to our children. We cannot sleep well the last sleep, nor will the pillow of dust be easy to our heads until we are assured that the God of our American institutions in the past, will be the God of our American institutions in the days that are to come. Oh, when all the rivers which empty into the Atlantic and Pacific seas shall pull on factory bands, when all the great mines of gold, and silver, and iron, and coal shall be laid bare for the nation, when the last swamp shall be reclaimed, and the last jungle cleared, and the last American desert Edenized, and from sea to sea the continent shall be occupied by more than twelve hundred million souls, may it be found that moral and religious influences were multiplied in more rapid ratio than the population. And then there shall be four doxologies coming from north, and south, and east, and westfour doxologies rolling toward each other and meeting mid-continent with such dash of holy joy that they shall mount to the throne.

TALMAGE.

Books! 'tis a dull and endless strife:
Come, hear the woodland linnet,
How sweet his music! on my life,
There's more of wisdom in it.
And hark! how blithe the throstle sings!
He, too, is no mean preacher;
Come forth into the light of things,
Let Nature be your teacher.WORDSWORTH.

She is sensible of my sufferings. This morning her look pierced to my very soul. I found her alone, and she was silent; she steadfastly surveyed me. I no longer saw in her face the charm of beauty or the fire of genius; these had disappeared. But I was affected by an expression much more touching, a look of the deepest sympathy and of the softest pity. Why was I afraid to throw myself at her feet? Why did I not dare to take her in my arms, and answer her by a thousand kisses? She had recourse to her piano for relief, and in a low and sweet voice accompanied the music with delicious sounds.

Her lips never appeared so lovely; they seemed but just to open, that they might imbibe the sweet tones which issued from the instrument, and return the heavenly vibration from her lovely mouth. Oh! who can express my sensations? I was quiteovercome, and, bending down, pronounced this vow: "Beautiful lips, which the angels guard, never will I seek to profane your purity with a kiss."

GOETHE.

The only happiness a brave man ever troubled himself with asking much about was happiness enough to get his work done. Not "I can't eat!" but "I can't work!" that was the burden of all wise complaining among men. It is, after all, the one unhappiness of a man. That he cannot work; that he cannot get his destiny as a man fulfilled. Behold, the day is passing swiftly over, our life is passing swiftly over; and the night cometh, wherein no man can work. The night once come, our happiness, our unhappiness,it is all abolished; vanished, clean gone; a thing that has been: not of the slightest consequence whether we were as happy as eupeptic Curtis, as the fattest pig of Epicurus, or unhappy as Job with potsherds, as musical Byron with Giaours and sensibilities of the heart. But our work,behold, that is not abolished, that has not vanished: our work, behold, it remains, or the want of it remains; for endless Times and Eternities, remains; and that is now the sole question with us forevermore.CARLYLE. Among the powers in man which suffer by this too intense life of the social instincts, none suffers more than the power of dreaming. Let no man think this a trifle. The machinery for dreaming planted in the human brain was not planted for nothing. That faculty, in alliance with the mystery of darkness, is the one great tube through which man communicates with the shadowy. And the dreaming organ, in connection with the heart, the eye, and the ear, composes the magnificent apparatus which forces the infinite into the chambers of a human brain, and throws dark reflections from eternities below all life upon the mirrors of the sleeping mind.

DE QUINCEY.

Thus with the year
Seasons return; but not to me returns
Day, or the sweet approach of even or morn
Or sight of vernal bloom, or summer's rose,
Or flocks, or herds, or human face divine;
But cloud instead and ever-during dark
Surrounds me, from the cheerful ways of men
Cut off, and, for the book of knowledge fair,
Presented with a universal blank

Of Nature's works, to me expunged and rased,
And wisdom at one entrance quite shut out.
MILTON.

It happened one day, about noon, going towards my boat, I was exceedingly surprised with the print of a man's naked foot on the shore, which was very plain to be seen in the sand. I stood like one thunder-struck, or as if I had seen an apparition. I listened, I looked around me, I could hear nothing, nor see anything. I went up to a rising ground to look farther. I went up the shore, and down the shore, but it was all one, I could see no other impressions but that one. I went to it again to see if there were any more, and to observe if it might not be my fancy; but there was no room for that, for there was exactly the very print of a foot, toes, heel, and every part of a foot. How it came thither I knew not, nor could in the least imagine.

DEFOE.

NOTE

It would be well to apply the critical principles of this chapter, and indeed of the entire Part Second, to some brief but complete work. For this purpose the teacher might assign Macaulay's "Essay on Milton," De Quincey's "Joan of Arc," Tennyson's "Enoch Arden," Webster's "First Bunker Hill Oration," or some other similar work. After determining the diction, prevailing type of sentences, and figures of speech, let the student divide the work, as far as possible, into its descriptive, narrative, expository, argumentative, and persuasive portions. In many cases the various kinds of discourse will be so interwoven that the classification will be doubtful and difficult. At the same time the student might point out the passages in which thought, imagination, feeling, or energy of will predominates in a marked degree. The effort should be made accurately to characterize the author's style as a whole.

PART THIRD KINDS OF LITERATURE

Chapter 7

Nature and Structure of Poetry

- Definition. We may approximately define poetry as the metrical expression of lofty or beautiful thought, feeling, or action, in imaginative and artistic form. Its metrical character distinguishes it from prose; for there is no such thing as prose poetry, though we sometimes find, as in the best passages of Ruskin, poetical prose.

  Its aesthetic idea or content, its exquisite diction, and its artistic form distinguish genuine poetry from mere verse, which is the mechanical or unartistic expression of commonplace thought, feeling, or incident. Poetry is, in large measure, a product of the creative imagination; and in its highest forms there must be energy of passion, intensity yet delicacy of feeling, loftiness of thought, depth and clearness of intuitive vision. It is the metrical expression of an exaltation of soul, which sometimes suffuses the objects of nature and the scenes of human life with a beauty and glory of its own, "The light that never was on sea or land, The consecration and the poet's dream."
- Poetry and Prose. Poetry occupies a region above prose. While prose in its highest flights approaches the plane of poetry, and poetry in its lowest descent touches the level of prose, they are yet essentially different. The one is commonplace, the other elevated or ideal. This truth is brought out clearly when we compare the same fact or incident of history as

related in poetry and prose. The "AEneid" is very unlike a prose account of the founding of Rome. We sometimes say in plain prose, "The evening passed pleasantly and quickly"; but when the poet describes it, there is an elevation of thought and glow of feeling that make it ideal:

"The twilight hours like birds flew by,
As lightly and as free;
Ten thousand stars were in the sky,
Ten thousand in the sea.
For every wave with dimpled face
That leaped upon the air,
Had caught a star in its embrace,
And held it trembling there."

- Sources of Poetry. Nature is filled with poetry. The great poet is God, and he has filled the universe with rhythm, harmony, beauty. Human poems are but faulty shells gathered on the shore of the divine ocean of poetry. The stars are the poetry of the skies. The planets and stellar systems that circle in their glorious orbits preserve a sublime harmony of movement. The light that reaches us from distant worlds comes to us in rhythmical wavelets. Every human life is a poem,often an amusing comedy, but still oftener a moving tragedy.

The tender friendships, the innocent joys, the noble aspirations, the high achievements of men, form the lyric poetry of human existence. The rippling of the forest stream within its shady banks of fern, the rhythmical roll and heavy roar of the ocean surges, are the poetry of the sparkling waters. The audible silence and mysterious whisperings of the dark and majestic forest, the modest hiding of the little violet that gives charm to some neglected spot,this is the poetry of the woods and fields. Whether we look upon earth, or air, or sky, we may be sure that the unwritten poetry of God is there. In our best moments we feel its presence,its mute yet eloquent appeal to our higher natures. It lifts us up into fellowship with Him who thus speaks to us.

- The Poet. When material interests dominate the life of a people, the poet is generally undervalued. He is apt to be regarded as an unpractical, or even an eccentric and valueless member of society. Too often the eccentricities of genius afford some basis for this prejudice; but it is wholly groundless in the case of the largest and most gifted of the poetic race. High poetic gifts are favorable to the noblest types of manhood. The great poet, beyond all other men, possesses an intuitive insight into truth, depth of feeling, and appreciation of beauty. These gifts lift the poet out of the rank of common men, and make him, in his moments of highest inspiration, a prophet to his people.

  In the language of Bailey in his "Festus," "Poetry is itself a thing of God; He made His prophets poets, and the more We feel of poesy, do we become Like God in love and powerunder makers." Among the greatest of every nation, whether ancient or modern, poets stand almost preeminent. In the Old Testament history there is no one greater than "the sweet Psalmist of Israel." Homer stands in almost solitary grandeur in the early annals of Greece. In the history of Italy, what name is to be placed above that of Dante? In England there are, perhaps, no names to be ranked above those of Chaucer, Shakespeare, Milton, Tennyson, whose imperishable works abide with us, and in no small degree mould the thought and feeling of each succeeding generation. And among the illustrious citizens of our own country there are few or none who have reached a higher nobility of character than its great singers,Longfellow, Bryant, Whittier, Hayne, and Lowell. Their lives were no less sane than beautiful.

- The Poet as Seer. The poet is preeminently a seer. He discerns the divine beauty and truth of life which escape the common sight; and because he reveals them to us in his melodious art he becomes an exalted teacher. In the midst of the tumults of greed and gain he lifts up his voice to witness of higher things. In the presence of what seemed to her a sordid generation, Mrs. Browning calls poets

"The only truth-tellers now left to God,
The only speakers of essential truth,
Opposed to relative, comparative,
And temporal truths; the only holders by
His sun-skirts, through conventional gray glooms;
The only teachers who instruct mankind,
From just a shadow on a charnel-wall,
To find man's veritable stature out,
Erect, sublimethe measure of a man."

The poet, with his intenser nature, gives expression to our deepest thoughts and feelings. What we have often felt but vaguely, he utters for us in imperishable forms. In how many things Shakespeare has voiced the human soul! While poetry has rippling measures suited to our smiles, it belongs, in its richest form, to the deeper side of our nature. Its loftiest numbers are given to truth and righteousness, to the tragic strivings and sorrows of life, and to the mysteries of deathless love.

- Versification. Versification is the science of making verse. The unit or starting point in versification is the syllable, which may be long or short, according to the time it requires in pronouncing, and accented or unaccented, according to the stress of tone with which it is pronounced. Quantity, by which is meant the length of syllables, formed the basis of versification in Latin and Greek poetry; but in English poetry it is used to give variety, music, or some other element of effectiveness to the verse. This may be illustrated in a well-known passage from Pope:

"When Ajax strives some rock's vast weight to throw,
The line, too, labors, and the words move slow;
Not so, when swift Camilla scours the plain,

Flies o'er the unbending corn, and skims along the main."

The first two lines occupy more time in reading than the last two, the sound in each case corresponding in some measure to the sense. An examination of the lines will show that the first two have more long vowel sounds than the last two, and that these and other vowel sounds are lengthened in pronunciation by the presence of difficult consonant combinations. "Ajax strives" and "rock's vast weight" are not phrases that slip quickly from the tongue. Furthermore, the second line is lengthened by no fewer than three pauses.

The principle of English verse is accent, and not quantity. In the line,

"The mossy marbles rest,"

It will be observed that every other syllable receives a stress of voice or is accented. The scheme of the verse may be represented as follows:

u-'|u-'|u-',

The line being broken up into three equal and similar parts, each of which is called a foot. The foot consisting of an unaccented followed by an accented syllable is called an iambus.

In the line,

"Home they brought her warrior dead,"

We observe that beginning with the first syllable every other one is accented, giving us the following as the scheme of the verse:

-'u|-'u|-'u|-'.

The last foot is obviously incomplete or catalectic. The foot that consists of two syllables, the first of which is accented, is called a trochee. It is the opposite of the iambus.

Again, in the line,

"This is the forest primeval; the murmuring pines and the hemlocks,"

it will be noticed that, beginning with the first, each

accented syllable is followed by two unaccented syllables, except in the last foot, which is a trochee. The scheme of the verse is as follows:

-'uu|-'uu|-'uu|-'uu|-'uu|-'u.

This foot, consisting of one accented syllable, followed by two unaccented syllables, is called a dactyl.

Once more, in the line,

"Through the depths of Loch Katrine the steed shall career," the third syllable is accented, and the scheme of the verse may be thus indicated:

uu-'|uu-'|uu-'|uu-'.

This foot, which is the opposite of the dactyl, is known as the anapest.

A spondee is a foot of two equally accented syllables; as, mainspring, sea-maid. There is still another foot, known as the amphibrach, which consists of three syllables, the second of which is accented, as in the word de-ni'-al. The scheme of the following line,

"The flesh was a picture for painters to study,"

may be indicated thus:

u-'u|u-'u|u-'u|u-'u.

But nearly all English poetry is based upon the four feet,iambus, trochee, dactyl, and anapest,first given.

- Meters. A verse is named from the number of prevailing feet. A verse containing one iambic foot is called iambic monometer; two feet, iambic dimeter; three feet, iambic trimeter; four feet, iambic tetrameter; five feet, iambic pentameter; six feet, iambic hexameter. The line, "The twilight hours like birds flew by," is made up of four iambic feet, and is therefore an iambic tetrameter. Iambic pentameter, in which Milton's "Paradise Lost," much of Pope's poetry, Shakespeare's dramas, and, indeed, a large proportion of English verse, are written, is called heroic measure. In like manner we have trochaic monometer, dimeter, trimeter, tetrameter, pentameter, and hexameter. The following line, "As unto the bow the cord is," is trochaic tetrameter, which is the meter of "Hiawatha." The foregoing are called dissyllabic meters; but the trisyllabic measures have the same names according to the number of feet. A verse consisting of a single dactyl is thus dactylic monometer; of two dactyls, dactylic dimeter; and so on up to dactylic hexameter, which is the meter of Homer's "Iliad," Vergil's "AEneid," and Longfellow's "Evangeline" and "Courtship of Miles Standish." The line, "Softly the breezes descend in the valley," is dactylic tetrameter, though the last foot is a trochee. In like manner we have anapestic lines of all lengths from monometer to hexameter.

The line, "How she smiled, and I could not but love," contains three anapests, and is therefore anapestic trimeter. But the time element of a poetic foot is important, as it explains the seeming irregularities often met with in verse. An additional syllable may be added to a foot or subtracted from it when the time of the foot or verse is not changed. By rapid utterance two syllables are often equal to one, and in this way an anapest is frequently used with the time value of an iambus. In like manner a pause may sometimes take the place of an unaccented syllable. Both cases are fully illustrated in Tennyson's well-known lyric, "Break, break, break, On thy cold gray stones, O sea!" In spite of the seeming irregularity of this poem, the presence of the proper time element, together with the regular accents, preserves its metrical harmony.

There are few poems without slight metrical irregularities. The meter is varied to prevent monotony, to give emphasis to a word, or to respond better to some turn of the thought or feeling. Take, for example, the following couplet from Wordsworth: "To me the meanest flower that blows can give Thoughts that do often lie too deep for tears." The meter is iambic pentameter; but the first foot of the second line is a trochee, and emphasizes thoughts with fine effect. The time of the line remains unchanged. In Milton we read, "Leviathan, which God of all his works Created hugest that swim the ocean stream." This is likewise iambic pentameter; but in the second line a clumsy anapestic foot is inserted to correspond to the nature of the monster described. No doubt irregularities sometimes occur by oversight or from lack of skill; but with our greater poets, whose thought and emotion instinctively assume the proper metrical form, the irregularities are motived.

- Rhyme. Rhyme, or as it is more correctly spelled rime, is a similarity of sound between words or syllables. Identity of sound, as heir, air, site, sight, is not rhyme. It usually occurs between words at the end of a verse, and serves to lend both beauty and emphasis to poetry. The order in which rhymes occur is various. They may be found
in succeeding lines; as,

"The tear down childhood's cheek that flows
Is like the dewdrop on the rose;
When next the summer breeze comes by,
And shakes the bush, the flower is dry."
They may occur in alternate lines; as,
"The sun has long been set;
The stars are out by twos and threes;
The little birds are piping yet
Among the bushes and the trees."

Or the rhymes may occur at longer intervals; as,

"I envy not in any moods
The captive void of noble rage,
The linnet born within the cage,
That never knew the summer woods."

In double rhyme the correspondence of sound extends to two syllables, and in triple rhyme to three. A double rhyme, as pleasure, measure, is also called feminine, while single rhymes are called masculine.

The following illustrates both double, or feminine, and masculine rhymes:

"'Tis the hour when happy faces
Smile around the taper's light;
Who will fill our vacant places?
Who will sing our songs to-night?"

The following from Hood illustrates triple rhyme:

"Take her up tenderly,
Lift her with care;
Fashioned so slenderly,
Young and so fair."

Triple rhyme is usually employed only in a light, satirical, or mocking vein. Byron uses it frequently in his frivolous or reckless moods; for example,

"O world that was and is! What is cosmogony?
Some people have accused me of misanthropy,
And yet I know no more than the mahogany
That forms this desk of what they mean; lycanthropy
I comprehend; for, without transformation
Men become wolves on any slight occasion."

Middle rhyme is that which exists between the middle and final words or syllables of a verse. It is frequently used in the *"The Ancient Mariner:"*

"The fair breeze blew, the white foam flew,
The furrow followed free;
We were the first that ever burst
Into that silent sea."

Sectional rhyme is that occurring in the first half or section of a verse; as,

Lightly and brightly breaks away
The morning from her mantle gray."

Alliteration is the use of the same letter at the beginning of two or more words or syllables in the same verse or successive verses. It was the determining principle in Anglo-Saxon poetry, and has remained ever since a source of harmony in English verse. Its effects are sometimes most pleasing when the alliteration turns on one or more internal syllables. The following from Mrs. Browning's "Romance of the Swan's

Nest" will serve for illustration:
"Little Ellie sits alone,
And the smile she softly uses
Fills the silence like a speech,
While she thinks what shall be done,
And the sweetest pleasure chooses
For her future within reach."

The light rippling melody of this stanza is due, in considerable measure, to its fine alliterative structure. Tennyson likewise makes effective use of alliteration, as may be noted especially in the matchless lyrics interspersed throughout "The

Princess." A single stanza will make this clear:
"The splendor falls on castle walls
And snowy summits old in story;
The long light shakes across the lakes
And the wild cataract leaps in glory.
Blow, bugle, blow, set the wild echoes flying,
Blow, bugle; answer, echoes, dying, dying, dying."

- Stanzas. A stanza is a separate division of a poem, and contains two or more lines or verses. A stanza of two lines is called a couplet; of three lines, a triplet; of four lines, a quatrain. Tennyson's "Locksley Hall" is in two-line stanza:

  "Men, my brothers, men the workers, ever reaping something new; That which they have done but earnest of the things that they shall do."

  His "Two Voices" is in the triplet stanza:

  "A still small voice spake unto me,
  'Thou art so full of misery,
  Were it not better not to be?'
  "Then to the still small voice I said,
  'Let me not cast in endless shade
  What is so wonderfully made.'"

Numerous examples of the four-line stanza have already been given. Rhyme royal is a seven-line stanza invented by Chaucer. As will be seen from the following example, it is made up of iambic pentameter lines, the first four forming a quatrain of alternate rhymes, the fifth line repeating the rhyme of the fourth, and the last two lines forming a rhyming couplet. Its scheme is a b a b b c c, in which the same letters indicate rhymes.

"For lo! the sea that fleets about the land,
And like a girdle clips her solid waist,
Music and measure both doth understand,
For his great crystal eye is always cast
Up to the moon, and on her fixeth fast;
And as she circles in her pallid sphere,
So danceth he about the centre here."

Ottava rima is composed of eight iambic pentameter verses with alternate rhymes, except the last two lines, which form a rhymed couplet. Byron's "Don Juan" is written in this stanza. The scheme of rhyme is a b a b a b a c.

"'Tis sweet to hear the watch-dog's honest bark
Bay deep-mouthed welcome as we draw near home;
'Tis sweet to know there is an eye will mark
Our coming, and look brighter when we come;
'Tis sweet to be awakened by the lark
Or lulled by falling waters; sweet the hum
Of bees, the voice of girls, the song of birds,
The lisp of children, and their earliest words."

The Spenserian stanza, invented by Edmund Spenser and employed by him in the "Faerie Queene," is a difficult but effective form of poetry. It consists of nine verses, the first eight being iambic pentameter, and the ninth line iambic hexameter, or Alexandrine. Its rhyme scheme is a b a b b c b c c. The following from Byron's "Childe Harold" will serve for illustration:

"To sit on rocks, to muse o'er flood and fell,
To slowly trace the forest's shady scene,
Where things that own not man's dominion dwell,
And mortal foot hath ne'er or rarely been;
To climb the trackless mountain all unseen,
With the wild flock that never needs a fold;
Alone o'er steeps and foaming falls to lean;

This is not solitude; 'tis but to hold Converse with Nature's charms, and view her stores unrolled." The principal hymn stanzas are known as long meter, common meter, and short meter. The long-meter stanza is composed of four iambic tetrameter lines, rhyming either alternately or in couplets; as,

"Wide as the world is Thy command;
Vast as eternity Thy love;
Firm as a rock Thy truth must stand,
When rolling years shall cease to move."

The common-meter stanza contains four iambic lines, the first and third being tetrameter, and the second and fourth trimeter. The rhymes are alternate; as,

"Eternity, with all its years,
Stands present to Thy view;
To Thee there's nothing old appears,
To Thee there's nothing new."

The short-meter stanza consists of four iambic lines, the first, second, and fourth being trimeter, and the third tetrameter. The rhymes are alternate; as,

"Let good or ill befall,
It must be good for me;
Secure of having Thee in all,
Of having all in Thee."

- Blank Verse. Unrhymed poetry, usually in iambic pentameter measure, is known as blank verse. It is our ordinary epic and dramatic verse, as exemplified in Shakespeare and Milton. Blank verse has greater freedom than rhymed verse, but the attainment of a high degree of excellence in it is scarcely less difficult. It approaches the ease and freedom of prose, and perhaps for that reason it is apt to sink below a high level of poetry. Apart from its diction and meter, the harmony of blank verse depends upon two things,namely, its pauses and its periods. The rhythmical pause occurring in a line is called a caesura. Though usually falling near the middle of the line, the caesural pause may occur at any point, and sometimes there may be two caesuras.

  There is generally a rhythmical pause at the end of a verse, and when this pause is stressed by a completion of the sense the line is said to be "end-stopt"; but if the sense awaits completion in the following verse, the line is said to be "run-on." The French name enjambement is sometimes used to designate a "run-on" line. The following extract from Thomson will serve to illustrate the caesural pauses, as well as

"end-stopt" and "run-on" lines:
"These as they change, | Almighty Father, | these
Are but the varied God. | The rolling year
Is full of thee. | Forth in the pleasant Spring
Thy beauty walks, | thy tenderness and love.
Wide flush the fields; | the softening air is balm;
Echo the mountains round; the forest smiles;
And every sense, | and every heart, is joy.
Then comes thy glory | in the summer months
With light and heat refulgent. | Then thy sun
Shoots full perfection | through the swelling year."

By period is meant the conclusion of the sentence. The period or end of a sentence may fall at the end of a line or at any point in it. The period serves to break up the poem into longer or shorter parts.

In Milton the sentences are generally long, and the periods thus break up the poem into a sort of stanza of varying length. "Run-on" lines are the prevailing type; and this fact, in connection with the length of the sentences and the constant shifting of the pauses, imparts to his "Paradise Lost" its peculiar organ roll. The following passage will serve to make this clear:

"Of man's first disobedience, | and the fruit
Of that forbidden tree, | whose mortal taste
Brought death into our world, | and all our woe,
With loss of Eden, | till one greater Man
Restore us, | and regain the blissful seat,
Sing, Heavenly Muse, | that on the secret top
Of Oreb, | or of Sinai, | didst inspire
That shepherd | who first taught the chosen seed
In the beginning | how the heavens and earth

Rose out of Chaos.
"Or, if Sion hill
Delight thee more, | and Siloa's brook that flowed
Fast by the oracle of God, | I thence
Invoke thy aid | to my adventurous song,
That with no middle flight | intends to soar
Above the Aonian mount, | while it pursues
Things unattempted yet | in prose or rhyme."

These sixteen lines practically make two stanzas. Twelve lines, or three fourths of the whole number, are "run-on." The caesural pause, as will be seen on counting the feet in connection with which they occur, is exceedingly varied. With the two foregoing extracts may be compared the following from Shelley's "Alastor," in which all the periods are "end-stopt," and divide the selection into clearly recognizable and almost regular stanzas. It will be noted that the movement and effect are very different from those of Thomson and Milton.

"There was a poet | whose untimely tomb
No human hand | with pious reverence reared,
But the charmed eddies | of autumnal winds
Built o'er his mouldering bones | a pyramid
Of mouldering leaves | in the waste wilderness.
"A lovely youth, | no mourning maiden decked
With weeping flowers | or votive cypress wreath
The lone couch | of his everlasting sleep;
Gentle and brave and generous, | no lorn bard
Breathed o'er his dark fate | one melodious sigh;
He lived, he died, he sang, | in solitude.
"Strangers have wept | to hear his passionate notes;
And virgins, | as unknown he passed, | have pined
And wasted | for fond love of his wild eyes.
"The fire of those soft orbs | has ceased to burn,
And Silence, | too enamored of that voice,
Locks its mute music | in her rugged cell."

It will be observed that not only all the periods, but also twelve out of the seventeen lines are "end-stopt."

- Poetic Style. By poetic style is meant the choice and arrangement of words peculiar to poetry. While in the main poetic and prose diction is the same, still there are words and verbal combinations admissible only in poetry. Poetry strives after concreteness and vividness of expression. Such words as steed, swain, wight, muse, Pegasus, yclept, a-cold, sprent, bower, meed, isle, a-field, dight, sooth, hight, and many others, are hardly ever met with in ordinary prose. Their prose equivalents are generally preferred. Poetry uses great freedom, called poetic license, in the order of words and construction of sentences. The principal deviations from the prose order are as follows:

— The verb may precede the subject for the sake of emphasis or meter; as, *"Came a troop with broad swords swinging."*
— The verb may follow its object; as,
"Thee, shepherd, thee the woods, and desert caves,
And all their echoes, mourn."
— The infinitive may precede the word on which it depends; as, *"When first thy sire, to send on earth*
Virtue, his darling child, designed."
— Prepositional phrases may precede the verbs they modify; as, *"Of man's first disobedience, sing, Heavenly Muse."*
— The preposition may follow the noun it governs; as, *"From peak to peak, the rattling crags among,*
Leaps the live thunder."
— Adverbs may precede the words they modify; as, *The plowman homeward plods his weary way."*
— Condensed expressions in the form of compound epithets are frequently used; as, *"O music, sphere-descended maid!"*
— An expletive pronoun may be used to throw the subject after the verb; as, *"It ceased, the melancholy sound."*
— The relative pronoun may be omitted; as,
"'Tis fancy, in her fiery car,
Transports me to the thickest war."

— Intransitive verbs are sometimes used with an objective case; as, *"Still in harmonious intercourse they lived The rural day, and talked the flowing heart."*

— Archaic or antiquated words and modes of expression may be used; as, *"Whilome in Albion's isle there dwelt a youth Who ne in virtue's ways did take delight."*

— The noun may precede the adjective modifying it; as, *"The willows, and the hazel copses green."*

Review Questions

- What is poetry? How is it distinguished from prose? What is the difference between poetry and verse?
- What is the relative position of poetry and prose? Illustrate the difference.
- What is the source of poetry? What is said of human life? What constitutes its lyric poetry? Mention some mental aspects of nature.
- How is the poet regarded in a materialistic age? With what is the great poet gifted? What is Bailey's estimate of poets? What is said of the rank of great poets? Mention some of the world's greatest poets.
- Why is the poet called a seer? What is his relation to his contemporaries? What does Mrs. Browning say of poets? What is said of Shakespeare? To what class of themes does the best poetry give itself?
- What is versification? What is its unit? How are syllables distinguished? What is the function of quantity in English verse? Illustrate. What is the principle of English verse? What is a metrical foot? Define iambus? Illustrate. Define a trochee, with example. When is a verse or foot catalectic? Define a dactyl, with illustration. Define an anapest, with example. Define a spondee; amphibrach, with example.
- How is a verse named? What is iambic trimeter? What is iambic pentameter called? What is trochaic

tetrameter? Illustrate. What is dactylic hexameter? Illustrate. Mention some well-known poems written in this meter. What is anapestic trimeter? Illustrate. On what principle may a syllable be added to a foot or omitted from it? Explain the irregularities in the first two lines of Tennyson's "Break, break, break." What is said of metrical irregularities? What is their purpose? Illustrate from Wordsworth and Tennyson.

- What is rhyme? Of what use is it? In what order may rhymes occur? Illustrate. What is a double rhyme? What other name has it? Illustrate. What is a triple rhyme? Illustrate. When is triple rhyme usually employed? What is middle rhyme? Illustrate. What is sectional rhyme? Illustrate. What is alliteration? What is said of it? Give illustrations from Mrs. Browning and Tennyson.
- What is a stanza? What is a stanza of two lines called? of three? of four? Illustrate. Explain rhyme royal; ottava rima; Spenserian stanza. Illustrate. Explain the usual hymn meters, illustrating in each case.
- What is blank verse? What is said of its freedom and difficulty? On what does its harmony depend? What is meant by caesura? What is an "end-stopt" line? A "run-on" line? What French name is used for the latter? What is meant by period? Into what does the period practically divide blank verse? On what does Milton's "organ roll" depend? Point out a notable difference between Milton's and Shelley's blank verse.
- What is meant by poetic style? What is said of poetic diction? Mention some poetic words. State some of the leading deviations in construction?

Illustrative and Practical Exercises

The following selections should be examined in the light of such questions as these:

Is it poetry or verse? What lifts it above prose?

Does it treat of nature, man, or God? Is it

intellectual, emotional, or both? What is the poet's idea? Is it commonplace, true, elevated, delicate, exquisite? What is the mood of the poet,serious, playful, humorous, calm, exalted? What imaginative features has it? What concrete pictures? What figures? Is it self-restrained and classic? Is it loose and voluble?

As to structure, what is the fundamental foot? Name each line. What irregularities may exist and for what purpose? Is the movement slow or rapid? Explain the source of slowness or rapidity. What is the order of rhymes? Are they perfect or defective? Are there double, triple, middle, or sectional rhymes? Point out the alliteration. What is the effect? Name the stanza. Is it blank verse? Where does the caesural pause fall in each line? Is there variety? Are the lines "end-stopt" or "run-on"? Point out the poetic words. What is their effect? What poetic constructions are there? Divide the selections into three classes,feeble, good, excellent.

Now all our neighbors' chimneys smoke,
And Christmas blocks are burning;
Their ovens they with baked meats choke,
And all their spits are turning.
Without the door let sorrow lie;
And if for cold it hap to die,
We'll bury it in a Christmas pie,
And evermore be merry.WITHER.
Silence in love betrays more woe
Than words, though ne'er so witty;
A beggar that is dumb, you know,
May challenge double pity.
Then wrong not, dearest to my heart,
My true, though secret passion;
He smarteth most that hides his smart,
And sues for no compassion.RALEIGH.
Father, thy hand
Hath reared these venerable columns, thou

Didst weave this verdant roof. Thou didst look down
Upon the naked earth, and forthwith rose
All these fair ranks of trees. They, in thy sun,
Budded and shook their green leaves in thy breeze,
And shot toward heaven. The century-living crow
Whose birth was in their tops, grew old and died
Among their branches, till at last they stood,
As now they stand, mossy, and tall, and dark,
Fit shrine for humble worshipper to hold
Communion with his Maker.BRYANT.
But since, O man! thy life and health demand
Not food alone, but labour from thy hand,
First, in the field, beneath the sun's strong rays,
Ask of thy motheı Earth the needful maize;
She loves the race that courts her yielding soil,
And gives her bounties to the sons of toil.BARLOW.
My days among the dead are passed;
Around me I behold,
Where'er these casual eyes are cast,
The mighty minds of old;
My never-failing friends are they,
With whom I converse day by day.
With them I take delight in weal,
And seek relief in woe;
And while I understand and feel
How much to them I owe,
My cheeks have often been bedewed
With tears of thoughtful gratitude.SOUTHEY.
It is a beauteous evening, calm and free;
The holy time is quiet as a nun
Breathless with adoration; the broad sun
Is sinking down in its tranquillity;
The gentleness of heaven is on the sea;
Listen! the mighty being is awake,
And doth with his eternal motion make
A sound like thundereverlastingly.
WORDSWORTH.
Lives of great men all remind us

We can make our lives sublime,
And departing leave behind us
Footprints on the sands of time;
Footprints, that perhaps another
Sailing o'er life's solemn main,
A forlorn and shipwrecked brother,
Seeing, shall take heart again.
Let us, then, be up and doing,
With a heart for any fate;
Still achieving, still pursuing,
Learn to labour and to wait.LONGFELLOW.
Beneath those rugged elms, that yew-tree's shade,
Where heaves the turf in many a mouldering heap,
Each in his narrow cell forever laid,
The rude forefathers of the hamlet sleep.
The breezy call of incense-breathing morn,
The swallow twittering from the straw-built shed,
The cock's shrill clarion, or the echoing horn,
No more shall rouse them from their lowly bed.
For them no more the blazing hearth shall burn,
Or busy housewife ply her evening care;
No children run to lisp their sire's return,
Or climb his knees the envied kiss to share.GRAY.
And slowly answered Arthur from the barge:
"The old order changeth, yielding place to new,
And God fulfils himself in many ways,
Lest one good custom should corrupt the world.
Comfort thyself: what comfort is in me?
I have lived my life, and that which I have done,
May He within himself make pure! but thou,
If thou shouldst never see my face again,
Pray for my soul. More things are wrought by prayer
Than this world dreams of. Wherefore, let thy voice
Rise like a fountain for me night and day.
For what are men better than sheep or goats
That nourish a blind life within the brain,
If, knowing God, they lift not hands of prayer
Both for themselves and those who call them friend?

For so the whole round earth is every way
Bound by gold chains about the feet of God."
TENNYSON.

All day thy wings have fanned
At that far height, the cold, thin atmosphere,
Yet stoop not, weary, to the welcome land,
Though the dark night is near.
And soon that toil shall end;
Soon shalt thou find a summer home, and rest,
And scream among thy fellows; reeds shall bend,
Soon, o'er thy sheltered nest.BRYANT.

Then from a neighboring thicket the mocking-bird, wildest of singers, Swinging aloft on a willowy spray that hung o'er the water, Shook from his little throat such floods of delirious music, That the whole air and the woods and the waves seemed silent to listen.

Plaintive at first were the tones, and sad; then soaring to
madnessSeemed they to follow or guide the revel of
frenziedBacchantes.
Single notes were then heard, in sorrowful, low
lamentation; Till, having gathered them all, he
flung them abroad in derision,
As when, after a storm, a gust of wind through
the tree-tops Shakes down the rattling rain in a
crystal shower on the branches.
LONGFELLOW.
Over his keys the musing organist,
Beginning doubtfully and far away,
First lets his fingers wander as they list,
And builds a bridge from Dreamland for his lay;
Then, as the touch of his loved instrument
Gives hope and fervor, nearer draws his theme,
First guessed by faint auroral flushes sent
Along the wavering vista of his dream.LOWELL.
And when I am stretched beneath the pines,
Where the evening star so holy shines,
I laugh at the lore and the pride of man,
At the sophist schools, and the learned clan;

For what are they all, in their high conceit,
When man in the bush with God may meet?EMERSON.
'Twas twilight and the sunless day went down
Over the waste of waters; like a veil
Which, if withdrawn, would but disclose the frown
Of one whose hate is masked but to assail.
Thus to their hopeless eyes the night was shown,
And grimly darkled o'er the faces pale,
And the dim desolate deep: twelve days had Fear
Been their familiar, and now Death was here.BYRON.
And oft the craggy cliff he loved to climb,
When all in mist the world below was lost
What dreadful pleasure! there to stand sublime,
Like shipwrecked mariner on desert coast,
And view the enormous waste of , tossed
In billows, lengthening to the horizon round,
Now scooped in gulfs, with mountains now embossed,
And hear the voice of mirth and song rebound,
Flocks, herds, and waterfalls, along the hoar profound!
BEATTIE.

NOTE

In addition to the foregoing poetical selections, those previously given may be analyzed with reference to form, content, and mood. Their beauty or excellence will now be more clearly understood. Furthermore, it is recommended that the teacher assign brief poems, either from our standard authors or from current literature, for full analysis and criticism. The blank verse of Tennyson, Shelley, Milton, and Shakespeare might be investigated and compared at considerable length in order to determine the average length of their sentences, the place of the caesural pause, and the proportion of "end-stopt" or "run-on" lines.

Chapter 8

Kinds of Poetry

- Classification. Poetry may be divided into four general types or classes:
  - Didactic poetry, which is chiefly concerned with instruction;
  - Lyric poetry, which generally gives expression to some emotion;
  - Epic poetry, which is devoted principally to narration; and
  - Dramatic poetry, which deals with direct representation. All these types or classes have variations and subdivisions, which call for consideration in some detail.
- Didactic Poetry. The term "didactic" as applied to poetry involves a seeming contradiction. Instruction is a function peculiar to prose; but in the hands of a genuine poet, didactic verse may be so adorned by the imagination and so warmed by the feelings as to lift it sometimes into the realm of genuine poetry. Thus Dryden's Religio Laici, the first didactic poem of special note in our language, is essentially prosaic in theme and purpose.

  But its opening lines, by a happy simile, are unmistakably poetic:

  "Dim as the borrowed beams of moon and stars
  To lonely, weary, wandering travellers,
  Is Reason to the soul; and as on high
  Those rolling fires discover but the sky,
  Not light us here, so Reason's glimmering ray

Was lent, not to assure our doubtful way,
But guide us upward to a better day."

A didactic poem, at its best, is apt to be more or less prosaic. In estimating its worth, three points are principally to be considered:

— To what extent has it a true poetic quality?
— To what extent is it complete, symmetrical, and true? and
— To what extent is it correct and skillful in versification?

• Our language is specially rich in didactic poems, among which may be mentioned Dryden's Religio Laici and "Hind and Panther," Pope's "Essay on Criticism" and "Essay on Man," Young's "Night Thoughts," Johnson's "Vanity of Human Wishes," Cowper's "Task," Akenside's "Pleasures of the Imagination," Rogers's "Pleasures of Memory," Campbell's "Pleasures of Hope," Wordsworth's "Excursion," and Pollok's "Course of Time."

— Satire is a species of didactic poetry. It is the use of wit, irony, and sarcasm to ridicule foibles, vices, or evils of any kind. Three kinds of satire may be distinguished: personal satire, which is directed against individuals, and usually springs from malignant or unworthy motives; partisan satire, which aims to make an opposing party or sect odious; and social satire, which seeks to improve the manners or morals of society. Dryden, himself a master of the dangerous art, says,

"Satire has always shone among the rest,
And is the boldest way, if not the best,
To tell men freely of their faintest faults,
To laugh at their vain deeds and vainer thoughts."

— The mood of satire may be various: it may be genial and pleasant; it may be earnest and just; or it may be personal, unjust, and malicious. Any species of satire may exhibit keenness of wit, but satire reaches its highest excellence only when it springs from upright motives and confines itself to truth. If there is exaggeration or caricature, as is generally the case, there still must be a substantial basis of fact. No amount of intellectual brilliancy or artistic skill can justify what is false and slanderous. Satirical poetry is very old. Aristophanes, Juvenal, Horace were distinguished satirists of antiquity. Satire is found in almost every period of English literature. Among our well-known satires are Butler's

"Hudibras," Dryden's "Mac Flecknoe" and "Absalom and Achitophel," Pope's "Dunciad," Byron's "English Bards and Scotch Reviewers" and "Waltz,"

Lowell's "Fables for Critics," Moore's "Fudge Family in Paris," and not a few others.

— Descriptive poetry, or the nature epic, as it has been called, may be classed under didactic poetry. It is devoted to the description not of successive events but of successive scenes in nature. It is sobre and reflective in character. Beginning with Chaucer, who delights in May time and the daisies, nature occupies a prominent place and displays an ever-unfolding richness in English poetry. Pope's "Windsor Forest" is an elaborate though artificial piece of description. Milton's "L'Allegro" and "Il Penseroso" are nature pictures that have never been surpassed in their graphic portraiture. Other celebrated descriptive poems are Goldsmith's "Traveller" and "Deserted Village," Thomson's "Seasons,"

Bryant's "Forest Hymn," Whittier's "Snow-Bound." But in poems of every class there are descriptions of nature, though occupying an incidental and secondary position. In these nature poems there should be truthfulness of description. They should be genuine; not coldly conventional, as Pope's "Windsor Forest," but real or idealized pictures from nature. The descriptions should be specific rather than general; and if, in addition to faithful portraiture, we have the warmth and elevation that come from human emotion or from the recognition of an all-pervading Presence, the result is the highest type of descriptive poetry. These finer descriptions of nature are found in all the great poets since the days of Wordsworth.

— Pastoral poetry is a species of descriptive poetry. It is devoted to a portrayal of country life and manners, and generally embodies a slight degree of dramatic action. "A pastoral," says Alexander Pope, "is an imitation of the action of a shepherd, or one considered under that character. The form of this imitation is dramatic or narrative, or mixed of both; the fable simple, the manners not too polite nor too rustic; the thoughts are plain, yet admit a little quickness and passion, but that short and flowing; the expression humble, yet as pure as the language will afford; neat but not florid; easy and yet lively." English literature is not rich in pastoral poetry. What we have is generally an imitation or translation of classical models. One of the best known English pastorals is Spenser's "Shepherd's Calendar," which contains imitations of Theocritus and Marot. Milton's "Comus" is a kind of pastoral. The purest examples of pastoral poetry are found in Pope, who has a series which he calls "Pastorals." Keats's "Endymion" has been classed with pastoral poetry, but it is not a pure example of the type.

- Lyric Poetry. Lyric poetry gives intense expression to thought and emotion. As the name indicates, it was originally accompanied by music. Though lyric poems are short, they constitute, in the aggregate, a large part of English poetry. At the present day didactic and epic poetry is rarely written; but lyric poetry continues to flourish. Its range of theme is practically without limits. There are numerous kinds or classes of lyric poetry, of which we may distinguish the following:

— Ballads,
— Songs,
— Odes,
— Elegies,
— Sonnets.

- These will now be considered in the order given.

— A ballad is a brief narrative poem in lyric form. The ballad was originally the production of wandering minstrels, and in its old English form it possessed a simplicity, directness, and charming crudeness that a more cultivated age cannot successfully imitate. The old English ballads, most of which were composed in the north of England, depict the lawlessness, daring, fortitude, and passion characteristic of life along the Scottish border. A group of ballads gathers about the name of Robin Hood, "the gentlest thief," as Scott calls him, "that ever was.

" A stanza or two will illustrate their general tone and style:

"He that hath neither beene kithe nor kin
Might have seen a full fayre sight,
To see how together these yeomen went
With blades both brown and bright.
"To see how these yeomen together they fought
Two hours of a summer's day,
Yet neither Robin Hood nor Sir Guy
Them fettled to flye away."

Recent poets have written ballads, among the best of which may be mentioned Longfellow's

"Skeleton in Armor" and "Wreck of the Hesperus," Tennyson's "Edward Gray" and "Lady Clare," and Goldsmith's "Hermit."

- These are all ballads of a pure type.
  - A song is a lyric poem intended to be sung. Songs may be classified according to sentiment or occasion. In this way we may distinguish love songs, convivial or drinking songs, political songs, war songs, national songs, religious songs or hymns. As with lyric poems in general, there is no thought or sentiment of the human soul that may not find expression in song. Burns is distinguished as one of the best of all song writers. Moore's "Irish Melodies" and "National Airs" are bright though somewhat artificial. Among the writings of nearly all our poets are pieces suitable for music. Our hymns do not as a rule reach a high degree of poetic excellence. The reason is, perhaps, not difficult to find. The hymn writers are concerned less with a free play of the imagination and emotions than with a strict regard to theological or even dogmatic truth. But notwithstanding the difficulties of the case, not a few hymn writers have given beautiful expression to their faith, adoration, and love. Keble, Watts, Wesley, Cowper, Bonar, and many others have written hymns that give satisfying expression to a deep religious fervor.
  - The ode, is a somewhat lengthy lyric, characterized by exalted feeling, dignity of theme, and irregular and complicated structure. Our literature contains a number of excellent and famous odes, among which may be mentioned Dryden's "Alexander's Feast," which the confident author thought would never be surpassed.

"'Twas at the royal feast, for Persia won
By Philip's warlike son:

Aloft in awful state
The godlike hero sate
On his imperial throne;
His valiant peers were placed around,
Their brows with roses and with myrtles bound;
(So should desert in arms be crowned).
The lovely Thais, by his side,
Sate like a blooming Eastern bride,
In flower of youth and beauty's pride.
Happy, happy, happy pair!
None but the brave,
None but the brave,
None but the brave deserve the fair."

Pope's "Ode on Saint Cecilia's Day" is scarcely inferior. Collins's "Ode on the Passions" is well known, though not equal perhaps to his "Ode to Evening." Gray's "Ode on a Distant Prospect of Eton College" and "Progress of Poesy" are deserving of mention. Shelley wrote an "Ode to Liberty" and an "Ode to the West Wind," both well worth reading and study. Coleridge's "Ode on France" deservedly ranks high, and Wordsworth's "Ode to Duty" and "Ode on the Intimations of Immortality" are almost unsurpassed. Lowell's "Commemoration Ode" is justly admired.

— The elegy is a meditative poem of sorrowful theme, usually lamenting the dead. English literature may boast of several elegies unsurpassed in any age or country. Spenser's "Astrophel" is a lament over the death of Sir Philip Sidney. Milton's "Lycidas" is a monody on the death of the poet's friend, Edward King. Gray's "Elegy in a Country Churchyard" is celebrated for its graphic description and beautiful thought. Shelley's "Adonais," a lament for Keats, belongs to the upper regions of song; and Tennyson's "In Memoriam" belongs to the great poetic achievements of the nineteenth century.

— The sonnet is a lyric poem consisting of fourteen iambic pentameter lines. It is divided into two parts: the first consisting of an octave or double quatrain, and the other of a sestet. The rhymes of the first two quatrains are usually the same; those of the sestet are variously arranged. The sonnet is an artificial and complicated poetic form; but it lends itself admirably to the development of a single poetic thought, and Shakespeare, Milton, Wordsworth, Mrs. Browning, Longfellow, Hayne, and many others have used it with great skill and power. The following sonnet by Mrs. Browning will serve for illustration:

"I thought once how Theocritus had sung
Of the sweet years, the dear and wished-for years,
Who each one in a gracious hand appears
To bear a gift for mortals, old or young;
And, as I mused it in his antique tongue,
I saw in gradual vision through my tears,
The sweet, sad years, the melancholy years,
Those of my own life, who by turns had flung
A shadow across me. Straightway I was 'ware,
So weeping, how a mystic Shape did move
Behind me, and drew me backward by the hair,
And a voice said in mastery while I strove,
'Guess now who holds thee?' 'Death,' I said.
But, there,The silver answer rang,
'Not Death but Love!'"

As will be seen on examination, the rhyme scheme is as follows: a b b a a b b a c d c d c d. But the quatrains may have alternate rhymes, and the sestet may consist of a quatrain and couplet or of interwoven triplets, as in the following schemes: a b a b a b a b c d c d e e; a b b a a b b a c d e c d e.

– Some Criteria. The brief lyric, above all other kinds of poetry, should be finished in form and expression. The imperfections of diction that might go unchallenged in a longer poem are inexcusable in a lyric. Delicacy of thought and intensity of feeling constitute its breath of life, and should mold for themselves a beauteous form. What is commonplace, harsh, or unmusical in expression should be avoided, unless such diction is wedded to the thought. Concrete and suggestive words are to be used rather than abstract and vague expressions. There is always a distinct gain when the poem evokes pleasing pictures. As a rule the thought and expression should be clear; the poet should not mystify the reader nor tax too far his efforts at comprehension. Browning sometimes grievously offends in this particular. While insisting on clearness, however, we should not forget that the mystical and the musical have their place in poetry. A poem may sometimes be pleasing through its melodious and mystical character, even when it is not clearly intelligible. Whether the poet has a distinct introduction, or whether he plunges into the midst of his theme, he should observe method and symmetry of structure; and in spite of the liveliest play of the imagination and sensibilities, he should impose a severe restraint upon himself. He should leave something to the imagination of the reader.

Review Questions

- Into how many classes is poetry divided? Name them, giving the general character of each class. 56.
- What contradiction is there in the term didactic poetry? How is it saved from this contradiction? Illustrate. What points are to be considered in estimating didactic poetry? Mention some principal didactic poems. What is poetic satire? What three species are mentioned? What is said of the mood of

satire? Mention some well-known satires. What is meant by descriptive poetry? What is said of nature in poetry? Mention some descriptive pieces, or nature epics. What are their criteria? What is pastoral poetry? What was Pope's conception of it? What is its place in English literature? Mention our principal pastorals.

- What is lyric poetry? Mention the principal kinds. What is a ballad? What is said of old English ballads? Mention some recent ballads. What is a song? Name the different kinds. Who are mentioned as song writers? What is said of hymns? Why are they not better? Name some prominent hymn writers? What is an ode? What place does it hold in our literature? Name a few famous odes. What is an elegy? Mention some famous elegies. What is a sonnet? How is it divided? What is the rhyme scheme of the sonnet? Name some of our great sonneteers.
- What are some of the criteria for judging lyric poetry? What was one of Browning's faults?

Illustrative and Practical Exercises

The following selections should be studied in the light of such questions as these:

To what division of poetry does it belong? Is it didactic, descriptive, pastoral, satirical? What is the spirit of the piece? Is it a ballad, song, hymn, ode, elegy, sonnet? Is it elevated and intense? Is it true in sentiment and thought? Is it well constructed and harmonious? Is it clear or hazy? Is it natural or affected? What is its meter?

Of all the causes which conspire to blind
Man's erring judgment, and misguide the mind,
What the weak head with strongest bias rules,
Is pride, the never-failing vice of fools.
Whatever nature has in worth denied,
She gives in large recruits of needful pride;
For as in bodies, thus in souls, we find
What wants in blood and spirits, swelled with wind:

Pride, where wit fails, steps in to our defence,
And fills up all the mighty void of sense.POPE.
Of these the false Achitophel was first,
A name to all succeeding ages cursed:
For close designs, and crooked counsels fit;
Sagacious, bold, and turbulent of wit;
Restless, unfixed in principles and place;
In power unpleased, impatient of disgrace:
A fiery soul, which, working out its way,
Fretted the pigmy-body to decay;
A daring pilot in extremity;
Pleased with the danger, when the waves went high,
He sought the storms; but, for a calm unfit,
Would steer too nigh the sands to boast his wit.
DRYDEN.
Deign on the passing world to turn thine eyes,
And pause awhile from letters to be wise;
There mark what ills the scholar's life assail,
Toil, envy, want, the patron, and the jail.
See nations, slowly wise, and meanly just,
To buried merit raise the tardy bust.
If dreams yet flatter, once again attend,
Hear Lydiat's life and Galileo's end.JOHNSON.
The groves of Eden, vanished now so long,
Live in description, and look green in song:
These, were my breast inspired with equal flame,
Like them in beauty, should be like in fame.
Here hills and vales, the woodland and the plain,
Here earth and water seem to strive again;
Not chaos-like together crushed and bruised,
But, as the world, harmoniously confused:
Where order in variety we see,
And where, though all things differ, all agree.
Here waving groves a chequered scene display,
And part admit, and part exclude the day;
As some coy nymph her lover's warm address
Nor quite indulges, nor can quite repress.POPE.
Right against the eastern gate,

Where the great sun begins his state,
Robed in flames, and amber light,
The clouds in thousand liveries dight;
While the plowman, near at hand,
Whistles o'er the furrowed land,
And the milkmaid singeth blithe,
And the mower whets his sithe,
And every shepherd tells his tale
Under the hawthorn in the vale.MILTON.
In this, our happy and "progressive" age,
When all alike ambitious cares engage;
When beardless boys to sudden sages grow,
And "Miss" her nurse abandons for a beau;
When for their dogmas Non-Resistants fight,
When dunces lecture, and when dandies write;
When spinsters, trembling for the nation's fate,
Neglect their stockings to preserve the state;
When critic wits their brazen lustre shed
On golden authors whom they never read;
With parrot praise of "Roman grandeur" speak,
And in bad English eulogize the Greek;
When facts like these no reprehension bring,
May not, uncensured, an Attorney sing?SAXE.

In the street I heard a thumping; and I knew it was the stumping Of the Corporal, our old neighbour, on that wooden leg he wore, With a knot of women round him,it was lucky I had found him, So I followed with the others, and the Corporal marched before. They were making for the steeple,the old soldier and his people; The pigeons circled round us as we climbed the creaking stair; Just across the narrow riverO, so close it made me shiver! Stood a fortress on the hill-top that but yesterday was bare. HOLMES.

Jenny kissed me when we met,
Jumping from the chair she sat in.
Time, you thief! who love to get
Sweets into your list, put that in.
Say I'm weary, say I'm sad;
Say that health and wealth have missed me:

Say I'm growing old, but add
Jenny kissed me.LEIGH HUNT.
Those evening bells! those evening bells!
How many a tale their music tells,
Of youth, and home, and that sweet time
When last I heard their soothing chime!
Those joyous hours are passed away;
And many a heart that then was gay,
Within the tomb now darkly dwells,
And hears no more those evening bells.MOORE.
There was a time when meadow, grove, and stream,
The earth, and every common sight,
To me did seem
Apparelled in celestial light,
The glory and the freshness of a dream.
It is not now as it hath been of yore;
Turn wheresoe'er I may,
By night or day,
The things which I have seen I now can see no more.
WORDSWORTH.
Abide with me! fast falls the even-tide;
The darkness deepens; Lord, with me abide!
When other helpers fail, and comforts flee,
Help of the helpless, oh, abide with me.
Swift to its close ebbs out life's little day;
Earth's joys grow dim; its glories pass away;
Change and decay in all around I see;
O Thou who changest not, abide with me!LYTE.
When I consider how my light is spent
Ere half my days in this dark world and wide,
And that one talent which is death to hide,
Lodged with me useless, though my soul more bent
To serve therewith my Maker, and present
My true account, lest he returning chide;
"Doth God exact day-labour, light denied?"
I fondly ask; but Patience, to prevent
That murmur, soon replies, "God doth not need
Either man's work or his own gifts; who best

Bear his mild yoke, they serve him best; his state
Is kingly: thousands at his bidding speed,
And post o'er land and ocean without rest;
They also serve who only stand and wait."MILTON.

Chapter 9

Epic and Dramatic Poetry

- The Epic. The epic is a long poem celebrating in stately verse some important and heroic event of the past. It may be based either on history or tradition, though in our greatest epics there is a commingling of the two. The method of the epic is chiefly narrative and descriptive. The theme is generally stated in the beginning, and the narrative, frequently interspersed with episodes, pursues an even course. Homer thus begins the "Iliad":

  "Of Peleus' son Achilles, sing, O Muse,
  The direful wrath, which sorrows numberless
  Brought on the Greeks, and many mighty souls
  Of youthful heroes, slain untimely, sent
  To Pluto's dark abode, their bodies left
  A prey to dogs and all the fowls of heaven."

  Vergil begins the "AEneid" in a similar manner, and the opening lines of "Paradise Lost" follow classic models. The structure of the epic may be determined from the fundamental conception of its nature. As a narrative of an important and heroic event, it should be simple, direct, and dignified in its treatment. The incidents should be introduced in a natural order, and their prominence should be regulated according to their relative importance. In an epic poem, as in every other creation of art, the law of symmetry should be observed. But the epic admits of episode. The poet may stop the flow of his narrative for a time to dwell upon some incident connected with or growing out of the main theme. Such an episode is the story of the destruction of Troy in the second and third books of the "AEneid." The episode may be employed to throw light on existing conditions or to add interest to the general narrative. In the "AEneid" it serves both purposes to an eminent degree. The epic makes extensive use of dialogue, and thus, in a measure, partakes of the nature of the drama. The introduction of the dialogue serves a double purpose: first, it lends greater vividness to the narrative; and second, it lends variety to the story, enabling the ancient minstrel, and in a less degree, the modern reader, to do a little acting. Often the dialogue is highly dramatic, as in the quarrel between Achilles and Agamemnon in the first book of the "Iliad." A large part of our greatest epics is in dialogue. The great epics of the world are all heroic. They celebrate great eventsthe Trojan war, the founding of Rome, the loss of Paradiseand bring before us a large number of heroes, divinities, and angels. The "Iliad" is made up chiefly of battle scenes, in which mighty heroes and Olympian deities take part. AEneas is the hero of the "AEneid"; but back of the tribulations through which he passes, we recognize the agency of contending divinities. And in "Paradise Lost" Milton introduces the mighty beings of heaven and hell. The epic is thus the stateliest and grandest form of poetry. There are minor varieties of the epic, which occupy an important place in modern poetry.

— The principal of these varieties is the metrical romance, of which Scott's "The Lady of the Lake" or Owen Meredith's "Lucile" may be taken as the type. It differs from the grand or heroic epic in confining itself to lowlier themes, and in introducing the passion of love. The metrical romance lends itself readily to every form of romantic story. In Scott it introduces the scenes and characters of mediaeval Scotland.

Byron, in "The Giaour," "The Siege of Corinth," "The Bride of Abydos," and others, works up oriental legends. Moore's "Lalla Rookh" is a beautiful oriental romance. Owen Meredith's "Lucile" is a modern love story, while Morris's "Story of Sigurd" is derived from Scandinavian legends.

– The metrical tale may be distinguished from the metrical romance by the absence of romantic love and adventure. It is naturally briefer in form. Byron's "Prisoner of Chillon" and Burns's "Tam O'Shanter" may be taken as types of the metrical tale. On the one side it approaches the metrical romance, and on the other the lyrical ballad. Since the days of Gower and Chaucer the metrical tale has added to English poetry some of its choicest pieces.

– The mock epic is, as the name suggests, a burlesque. It narrates trivial incidents in a stately manner. It is not to be taken seriously, and may be employed either to satirize or to amuse. Butler's "Hudibras" is a mock heroic satire, while Pope's "The Rape of the Lock" was intended to amuse with its pleasant conceits and to effect a reconciliation between two alienated families among the nobility. Here are the opening lines of Canto III:

Close by those meads, forever crowned with flowers, Where Thames with pride surveys hisrising towers,

There stands a structure of majestic frame,
Which from the neighboring Hampton
takes its name.
Here Britain's statesmen oft the fall foredoom
Of foreign tyrants, and of nymphs at home;
Here thou, great Anna, whom three realms obey,
Dost sometimes counsel takeand sometimes tea."

• The Drama. The drama is a composition in prose or

verse usually intended to be acted on the stage. Representation takes the place of narration. In order to add to the reality and interest of the representation, the accessories of dress and scenery are carefully employed. Whether in prose or verse, the laws of dramatic structure are the same. The two principal divisions of the drama are tragedy and comedy. Tragedy represents an important and serious action, which usually has a fatal termination; it appeals to the earnest side of our nature, and moves our deepest feelings. Comedy consists in a representation of light and amusing incidents; it exhibits the foibles of individuals, the manners of society, and the humorous phases of life. The name tragi-comedy is applied to a drama in which tragic and comic scenes are intermingled. A farce is a short comedy distinguished by its slight thought and ridiculous caricature or extravagance. A melodrama is a drama with a romantic story or plot, and sensational situations and incidents. An opera is a musical drama, the higher forms of which are known as grand opera, and the lower or farcical forms as opera bouffe. The laws of the drama are substantially the same for all forms. There should be unity of dramatic action; that is, the separate scenes and incidents should contribute in some way to the development of the plot and to the final result or denouement. A collection of disconnected scenes, no matter how interesting in themselves, would not make a drama. In addition to unity of action, which is obviously the one indispensable law of the drama, two other unities were prescribed by ancient authorities. The one is unity of time, which requires that the action fall within the limits of a single day; the other is unity of place, which requires that the action occur in the same locality. While evidently artificial and dispensable, these latter unities conduce to clear and concise treatment. Among the Greeks and Romans the three unities, as they are called, were strictly observed; they have been followed also by the older French drama; but the English stage, breaking away in the days of Elizabeth from every artificial restriction, recognizes unity of action alone. The action of the drama should exhibit movement or progress, in which several stages may be clearly marked. The introduction acquaints us, more or less fully, with the subject to be treated. It usually brings before us some of the leading characters, and shows us the circumstances in which they are placed. After the introduction follows the growth or development of the action toward the climax.

From the days of Aristotle this part of the drama has been called "the tying of the knot," and it needs to be managed with great care. If the development is too slow, the interest lags; if too rapid, the climax appears tame. The interest of a drama depends in a large measure upon the successful arrangement of the climax, or the point in which the opposing forces immediately confront each other. In our best dramas it usually occurs near the middle of the piece. From this point the action proceeds to the close or denouement. The knot is untied; the complications in which the leading characters have become involved are either happily removed or lead to the inevitable catastrophe. Avoiding every digression, the action should go forward rapidly, in order not to weary the patience and dissipate the interest of the spectator. The denouement should not be dependent upon some foreign element introduced at the last moment, but should spring naturally from the antecedent action.

In addition to the five principal parts just indicatedintroduction, rise or tying of the knot, climax, fall or untying of the knot, and denouementthere are three other elements or factors that need to be pointed out. The first is the cause or exciting impulse of the dramatic action, and naturally stands between the introduction and the rise or tying of the knot. The second is the cause or tragic impulse of the counteraction, and stands between the climax and the fall or untying of the knot. The third is the cause or impulse that sometimes holds the action in check for a moment before reaching its final issue, and stands between the fall and the denouement. The structure and eight component parts of a complete or ideal drama may be represented in a diagram as follows. C A = Introduction. / \ B = Rise or tying of knot. / \b C = Climax. / \ D = Fall or untying of knot. / B \ E = Denouement. / \ D a = Cause or exciting impulse. / \ b = Tragic impulse. /a \c c = Impulse of last suspense. / \ /A \E

- Characters and Manners. Apart from the plot or story the interest of a drama depends to a large extent on the dramatis personae. In the classic drama the characters are few and dignified; in the romantic drama, as first developed in the age of Shakespeare, the characters are numerous and drawn from every class of society. The same difference is found in the classic school of France, represented by Corneille, Moliere, and Racine, and the romantic school founded by Victor Hugo. The characters should be clearly drawn and sufficiently differentiated. Each one should have his peculiar individuality, and be reasonably consistent with himselt in all parts of the dramatic action.

The whole world of mankind is at the service of the dramatist, and there is no type of humanity that may not be brought upon the stage. The ancient world of history or of tradition may be represented, or the stage may hold up the mirror to contemporary manners and society. The drama should be true to the time and locality in which the action is placed. The dress and manners should be in keeping with the conditions assumed, and the tone of thought and expression should not do violence to time or place. A Carthaginian nobleman, for example, should not ascertain the time of day by means of a gold watch, nor should an unlettered rustic speak in strains of eloquent poetry. A violation of the truth in time is called an anachronism. But "in some dramas, and in some species of drama," as Ward has said, "time and place are so purely imaginary and so much a matter of indifference that the adoption of a purely conventional standard of manners, or at least the exclusion of any definitely fixed one, is here desirable." This is shown in Shakespeare's "A Midsummer Night's Dream."

The drama should be moral both in tone and teaching. We may apply to the drama, as to every other species of composition, Pope's well-known couplet: "Immodest words admit of no , For want of decency is a want of sense." Indecent language and grossly immoral situations should be excluded from the stage. When this is not done, as is frequently the case, the drama, instead of uplifting, degrades humanity. This fact has brought the stage into disrepute with many excellent people. In its close or denouement the drama should not let vice triumph over virtue, nor should it make the impression that wickedness ever escapes unpunished. Such teaching places the stage in contravention with the moral order of the world, according to which, even when the punitive consequences are not openly manifest, wickedness is inevitably accompanied with some form of internal or external retribution.

Review Questions

- What is an epic? On what may it be based? What is the method of the epic? Where is the theme stated? Illustrate. What should be the structure of the epic? What is meant by symmetry? What is an episode? Why may it be introduced? Illustrate. What is said of the use of dialogue? What is the nature of the great epic? What is meant by heroic here? Illustrate. What is a metrical romance? How does it differ from the grand epic? What is said of the adaptability of the metrical romance? Illustrate. What is a metrical tale? Name an example or two. What is a mock epic? For what ends may it be used? Mention a mock epic.

- What is a drama? What is said of the laws of the drama? Name the two chief divisions. Define tragedy; comedy. What is tragi-comedy? farce? melodrama? opera? What is the difference between grand opera and opera bouffe? What is meant by unity of action? What other two unities are there? What is meant by unity of time? What is meant by unity of place? Where are the three unities strictly observed? Which is observed on the English stage? Mention the successive steps of dramatic action. What is the function of the introduction? What follows the introduction? What name did Aristotle give it? What is the climax? What is said about the arrangement of the climax? What is the fall or untying of the knot? Why should it not be protracted? What is meant by the denouement? What are the three other dramatic elements? What is meant by the cause or exciting impulse? What is meant by the tragic impulse? By the impulse of last suspense?
- On what does the interest largely depend? What is the difference in the characters of the classic and the romantic drama? What is said of each character? Whence may the drama draw its characters? Where may the dramatist get his materials? To what should the drama be true? What is an anachronism? Illustrate. Is conformity to time and place always to be adhered to? What is said of the moral tone of the drama? What is Pope's opinion? In what two ways should the stage be moral?

Chapter 10

Nature and Forms of Prose

- Definition. Prose is the ordinary form of discourse. It is distinguished from poetry not only by more commonplace thought but also by the absence of regular metrical structure. Prose and poetry together constitute the great body of literature; but at the present time, which is characterized by the predominance of material and commercial interests, prose forms by far the larger part. In our popular magazines, poetry is relegated to a very subordinate place. The forms of prose are various. They may be approximately classified under history, essays, oratory, fiction, science, philosophy, and epistolary correspondence. These classes, as will be seen later, are subject to numerous subdivisions. The last three classesscience, philosophy, and epistolary correspondencedo not come within the scope of the present work, but in general it may be said that they are subject to the same laws of truth and beauty that govern other forms of literary composition.
- History. History is a systematic record of past events. It rests upon contemporary testimony, which may exist in the form of written documents or of oral tradition. History passes into mythology when it treats of legendary heroes and divinities, and into fiction when it treats of imaginary events. Metrical chronicles, however valuable may be the historical materials they contain, are not to be regarded as history in the true sense of the word. History

presupposes change, which may take the form of progress or decadence. Without the element of change, there is nothing to relate beyond the existing state of things. English literature is very rich in historical writing of every kind, and in the century that has just passed, we meet in England with the names of Macaulay, Carlyle, and Froude, and in America with the names of Bancroft, Prescott, and Motley. As to time, history has a well-defined and generally accepted division. This division recognizes three great periods,namely, ancient, mediaeval, and modern. In each of these periods a general type of social condition, varying somewhat in different countries, prevailed without essential change.

Ancient history extends from the beginning of trustworthy records to the fall of the Roman empire in A.D. 476; mediaeval history extends from that date to the revival of learning and the beginning of the Protestant Reformation in 1517; and modern history embraces the period extending from that time down to the present. As to subject-matter, history has been variously divided. When it treats of human progress in all nations and ages it is called general or universal history. When it deals with a single country it becomes national history; thus we have histories of England and of the United States. When it treats of separate institutions or interests it may be regarded as special history,as church history or a history of literature.

Again, history may be divided according to the sources from which it derives its data. When based on the facts supplied in the Scriptures it is known as sacred history; when based on other sources of information it is called profane or secular history. This, however, is only an arbitrary though convenient distinction; for all history, as a record of the unfolding purposes of God, is sacred. As to form, history is divided into several classes. A chronicle is a register of facts and events in the order of time in which they occurred. It does not enter into a discussion either of causes or effects. It is rather a source of historical materials than history itself. The "Anglo-Saxon Chronicle," for example, contains valuable facts, but can hardly be regarded as a history of the Anglo-Saxons. Annals are chronicles that give the events year by year. As to method, history may be divided into narrative, descriptive, and philosophical. Each has its definite object, by which its treatment of materials is determined. Narrative history is chiefly concerned with a systematic presentation of the facts. It is satisfied when these are clearly presented in due perspective, and afford a comprehensive survey of the period or subject treated of. Nearly all the manuals of history in common use belong to this class. Descriptive history aims at presenting a graphic portraiture of the past. Its method is not so much narration as description. Men and events are brought forward in vivid colors. It makes the past live again before our eyes like a moving pageant; and better to accomplish this result, perspective, and even a full statement of events, are sometimes sacrificed. While narrative history is concerned mostly with the succession of important public events,wars, changes of administration, and far-reaching legislative enactments,descriptive or scenic history introduces, in large measure, the social life and manners.

Macaulay is a prince among descriptive historians, though no better example of scenic history can be found than Carlyle's "French Revolution." Philosophic history is concerned less with narration and description than with the underlying causes and effects of events. It regards all human events as an outward movement or evolution, which proceeds according to fixed and ascertainable laws. It looks upon history, to use the words of Macaulay, as "philosophy teaching by example." Philosophic history is a product of recent times; and among the best examples are Hegel's "Philosophy of History," Guizot's "History of Civilization," and Lecky's "History of European Morals." It is evident that an ideal history will be a combination of the narrative, descriptive, and philosophic.

The first gives the events in due order and proportion; the second clothes them in living reality; and the third explains their causes and results. But the production of such a history requires a rare combination of mental gifts; the vivid imagination required in scenic description is not usually found associated with philosophic depth. Perhaps Green's "History of England" and Bancroft's "History of the United States" are as good examples of the highest type of historical writing as can be found. There is a very noticeable difference between the methods of ancient and modern historians. The former, it has been said, were artistic, and the latter sociological. These terms, while aiming at the facts, are neither accurate nor happy. The ancient historians, as Herodotus and Thucydides, aimed at a pleasing narrative. To attain this end, neither an exhaustive investigation of facts nor a conscientious abstention from fiction was necessary.

Hence we find the works of the one filled with impossible events, and those of the other with orations confessedly fictitious; but in both cases the introduction of legend and fiction has imparted an interest that would otherwise be lacking in their works. With modern historians, especially in the presence of the existing dominant scientific spirit, it is different. The first requisite of historical writing at the present day is absolute truth, as nearly as it can be ascertained. The modern historian is not allowed to draw upon his imagination for facts; he is held to a laborious and exhaustive investigation of the sources of information. He writes out of abundant stores of accurate information; and not content with the mere chronological narration of facts, he seeks beneath them the principles or laws that bind them together as a whole. Modern history, particularly that of the last fifty years, has a breadth, accuracy, and depth, of which the historians of Greece and Rome hardly dreamed. 64. Biography.Biography is that department of history that gives the facts and events of an individual life.

It is at once an interesting and important form of history. We have a natural desire to know the lives and characters of the men who have in any way risen above their fellows, and been associated with great social, literary, or political movements. While great men are in large measure the creatures of mighty movements, they at the same time give direction to historic development. There is truth in Carlyle's idea that universal history "is at bottom the history of the great men who have worked there." There are three general types of biography, corresponding to the three kinds of history. The first is narrative biography, which is concerned chiefly with an orderly statement of the leading factsbirth, parentage, education, marriage, and achievementsin a person's life. The second is scenic or descriptive biography, which aims at interest by means of characteristic incidents or anecdotes.

The third is philosophic, which tries to trace the relation of a person's life to the age in which he lived, and to estimate the influence he exerted on his own and subsequent ages. The first is more common, the second more interesting, the third more instructive; but it is evident that the best biographies present a judicious combination of all three types. The first essential of biography, as of history in general, is truth. When we are studying a man's life we want to know the facts; otherwise we shall not be able to judge correctly of his life and work. There are two principal sources of error in writing biography: the first is ignorance, which leads to the omission of important particulars or to a misinterpretation of those that are known; the other source of error is prejudice for or against the person whose life is portrayed. This prejudice leads, on the one hand, to such a presentation of the biographical facts as to magnify the merits of the man; and on the other, it leads to such a suppression or distortion of the facts as to detract from his just deserts.

Both faults are illustrated in Johnson's "Lives of the Poets," which, though excellent in the main, are sometimes defective for lack of research, and colored by the writer's strong Tory and Anglican sentiments.

Autobiography is the story of a man's life written by himself. It is perhaps the most interesting form of biography. In autobiography the writer has the advantage of an intimate acquaintance not only with the outward facts but also with the secret influences and motives by which his life has been controlled. It takes us, as it were, behind the scenes of history; but at the same time there is inevitably the error that springs from undue partiality.

And though men like Rousseau, Gibbon, and Franklin attempt to divest themselves of this prejudice, and even succeed in a remarkable degree, there is reason to suspect the omission of facts and motives that would reflect too unfavorably upon the character. A diary is a record of one's daily occupations and experiences. It sustains the same relation to biography that chronicles or annals do to history: it furnishes the materials out of which biography is made. When the diarist is a man of prominence, as in the case of Dean Swift, his journal throws an interesting light not only upon his own life but also upon the times in which he lives. It introduces us to men in the freedom and frankness of private life. When the diary is kept, not with a view to subsequent publication but merely to aid one's memory, it becomes a valuable record of facts.

- Some Criteria. In judging a historical work three principal points are to be taken into consideration.
  - The first is concerned with the mode of execution. Is the outward form of the work such as is required by the laws of art? The diction should be conformable to the subject, and marshaled in correct, varied, and forcible sentences. The style should bend to suit the changing themes. The interest and impressiveness of a work, as may be seen in Macaulay and Irving, depend in no small measure upon its literary quality. Furthermore, there should be movement and symmetry. The progress of events should be followed in a natural order, and the place and treatment of each should be according to its relative importance. As in a drama, there should be a beginning, middle, and end.
  - The second point to be considered in a history is the subject-matter. Obviously this is of prime importance, for the object of history is the preservation and communication of truth. In weighing a historical work, we should consider both the writer's sources of information and the use he has made of them. Has he gone to original and trustworthy sources of information or has he taken his materials at secondhand? Has he given them thorough or only partial examination? Has he well digested his materials, so that he writes from the fullness of assimilated knowledge, or does he present only the raw materials of history? While delightful and useful histories may be written largely of secondhand materials, it is evident that monumental historic achievements, like Gibbon's "Decline and Fall"

or Carlyle's "Oliver Cromwell," must be based on exhaustive original investigation. And however useful may be the works that serve up undigested materials, they cannot be regarded as constituting history in a literary sense, for they lack the element of art.

— The third point to be considered in judging a historical work is the personality of the author. What is his mental caliber? He should have the breadth of view that enables him to grasp the subject in its entirety, and to cooerdinate the facts according to their relative importance. Otherwise he will dwell on insignificant details, lack largeness of movement, and, instead of sweeping forward like a river, spread out aimlessly like a dreary marsh.

He should have the breadth of culture that will enable him to weigh the facts he uses. This requires familiarity with various systems of belief. Whether a theologian or a scientist, a Protestant or a Romanist, he should be able to do justice to the facts and motives of the opposite party. His love of truth should be supreme. He should have soundness of judgment in connection with a clear logical sense. He must not jump at conclusions, but base them on sufficient evidence. And then the mood, attitude, and prejudices should be ascertained. This constitutes his standpoint. Most writers have convictions or belong to schools of belief that consciously or unconsciously influence their work. A skeptic like Gibbon could hardly do justice to the rise and progress of Christianity.

Review Questions

- What is prose? How is it distinguished from poetry? What is said of prose in this age? Name the principal forms of prose. Which do not come within the scope of this book?

- What is history? On what does it rest? How is it different from mythology? from fiction? What is the relation of history to change? What is said of history in English literature? What threefold division of history is there in regard to time? Name the limits of each. As to subject-matter, how is history divided? What division is based on the sources of information? Define a chronicle; annals. As to method, what threefold division of history is there? Define narrative, descriptive, and philosophic history. What method does the best history follow? What difference is there between ancient and modern methods in history? What is the first requisite of historic writing to-day?
- What is biography? Why is it interesting? What was Carlyle's idea? What three different types exist? What is the chief requisite? What are the two principal sources of error? What is autobiography? What advantage has autobiography? what source of error? What is a diary? Of what use is a diary?
- In judging a history, what is the first point to be considered? What is required by the laws of art? What is said of style? What is meant by symmetry? What is the second point to be considered? What two inquiries should be made? On what are the greatest historical works based? What is the third point to be considered? What should be the historian's mental equipment? Why is it important to know his fundamental philosophical or religious beliefs?

Chapter 11

Essays and Oratory

- Essays. An essay is a brief dissertation on some special subject. It aims to present its statements in a clear and interesting manner, and this careful regard for a finished form brings the essay within the scope of literature in the strict sense of the word. The essay does not usually aim at an elaborate discussion of a subject in all its phases, and it is thus distinguished from the treatise. Its origin dates from the French author Montaigne in the latter part of the sixteenth century; but since the vast multiplication of periodicals in recent years, the essay has become a prominent department of literature. There is scarcely any subject of human interest that may not be discussed in an essay. The principal forms of the essay are as follows:
  - The tract, which is usually a brief discussion of some religious or moral subject.
  - The editorial, which is an editor's discussion of some theme of public interest.
  - The review or critique, which is a critical examination and discussion of some literary work.

Two general and well-defined types of essays may be profitably distinguished. The first may be called the personal essay. It allows great freedom of treatment, and in large measure reflects the personality of the author. It has something of the ease and charm of conversation. The essays of Montaigne, of Addison, and of Lamb are of this personal type. The other kind may be designated as the didactic essay. Its aim is the impartation of knowledge and the formation of public opinion. The personality of the author is concealed behind his statements and arguments. He does not write in the first person. In our best writing of this kind there is a careful treatment of the subject. The method of the essay is chiefly exposition. It uses narration and description only in a subordinate way.

The essayist usually has some information to impart, some argument to present, or some conclusion to be reached. His purpose naturally determines the mode of treatment. Generally there will be a beginning or introduction, a middle containing the body of treatment, and a conclusion. Very frequently, however, the writer plunges at once into his subject without the formality of an introduction. In estimating the worth of an essay three things are to be chiefly taken into account. The first is its form, including diction, sentences, paragraphs, and arrangement. The various points brought forward should be in a natural order, and each should have the prominence to which its relative importance entitles it. There should be movement or progress in the treatment, and the essay should gain in weight as it advances to the conclusion. The second point is the subject-matter of the essay.

As the essay is not intended to be exhaustive, there should be judgment in the selection of points to be presented. A skillful writer will be recognized as much by what he leaves in the inkstand as by what he says. In the presentation of facts there should be a conscientious regard for truth. The author's originality, force, culture will be reflected in the matter and manner of his discussion. Then, last of all, the writer's mood and standpoint should be considered. Is he serious, satirical, humorous? Is he writing from the standpoint of party or sect, or is he seeking only to know and present the truth? Is he thoroughly acquainted with the subject that he discusses? Only as we answer questions like these can we enter into full sympathy with an author and form a just and adequate conception of his work.

- Oratory. Oratory is that form of discourse that is primarily intended not to be read but to be spoken. Its object is mingled instruction and persuasion, and it may be defined as instruction suffused with feeling. In its lofty and impassioned forms oratory attains to eloquence,that quality which profoundly moves the hearts and wills of the hearers. But it is well to recognize the source of eloquence, which is to be distinguished from bombast and fustian. Eloquence is not a trick of rhetoric; it springs from the moral character of the speaker, from his gifts and attainments, and from the subject and occasion. "Mere eloquence," said Webster, "does not consist in speech. It cannot be brought from far. Labour and learning may toil for it, but they will toil in vain. Words and phrases may be marshaled in every way, but they cannot compass it. It must exist in the man, in the subject, and in the occasion. Affected passion, intense expression, the pomp of declamation, all may aspire to it; they cannot reach it. It comes, if it come at all, like the outbreaking of a fountain from the earth, or the bursting of volcanic fires, with spontaneous, original, native force." Oratory is variously divided, but perhaps no other division is better than that of Aristotle. He distinguishes three species of oratory:
  - Deliberative oratory, which has its place in deliberative bodies. In Parliament or Congress it is concerned with questions of legal enactment, finance, or administration; in religious bodies, with ecclesiastical questions; in scientific bodies, with questions of science. At

the present day a large part of oratory is deliberative in character.

- Judicial or forensic oratory, which is heard before courts of justice. It is chiefly concerned with human conduct in relation to law, and its aim is to determine what is legally right and just.
- Demonstrative oratory is chiefly occupied with the presentation of abstract or practical truth. It is heard in lectures, sermons, and other public addresses. It draws its themes from any department of human knowledge, and aims at imparting instruction, uplifting character, or influencing conduct. A finished oration is a work of art. Ancient rhetoricians distinguished six parts, which may still be found in some elaborate specimens of pulpit or forensic eloquence. These six parts were
  a. The exordium or introduction,
  b. The division of the subject,
  c. The statement of what is to be established,
  d. The argumentation,
  e. The appeal to the feelings, and
  f. The peroration or conclusion.

- It is evident that this scheme for an oration is, as a rule, much too artificial and elaborate for use at the present day. Modern intelligence and modern intensity of life demand greater brevity and directness. An audience of the present time rarely has patience with a discourse of more than an hour, and it generally prefers one of half that length. In a modern discourse we may generally recognize a threefold division:
  - The introduction, which points out the relation of the subject to the occasion, or otherwise prepares the audience better to appreciate the discussion that is to follow. It should be natural, and not so lengthy as to be out of keeping with the main body of the discourse.

- The discussion of the subject in hand. This consists of a statement of the theme and the various facts, arguments, and illustrations that are designed to throw light upon it and establish its truth. This is the main part of the discourse, and great care should be exercised in the statement of facts and the arrangement of arguments. Personal conviction should be back of what is said, for without this tone of sincerity the most brilliant rhetoric and eloquent declamation will be in vain.
- The conclusion, in which the results of the discussion are presented. It should be clear and claim no more than has been fairly established in the preceding discussion. On the basis of the truth previously presented it may contain an appeal to the feelings and the will, urging the course of action that has been shown to be advisable, wise, or obligatory.

• Argumentation may seek to establish the truth of a proposition in four different ways:
  - There may be the introduction of testimony. By testimony is meant the statements of actual observers or witnesses. It rests on experience, and may be given orally or in writing; hence we have oral and written testimony.
  - A proposition may be supported or established by analogy. Reasoning from analogy is that process by which we infer that when two objects resemble each other in several known particulars they will also resemble each other in a certain unknown particular. The planet Mars, for example, resembles the earth in shape, motion, atmosphere, change of seasons, and relation to the sun; and from the resemblance in these known particulars some persons have inferred that, like the earth, it is also inhabited. Analogical reasoning has a prominent place in

our mental operations. Analogy lies at the basis of simile, metaphor, and personification, which are often used in argumentation. We frequently use analogical processes in the practical affairs of life, inferring, for example, that there will be rain to-day because the temperature, appearance of the clouds, and the condition of the atmosphere resemble those of a rainy day last week.

But it is to be observed that the arguments from analogy give us at the best only probable truth. The degree of probability depends upon the nature and number of the resemblances upon which the conclusion is based. There must be no point of dissimilarity that would disprove the conclusion inferred.

— We may establish a conclusion by an array of facts. This is called inductive reasoning. We observe, for example, that A, B, C, and all other men of the past, so far as our knowledge goes, have died; and in view of these individual cases we draw the comprehensive conclusion that all men are mortal.

But this mode of reasoning, common and indispensable as it is, needs to be employed with caution. There is always danger of inferring more than the facts warrant. When the inference is based on an inadequate induction of facts, the process is called "jumping at a conclusion," a mistake that is frequently made. Even large inductions are not always safe. We might conclude, for instance, that, because the bulldog, hound, mastiff, setter, spaniel, terrier, and other species we have known, are accustomed to bark, therefore all dogs bark. Yet this apparently well-founded conclusion is erroneous, for there is a non-barking species in Greenland.

— Again, we may establish a truth by showing that

it comes within an established and recognized principle. This process is known as deductive reasoning. The principle on which deductive reasoning depends is the self-evident truth that "whatever is true of the whole is true of the parts." Starting from the general truth that all men are mortal, we may conclude that A, B, and C are mortal. The general truth that supplies the basis of deductive reasoning may be taken from various sources. Sometimes the truth is self-evident or intuitive, as the axioms that lie at the basis of mathematical reasoning. Sometimes they are truths arrived at by inductive processes. Sometimes they are maxims that have gained the assent of mankind; and again, they are the statements of an accepted philosophy, creed, code, or other recognized source of authority.

In deductive reasoning two points need particular attention:

- The fundamental principle on which the argument is based should be well established or recognized as true; and
- The conclusion should necessarily follow from the truth assumed in the beginning, and not embrace more than is duly warranted by it. The general structure of an oration is determined by its object. There should be, in large measure, simplicity, unity, and progress. The language should be within the comprehension of the average hearer; the sentences, as a rule, should be brief and forcible; and the general style should be concrete rather than abstract. All parts of the oration should be bound together by the single truth and purpose at which the orator aims. The arguments should not be abstruse but clear and striking. Irrelevant matter of every kind, no matter how brilliant in itself, should be excluded; and every fact and principle should be scrupulously correct. Understatement is better than overstatement. The

orator should continually advance toward his conclusion; the auditor should feel himself borne along not on a circling eddy but on the bosom of a full, strong current of thought and feeling.

It was Cicero who said that the orator should know everything. However desirable such attainments might be, they are no longer possible; but the orator should have a wide range of culture and experience. This is necessary to give breadth and proportion to his outlook upon the world. In addition to this general culture he should, as far as possible, be master of his subject; and to this end he should bestow upon his discourse careful and even laborious preparation. Without these requisites the orator is apt to prove uninteresting, inconclusive, and unsuccessful.

Review Questions

- What is an essay? What brings it within the range of art? How is it distinguished from a treatise? With whom did it originate? What gives it prominence now? Name its principal forms. What is a tract? an editorial? a critique or review? Name two types of essay. What is the character of the personal essay? Give examples. Define the didactic essay. What is the method of the essay? What parts may usually be distinguished? What three things are to be considered in estimating the worth of an essay? How should the successive points be presented? How is a skillful writer recognized? What is said of the essayist's mood and standpoint?
- What is oratory? What is its object? What is eloquence? Whence does it rise? What is the substance of Webster's view? How did Aristotle divide oratory? What is deliberative oratory? judicial or forensic? demonstrative? What parts were anciently distinguished? What is said of this scheme? What three parts are now generally recognized? What is the purpose of the

introduction? What is said of the discussion? What is said of the speaker's convictions? What is the nature of the conclusion? What four methods of proof may be used? What is meant by testimony? What are the two kinds of testimony? What is meant by reasoning from analogy? Illustrate. What is said of its use? What sort of truth is furnished by analogical reasoning? On what does the degree of its probability depend? What is inductive reasoning? Illustrate. What is meant by "jumping at a conclusion"? Give a case of erroneous conclusion. What is deductive reasoning? Illustrate. Whence may come the general truth lying at the basis of deduction? What two points must be attended to carefully? What qualities should an oration have? Why should the diction and sentence structure be simple? What should give unity to the oration? What is said of irrelevant matter? of movement or progress? What was Cicero's view of an orator's attainments? What is the advantage of broad culture? What is said of special preparation?

Chapter 12

Nature and Classification of Fiction

- Definition. Fiction is that form of prose narrative in which the characters, scenes, and incidents are partly or entirely imaginary. In its highest form it is a sort of prose epic; and Homer's "Odyssey" finds a parallel in Fenelon's "Telemachus." In the arrangement of characters and incidents to form a plot, fiction resembles the drama; and at the present time every notable work of fiction is apt to make its way to the stage. Like poetry in general, fiction has its principal source in the creative imagination, which, working on the basis of experience, modifies or produces character, scene, and incident. A common division of fiction, though not consistently observed, is the novel and the romance. The novel is a fictitious narrative in which the characters and incidents are in keeping with the ordinary train of events in society. Goldsmith's "Vicar of Wakefield," which brings before us the simple life of a country pastor, may be taken as a type. A romance is a fictitious narrative in which the characters and scenes and incidents are uncommon, improbable, or marvelous. Scott's "Ivanhoe" may be taken as a representative of the best type of romance. The one form of fiction may readily shade into the other, and it becomes difficult in some cases to determine the classification; but in general the two species are clearly marked.

- Romanticism. During the past century there were two far-reaching movements in the field of fiction. Both came in the character of a reaction; taken together they have given greater breadth and depth to this department of literature. The first movement, which dates near the beginning of the last century, is known as romanticism. It was a reaction against the formal and the conventional. Romanticism may be defined as liberalism in literature; it is a breaking away from authority and a return to nature. It manifested itself in two particulars both in fiction and poetry: first, there was greater freedom in subject, form, and character; and second, there was a return to the past, particularly to an idealized age of chivalry in the Middle Ages. Scott was the great leader of the romantic movement both in poetry and in fiction. In their wide range of character and incident, and in their idealization of the past, the Waverley Novels are in general perfect types of romanticism.
- Realism. Realism came about the middle of the Victorian era as a reaction against romanticism. It was born of the scientific spirit, which rendered the public dissatisfied with fanciful pictures of past ages and with the impossibilities of wild romance. Realism, as the word indicates, adheres to reality. Discarding what is idealistic or unreal in characters and situations, it aims at being true to life. All the great novelists of this periodDickens, Thackeray, George Eliotwere in the best sense of the word realists. As an effort to represent life as it is, the worth of realism must be acknowledged. In its proper application it places the novel on an immovable basis. While idealism shows us how life might be or ought to be, realism shows how it actually is. Unfortunately, realistic writers have not, in many cases, been true to their fundamental principles. The great continental leaders of realismTolstoi, Zola, Ibsenhave been tainted with a fatal pessimism. Realists of this type

seem to see only one side of life,the darker side of sin and wretchedness and despair. They often describe what is coarse, impure, obscene. No doubt their pictures are true as far as they go; but the fatal defect of their work is that it does not reflect life as a whole. It does not portray the pure and noble and happy side of life, which is just as real as the other. Except in the hands of genius, realism is apt to be dull. It gives us uninteresting photographs.

There are times when we do not care so much for instruction as for amusement and recreation. This fact opens a legitimate field for the imaginative story-teller. There is to-day a decided reaction against realism in the form of what has been called the new romanticism. It does not present to us elaborate studies of actual life, but entertains us with an interesting or exciting story. Stevenson, Weyman, Hope, and Doyle have been leaders in this movement, and some of the most widely read novels of the past few years have belonged to this new romanticism.

- Idealism. The influence of idealism in fiction should be recognized. It may tinge the work both of romanticism and of realism. It is, perhaps, to be regarded as an atmosphere rather than as a method. The aim of idealism is to soften the hard realities of life. It in a measure portrays things not as they are but as they should be; and as far as it definitely pursues this course it presents a contrast to realism. It naturally chooses for the most part the nobler types of character; and to the villains that may be introduced it metes out in due time a merited punishment. The trials of life are brought to happy issue. The hero and heroine, both somewhat above the characters of ordinary life, at length triumph over all the obstacles that beset their path. Kept within due bounds, idealism gives a hopeful and uplifting tone to fiction; but without careful restraint it is in danger of becoming false and injurious. It presents to the young a caricature of the world, and exposes them, at a later period, to bitter and dangerous disillusionment. Among our greatest novelists an idealistic tendency is very perceptible in Scott and Dickens.

- Component Elements. In every important work of fiction there are six things to be considered, namely, the characters, the incidents, the environment, the plot, the purpose, and the view or philosophy of life. The first three elements constitute the materials out of which the novelist builds his work; the last three supply the general plan by which he builds it. The excellence of the work, as in architecture, depends both on the character of the materials and on the manner in which they are put together. When Solomon constructed his famous temple he not only used cedar and gold but also joined them together according to a wise design and noble purpose. These various elements are worthy of separate consideration.
  - The characters of a novel are of prime importance. As in actual life, they give tone to the society to which we are introduced. They should be clearly individualized, as in the drama, and maintain throughout a reasonable consistency. They may be taken from any class of society; and writers of large creative genius, like Shakespeare, Scott, Dickens, Balzac, will be distinguished both for the number and for the variety of their characters. It is not enough that the characters be described in their outward appearance and experiences. In all profounder work, as in George Eliot, there will be an unveiling of the hidden springs of motive and disposition. The great potentialities of human nature both for good and evil will be brought to light, and thus the mimic world of the

novelist will reflect the life of the great real world in its more tragic aspects.

— By the incidents of a novel we mean the acts and experiences of the characters. They make up the connected and progressive story. The incidents may be as varied, as the occurrences of human life, sweeping the whole range of toil, sorrow, and joy. They may be either comic or tragic. The interest of a work of fiction depends largely upon its incidents. Separately they may be entertaining, absorbing, or thrilling; and taken together in their sequence they may carry us forward irresistibly to the conclusion. They should be in keeping with the time and place, and the several acts of the personages should be in harmony with their character and culture.

— As in real life, the personages of a novel or romance live and move in the midst of an environment. They are placed in the midst of circumstances, upon which they act and by which they are acted upon. They may live on land or sea, in the country or in the city, amid the wildness of unsubdued forests or the culture of long-established communities.

They may be surrounded by intelligence and luxury or by ignorance and squalor. The environment is brought before us by description, which necessarily constitutes no inconsiderable part of every work of fiction. The descriptive passages should be true to fact, and graphic enough to enable the reader to picture the scenes in his mind; but they should not be so long drawn as to encumber or impede the story. Description is subordinate in fiction; instead of being an end in itself, its purpose is to throw light upon the characters and incidents of the story.

— By plot, we mean the manner in which the

incidents of a story are arranged with reference to the final issue. The incidents may be loosely connected or they may be so skillfully ordered as to arouse the reader's breathless interest. A skillful plot presupposes dramatic talent. This is not always found in union with a strong creative imagination; and thus it happens that some of our greatest novelists, as Thackeray and George Eliot, are defective in dramatic plots. While a skillfully arranged plot is not an essential element in a work of fiction, it is always a source of interest and power.

– Every work of fiction has an aim or purpose. Sometimes the author merely aims at telling an interesting story which has no other significance than to provoke a smile or a tear. Sometimes it may be intended to illustrate a period in history or the manners of a particular locality. Sometimes it is designed to throw light on some phase of human character or human experience. And again, it may be a vehicle for conveying some form of teaching or for illustrating the growth of culture and character. In studying a work of fiction the purpose should be clearly apprehended, for the merit of a novel or romance depends in a measure upon the author's aim and his degree of success in realizing it.

– Every work of fiction, consciously or unconsciously to the author, is apt to embody a particular view or philosophy of life. Every thoughtful person has convictions in regard to God, nature, and man. He may believe in a personal deity or an unconscious force as the source of all things. He may think of nature as a creation or as a product of impersonal natural law. He may think of man as an immortal being or as a creature whose existence ceases with death. But whatever may be an author's fundamental beliefs, they will inevitably colour his work.

- Kinds of Novels. Novels may be divided into various classes according to subject or method of treatment. As to method, we have already had the general division of romanticism and realism. Another generic classification has been proposed: first, novels of life, which include the works portraying both past and contemporary life; and second, novels of idea, which include didactic and artistic works of fiction. The didactic novel discusses some practical problem or advances some social or moral theory; the artistic novel subordinates the story to perfection of form. It will be helpful to the student to distinguish the following classes:
  - The society novel is devoted to a portrayal of existing men and manners. The field is a wide one. The characters may be taken from any class of society. The society novel may bring before us, as in Thackeray's "Vanity Fair," what is known as fashionable life. It may again, as in George Eliot's "Adam Bede" or Goldsmith's "Vicar of Wakefield," introduce us to the lives of plain people. It may acquaint us, as in Du Maurier's "Trilby," with the Bohemian or artist class in our great cities. It may deal, as in Dickens's "Oliver Twist" or Bulwer's "Paul Clifford," with the criminal class. In short, there is no class of society or type of character that may not become the subject of treatment in novels of this class.
  - Local novels are devoted to the portrayal of the life and manners of a well-marked locality. They are social novels within a restricted field. Differences of race, of language, of pursuit, and of intelligence, as seen in particular localities, are reflected in novels of this kind. There is scarcely

any portion of England that has not been described in some work of fiction. Charlotte Bronte brings Yorkshire scenery and character before us in "Shirley"; George Eliot portrays the scenes of her native Warwick in "The Mill on the Floss"; Blackmore's "Lorna Doone" portrays the scenery, life, and language of Devonshire. America has afforded a very rich field for the local novel. Not a few of its choicest works belong to this class. Scarcely any part of our wide country or any special phase of its life has escaped the eyes of the enterprising story-teller. In his "Grandissimes," for example, George W. Cable gives us a glimpse of the Creole life of Louisiana. In the "Hoosier Schoolmaster" Edward Eggleston describes pioneer life in Indiana. In "Gabriel Conroy" Bret Harte brings before us the wild and lawless life of California a half century ago. In various works Miss Murfree has described the dwellers in the Tennessee mountains. New England and the South have been portrayed by various writers.

The historical novel is devoted to the description of life in the past. It should be based on a careful study of the period to be portrayed. It may deal with the scenes of a hundred years ago or it may go back a thousand years before the Christian era. No other department of fiction has a prouder array of great books. Historical fiction has gone hand in hand with a revived interest in historical and archaeological research. The greatest of all historical novelists is Scott, whose Waverley series covers the centuries between the crusades, which "Ivanhoe" describes, and the rebellion of Prince Edward Charles in 1745, which "Waverley" describes. But other great namesGerman, English, Americanbelong to this class of fiction. "Uarda," for example, by George

Ebers, describes life in Egypt a thousand years before Christ. Kingsley's "Hypatia" takes us back to the city of Alexandria in the fifth century of our era. In the "Last Days of Pompeii" Bulwer Lytton describes the life of the Roman city at the time of its destruction. George Eliot's "Romola" portrays the spirit and manners of the city of Florence in the days of Savonarola and the revival of learning. "Ben Hur" by Lew Wallace is a tale of the Christ. "The Schoenberg-Cotta Family" by Mrs. Elizabeth Charles is a graphic portrayal of movements and scenes in Germany at the period of the Reformation. Recently there has been a notable revival in historical fiction. It has come, perhaps, as a reaction against a hard realism and empty romanticism. It probably strikes its roots in the desire for knowledge which at the present time is so generally characteristic of the American people. Not a few of the recent books of phenomenal popularityChurchill's "Richard Carvel," Miss Johnson's "To Have and to Hold," Ford's "Janice Meredith," Page's "Red Rock," Thompson's "Alice of Old Vincennes"deal with interesting periods in the history of our country.

— The problem or purpose novel has been prominent in recent fiction. It has been a natural product of this restless, intellectual age. Fiction has been made the medium for the discussion of political, social, and religious problems. Not a few of them, as Bellamy's socialistic "Looking Backward," have had an enormous circulation. "Uncle Tom's Cabin" by Mrs. Stowe was a severe arraignment of slavery, and exerted a strong influence in molding the sentiment of a large part of our country. Recent theological unrest is reflected in Mrs. Ward's "Robert Elsmere" and in Margaret Deland's "John Ward,

Preacher." The nature and influence of labour organizations are presented in Charles Reade's "Put Yourself in His Place," and in the anonymous American story "The Bread Winners." Hall Caine's "Christian" involves a serious indictment against the church in England. Disraeli traversed the field of English politics in his "Coningsby" and "Endymion," as did Trollope in his "Phineas Finn" and "Prime Minister." In his "Guardian Angel" and "Elsie Venner" Oliver Wendell Holmes traces the effects of heredity, a subject previously handled by Hawthorne in his "House of Seven Gables." In this way we see that nearly every great practical question of general interest may be discussed or portrayed in fiction.

— The love story and the story of adventure embrace a considerable though unambitious part of fiction. The love story deals with courtship and marriage. As a rule, after encountering more or less opposition or difficulty, the lovers are at last happily united. A thread of love usually runs through all the more ambitious types of fiction, for it is a source of universal interest that cannot lightly be set aside; but in the love story it is the central and dominant interest. The story of adventure consists of a succession of interesting or thrilling incidents. The type of this species of fiction is Defoe's "Robinson Crusoe." The new romantic movement already referred to lays much stress on a rapid succession of exciting incidents. This is illustrated by Hope's "Prisoner of Zenda" or by most of R. L. Stevenson's works, of which "Kidnapped" and "The Master of Ballantrae" may be taken as fair examples.

— Naval fiction belongs to the sea. It is an interesting field, though somewhat limited in its range of character and incident. The sea itself, with its magnificent and changing moods, is a sublime object. The restricted life on shipboardthe telling of yarns beneath the starlit skies, the spirit of mingled superstition and daring, the prompt and brave activities attending a storm, and, above all, the excitement and dangers of battlehas for the landsman a peculiar charm. Novelists of the sea are not numerous; for, in order to be in the best sense successful, the writer must have had a seafaring experience. James Fenimore Cooper, who had been in the navy, criticised Scott's "Pirate" as the work of a landsman. He undertook to produce a genuine story of the sea in his "Pilot," which, whatever else may be its defects, is correct in sailor's lingo and briny flavour. He was no less successful in "The Red Rover," the scenes of which antedate the Revolution. But the prince of marine novelists is unquestionably Frederick Marryat, whose "Peter Simple," "Jacob Faithful," and "Mr. Midshipman Easy" are perhaps unsurpassed in their sphere.

— The psychologic novel is concerned chiefly with mental analysis. It traces the workings of the soul under different circumstances and different influences. It follows the character in its ascent to higher goodness or in its descent to lower degradation. Stevenson's "Dr. Jekyll and Mr. Hyde," for example, is a powerful exhibition of the dualitythe brute and the divinityin human nature. Hawthorne's "Scarlet Letter," while in one sense a historical novel, is an incomparable study of the human soul under the weight of guilt and remorse. Throughout George Eliot's novels there is a constant portrayal of mental and moral conditions that give to her works an unusual depth and power. Her method has been justly called psychologic realism. Under this head we may place what has been called the "art and culture novel," the object of which is to exhibit the gradual development of individual character by means of a changing environment. The type of this sort of fiction is Goethe's "Wilhelm Meister." The short story, which our magazines have rendered so popular in recent years, is a novel in miniature. It paints on a small canvas but with exceeding delicacy. Like the novel or the romance, it may find its materials in any age or in any class of society; and in its general method it conforms to the laws of fiction in general.

Review Questions

- What is fiction? How does it resemble the drama? What is said of dramatized novels? Define novel and romance. Give examples of each.
- What is romanticism? When did it manifest itself? In what two particulars?
- What is realism? Whence did it spring? What are its merits? What tendency of realistic writers is noted? What is the danger of realism? What is meant by the new romanticism? Mention some of its representative writers.
- What is the aim of idealism? How does it do this? What two great novelists show idealistic tendencies?
- What six things are to be noted in every novel? What two groups are distinguished among them? On what does the excellence of a novel depend? What is said of the characters? Whence may they be drawn? How are great writers distinguished? What characterizes profound novels? What is meant by incidents? What is said of their variety? How should they be arranged? What is meant by environment? What environments may be used? How may they be brought before us? What should be the character of

this description? What is its place? What is meant by plot? What is presupposed in a skillful plot? What great writers are lacking in dramatic power? What purposes may be aimed at? Why should the purpose be apprehended? About what have thoughtful persons convictions? What is the effect of these convictions? Why should the writer's aim or purpose be understood?

- How may novels and romances be divided? What are novels of life? novels of idea? What seven classes are distinguished? What is a society novel? What may it portray? What are local novels? What is said of them in America? Mention some well-known local novels. What is a historical novel? On what should it be based? What is said of historical fiction? Who is the greatest of historical novelists? Mention some others. What is said of recent tendencies? Mention some recent historical novels. What is meant by problem or purpose novels? Illustrate by various examples. What is the nature of the love story? of the story of adventure? Illustrate. What is naval fiction? Why are sea novelists not numerous? What is said of Cooper? Who is the chief of marine novelists? With what is the psychologic novel principally concerned? Give examples. What gives George Eliot's novels their depth? What is said of the short story? To what laws is it subject?

Chapter 13

Development of Criticism

In England, as elsewhere, criticism was a late birth of the literary spirit. English poets had sung and literary prose been written for centuries before it struck men to ask themselves, What is the secret of the power that these things have on our mind, and by what principles are they to be judged? And it could hardly have been otherwise.

Criticism is a self-conscious art, and could not have arisen in an age of intellectual childhood. It is a derivative art, and could scarcely have come into being without a large body of literature to suggest canons of judgment, and to furnish instances of their application.

The age of Chaucer might have been expected to bring with it a new departure. It was an age of self-scrutiny and of bold experiment. A new world of thought and imagination had dawned upon it; and a new literature, that of Italy, was spread before it. Yet who shall say that the facts answer to these expectations? In the writings of Chaucer himself a keen eye, it is true, may discern the faint beginnings of the critical spirit. No poet has written with more nicely calculated art; none has passed a cooler judgment upon the popular taste of his generation. We know that Chaucer despised the "false gallop" of chivalrous verse; we know that he had small respect for the marvels of Arthurian romance. And his admiration is at least as frank as his contempt. What poet has felt and avowed a deeper reverence for the great Latins? What poet has been so alert to recognize the master-spirits of his own time and his father's? De Meung and Granson among the FrenchDante, Petrarch and Boccaccio of the Italianseach comes in for his share of praise from Chaucer, or of the princely borrowings which are still more eloquent than praise. Yet, for all this, Chaucer is far indeed from founding the art of criticism. His business was to create, and not to criticise. And, had he set himself to do so, there is no warrant that his success would have been great. In many ways he was still in bondage to the mediaval, and wholly uncritical, tradition. One classic, we may almost say, was as good to him as another. He seems to have placed Ovid on a line with Virgil; and the company in his House of Fame is undeniably mixed. His judgments have the healthy instinct of the consummate artist. They do not show, as those of his master, Petrarch, unquestionably do, the discrimination and the tact of the born critic.

For this, or for any approach to it, English literature had to wait for yet two centuries more. In the strict sense, criticism did not begin till the age of Elizabeth; and, like much else in our literature, it was largely due to the passion for classical study, so strongly marked in the poets and dramatists of Shakespeare's youth, and inaugurated by Surrey and others in the previous generation. These conditions are in themselves significant. They serve to explain much both of the strength and the weakness of criticism, as it has grown up on English soil. From the Elizabethans to Milton, from Milton to Johnson, English criticism was dominated by constant reference to classical models. In the latter half of this period the influence of these models, on the whole, was harmful.

It acted as a curb rather than as a spur to the imagination of poets; it tended to cripple rather than give energy to the judgment of critics. But in earlier days it was not so. For nearly a century the influence of classical masterpieces was altogether for good. It was not the regularity but the richness, not the self-restraint but the freedom, of the ancients that came home to poets such as Marlowe, or even to critics such as Meres. And if adventurous spirits, like Spenser and Sidney, were for a time misled into the vain attempt to graft exotic forms upon the homely growths of native poetry, they soon saw their mistake and revolted in silence against the ridiculous pedant who preferred the limping hexameters of the Arcadia to

Sidney's sonnets, and the spavined iambics of Spenser to the Faerie Queene. In the main, the worship of the classics seems to have counted at this time rather for freedom than restraint. And it is well that it was so. Yet restraint too was necessary; and, like freedom, it was found though in less ample measurethrough devotion to the classics. There can be little doubt that, consciously or no, the Elizabethans, with their quick eye for beauty of every kind, were swayed, as men in all ages have been swayed, by the finely chiselled forms of classical art.

The besetting sin of their imagination was the tendency to run riot; and it may well be that, save for the restraining influence of ancient poetry, they would have sinned in this matter still more boldly than they did. Yet the chastening power of classical models may be easily overrated. And we cannot but notice that it was precisely where the classical influence was strongest that the force of imagination was the least under control. Jonson apart, there were no more ardent disciples of the ancients than Marlowe and Chapman. And no poets of that age are so open to the charge of extravagance as they. It is with Milton that the chastening influence of the ancients first makes itself definitely felt. But Milton was no less alive to the fervour than to the self-mastery of his classical models. And it was not till the Restoration that "correctness" was recognized as the highest, if not the only, quality of the ancients, or accepted as the one worthy object of poetic effort. For more than a century correctness remained the idol both of poetry and of criticism in England; and nothing less than the furious onslaught of the Lyrical Ballads was needed to overthrow it. Then the floodgates were opened. A new era both of poetic and critical energy had dawned.

Thus the history of English criticism, like that of English literature, divides itself roughly into three periods. The first is the period of the Elizabethans and of Milton; the second is from the Restoration to the French Revolution; the third from the Revolution to the present day. The typical critic of the first period is Sidney; Dryden opens and Johnson closes the second; the third, a period of far more varied tendencies than either of the others, is perhaps most fitly represented by Lamb, Hazlitt, and Carlyle. It will be the aim of the following pages to sketch the broader outlines of the course that critical inquiry has taken in each.

The first thing that strikes us in the early attempts of criticism is that its problems are to a large extent remote from those which have engrossed critics of more recent times. There is little attempt to appraise accurately the worth of individual authors; still less, to find out the secret of their power, or to lay bare the hidden lines of thought on which their imagination had set itself to work. The first aim both of Puttenham and of Webbe, the pioneers of Elizabethan criticism, was either to classify writers according to the subjects they treated and the literary form that each had made his own, or to analyse the metre and other more technical elements of their poetry.

But this, after all, was the natural course in the infancy of the study. All science begins with classification; and all classification with the external and the obvious. The Greek critics could take no step forward until they had classified all poems as either lyric, epic, or dramatic. And how necessary that division was may be seen from the length at which Plato discusses the nature of the distinction in the second book of the Republic. Even Aristotle, in this as in other things the 'master of those who know', devotes no inconsiderable space of the Poetics to technical matters such as the analysis of vocal sounds, and the aptness of different metres to different forms of poetic thought.

There is another matter in which the methods of Elizabethan critics run side by side with those of the early Greeks. In Plato and Aristotle we are not seldom startled by the sudden transition from questions of form to the deepest problems suggested by imaginative art. The same is true of the Elizabethan critics. It is doubtless true that the latter give a proportionally larger space to the more technical sides of the subject than their Greek forerunners. They could not reasonably be expected to write with the width of view that all the world has admired in Aristotle and Plato. Moreover, they were from the first confronted with a practical difficulty from which the Greek critics were so fortunate as to be free. Was rhyme a "brutish" form of verse? and, if so, was its place to be taken by the alliterative rhythm, so dear to the older poets, or by an importation of classical metres, such as was attempted by Sidney and Spenser, and enforced by the unwearied lectures of Harvey and of Webbe?

This, however technical, was a fundamental question; and, until it was settled, there was but little use in debating the weightier matters of the law. The discussion, which might have raged for ever among the critics, was happily cut short by the healthy instinct of the poets. Against alliteration the question had already been given by default. Revived, after long disuse, by Langland and other poets of the West Midlands in the fourteenth century, it had soon again been swept out of fashion by the irresistible charm of the genius of Chaucer. The Tale of Gamelyn, dating apparently from the first quarter of the fifteenth century, is probably the last poem of note in which the once universal metre is even partially employed.

And what could prove more clearly that the old metrical form was dead? The rough rhythm of early English poetry, it is true, is kept; but alliteration is dropped, and its place is taken by rhyme. Nor were the efforts to impose classical measures on English poetry more blest in their results. The very men on whom the literary Romanizers had fixed their hopes were the first to abandon the enterprise in despair. If any genius was equal to the task of naturalizing hexameters in a language where strict quantity is unknown, it was the genius of Spenser. But Spenser soon ranged himself heart and soul with the champions of rhyme; his very name has passed down to us as a synonym for the most elaborate of all rhyming stanzas that have taken root in our verse.

For the moment, rhyme had fairly driven all rivals from the field. Over the lyric its sway was undisputed. In narrative poetry, where its fitness was far more disputable, it maintained its hold till the closing years of Milton. In the drama itself, where its triumph would have been fatal, it disputed the ground inch by inch against the magnificent instrument devised by Surrey and perfected by Marlowe.

It was during the ten years preceding the publication of Webbe's Discourse (1586) that this controversy seems to have been hottest. From the first, perhaps, it bulked more largely with the critics than with the poets themselves. Certainly it allowed both poets and critics sufficient leisure for the far more important controversy which has left an enduring monument in Sidney's Apologie for Poetrie.

The historical bearing of Sidney's treatise has been too commonly overlooked. It forms, in truth, one move in the long struggle which ended only with the restoration of Charles II.; or, to speak more accurately, which has lasted, in a milder form, to the present day. In its immediate object it was a reply to the Puritan assaults upon the theatre; in its ultimate scope, a defence of imaginative art against the suspicions with which men of high but narrow purpose have always, consciously or unconsciously, tended to regard it. It is a noble plea for liberty, directed no less against the unwilling scruples of idealists, such as Plato or Rousseau, than against the ruthless bigotry of practical moralists and religious partisans.

From the first dawn of the Elizabethan drama, the stricter Protestants had declared war upon the stage. Intrenched within the city they were at once able to drive the theatres beyond the walls (1575); just as seventy years later, when it had seized the reins of central government, the same party, embittered by a thousand insults and brutalities, hastened to close the theatres altogether. It would be an evident mistake to suppose that this was merely a municipal prejudice, or to forget that the city council was backed by a large body of serious opinion throughout the country. A proof of this, if proof were needed, is to be found in the circumstances that gave rise to the Apologie of Sidney.

The attack on the stage had been opened by the corporation and the clergy. It was soon joined by the men of letters. And the essay of Sidney was an answer neither to a town councillor, nor to a preacher, but to a former dramatist and actor. This was Stephen Gosson, author of the School of Abuse. The style of Gosson's pamphlet is nothing if not literary. It is full of the glittering conceits and the fluent rhetoric which the ready talent of Lyly had just brought into currency. It is euphuism of the purest water, with all the merits and all the drawbacks of the euphuistic manner. For that very reason the blow was felt the more keenly. It was violently resented as treason by the playwrights and journalists who still professed to reckon Gosson among their ranks.

A war of pamphlets followed, conducted with the usual fury of literary men. Gosson on the one side, Lodge, the dramatist, upon the other, exchanged compliments with an energy which showed that one at least of them had not in vain graduated in "the school of abuse". "Raw devises", "hudder mudder", "guts and garbage", such are the phrases hurled by Gosson at the arguments and style of his opponents; "bawdy charms", "the very butchery of Christian souls", are samples of the names fastened by him upon the cause which they defended. From this war of words Sidney turned loftily aside. Pointedly challenged at the outsetfor the first and second pamphlets of Gosson had, without permission, been dedicated to "the right noble gentleman, Maister Philip Sidney"he seldom alludes to the arguments, and never once mentions the name of Gosson.

He wrote to satisfy his own mind, and not to win glory in the world of letters. And thus his Apologie, though it seems to have been composed while the controversy was still fresh in men's memory, was not published until nearly ten years after his death (1595). It was not written for controversy, but for truth. From the first page it rises into the atmosphere of calm, in which alone great questions can be profitably discussed. The Apologie of Sidney is, in truth, what would now be called a Philosophy of Poetry. It is philosophy taken from the side of the moralist; for that was the side to which the disputants had confined themselves, and in whichaltogether apart from the example of othersthe interest of Sidney, as man of action, inevitably lay. It is philosophy as conceived by the mind of a poet. But, none the less, it pierces to the eternal problems which underlie the workings of all creative art, and presents them with a force, for the like of which we must go back to Plato and Aristotle, or look forward to the philosophers and inspired critics of a time nearer our own. It recalls the Phadrus and the Ion; it anticipates the utterance of a still more kindred spirit, the Defence of Poetry by Shelley. Philosopher as he was, Sidney arranges his thoughts in the loose order of the poet or the orator. It may be well, therefore, to give a brief sketch of his argument; and to do so without much regard to the arrangement of the Apologie itself. The main argument of the Apologie may indeed be called a commentary on the saying of Aristotle, cited by Sidney himself, that "Poetry is more philosophical and more studiously serious than History"that is, as Sidney interprets it, than the scientific fact of any kind; or again, on that yet more pregnant saying of Shelley, that "poets are the unacknowledged legislators of the world". Gosson had denounced poetry as "the vizard of vanity, wantonness, and folly"; or, in Sidney's paraphrase, as "the mother of lies and the nurse of abuse". Sidney replies by urging that of all arts poetry is the most true and the most necessary to men.

All learning, he pleads, and all culture begin with poetry. Philosophy, religion, and history herself, speak through the lips of poetry. There is indeed a sense in which poetry stands on higher ground than any science. There is no science, not even metaphysics, the queen of all sciences, that does not "build upon nature", and that is not, so far, limited by the facts of nature. The poet alone is "not tied to any such subjection"; he alone "freely ranges within the zodiac of his own wit".

This, no doubt, is dangerous ground, and it is enforced by still more dangerous illustrations. But Sidney at once guards himself by insisting, as Plato had done before him, that the poet too is bound by laws which he finds but does not make; they are, however, laws not of fact but of thought, the laws of the ideathat is, of the inmost truth of things, and of God. Hence it is that the works of the poet seem to come from God, rather than from man. They stand rather on a level with nature, the material of all sciences, than with the sciences themselves, which are nothing more than man's interpretation of nature. In some sense, indeed, they are above nature; they stand midway between nature and him who created nature. They are a first nature, "beyond and over the works of that second nature". For they are the self-revelation of that which is the noblest work of God, and which in them finds utterance at its best and brightest.

Thus, so far from being the "mother of lies", poetry is the highest form of truth. Avowedly so, in what men have always recognized to be the noblest poetry, the psalms and parables and other writings that "do imitate the inconceivable excellences of God". To a less degree, but still avowedly, in that poetry whose theme is philosophy or history. And so essentially, however men may overlook it, in that poetry which, professedly dealing with human life as we know it, does not content itself with reproducing the character of this man or that, but "reined only with learned discretion, ranges into the divine consideration of what may be and should be"of the universal and complete rather than the individual and imperfect. But, if truth be the essence of the poet's work, "the right describing note to know a poet by", it would seem that the outward form of it, the metre and the ornament, are of little moment. "There have been many most excellent poets that never versified."

And verse is nothing more than a means, and not the only means, of securing a "fitting raiment" for their matter and suiting their manner "according to the dignity of their subject". In this suggestionthat harmonious prose may, for certain forms of poetic thought, be hardly less suitable than verseSidney is at one with Shelley. And neither critic must be taken to disparage verse, or to mean more than that the matter, the conception, is the soul of poetry, and that the form is only of moment so far as it aidsas undoubtedly it does aidto "reveal the soul within". It is rather as a witness to the whole scope of their argument than as a particular doctrine, to be left or taken, that the suggestion is most profitably regarded.

Having settled the speculative base of poetry, Sidney turns to a yet more cherished theme, its influence upon character and action. The "highest end" of all knowledge, he urges, is "the knowledge of a man's self, with the end of well doing and not of well knowing only". Now by no artist is this end served so perfectly as by the poet. His only serious rivals are the moral philosopher and the historian. But neither of these flies so straight to his mark as the poet. The one gives precepts that fire no heart to action; the other gives examples without the precepts that should interpret and control them. The one lives in the world of ideas, the other in the world of hard and literal fact. Neither, therefore, has power to bridge the gulf that parts thought from action; neither can hope to take hold of beings in whose life, by its very nature, thought and action are indissolubly interwoven.

"Now doth the peerless poet perform both. For whatsoever the philosopher saith should be done, he giveth a perfect picture of it in some one, by whom he presupposeth it was done. So as he coupleth the general notion with the particular example.... Therein of all sciences is our poet the monarch." Once more we feel that Sidney is treading upon dangerous ground. But once more he saves himself by giving a wider definition both to thought and action, both to "well knowing and to well doing", than is common with moralists. By the former most moralists are apt to understand the bare "precept", thought as crystallized in its immediate bearing upon action. By the latter they commonly mean the passive rather than the active virtues, temperance and self-restraint rather than energy and resolve. From both these limitations Sidney, on the whole, is nobly free.

To him the "delight which is all the good fellow poet seemeth to promise", "the words set in delightful proportion and prepared for the well enchanting skill of music", "the tale which holdeth children from play and old men from the chimney corner"all these, its indefinable and purely artistic elements, are an inseparable part of the "wisdom" which poetry has to offer. In other words, it is the frame of mind produced by poetry, the "thought hardly to be packed into the narrow act", no less than the prompting to this action or to that, which Sidney values in the work of the poet. And if this be true, none but the most fanatical champion of "art for art's sake" will dispute the justice of his demands on poetry. None but such will deny that, whether by attuning the mind to beauty and nobleness, or by means yet more direct and obvious, art must have some bearing upon the life of man and on the habitual temper of his soul. No doubt, we might have wished that, in widening the scope of poetry as a moral influence, Sidney had been yet more explicit than in fact he is. We cannot but regret that, however unjustly, he should have laid himself open to the charge of desiring to turn poetry into sermons. But it is bare justice to point out that such a charge cannot fairly be brought against him; or that it can only be brought with such qualifications as rob it of its sting.

On the other matter the record of Sidney is yet clearer. By "well doing" he does not mean, as is too often meant, mere abstinence from evil, but the active pursuit of whatsoever things are manly, noble, and of good report. It is not only the "temperance of Diomedes" though temperance too may be conceived as an active virtuebut the wisdom of Ulysses, the patriotism of Aneas, "the soon repenting pride of Agamemnon", the valour of Achillesit is courage, above all courage, that stirs his soul in the great works of ancient poetry. It is the same quality that moves him in the ballads and romances of the moderns. "Certainly I must confess my own barbarousness; I never heard the old song of Percy and Douglas that I found not my heart moved more than with a trumpet." And again: "Truly I have known men that, even with reading Amadis de Gaule (which, God knoweth, wanteth much of a perfect poesy), have found their hearts moved to the exercise of courtesy, liberality, and especially courage." The man who wrote these words had no starved conception of what poetry should be. Once again. Sidney has small patience with those who would limit art by the banishment of all that recalls the baser side of life. "Now, as in geometry, the oblique must be known as well as the right. So in the actions of our life, who seeth not the filthiness of evil, wanteth a great foil to perceive the beauty of virtue. This doth the comedy handle so... as with hearing it we get, as it were, an experience....

So that the right use of comedy will, I think, by no body be blamed." No doubt, the moral aspect of comedy is here marked with what must be called immoderate stress. Here, too, as when he deals with the kindred side of tragedy, Sidney demands that the poet shall, in his villains, "show you nothing that is not to be shunned"; in other words, that, so far as it paints evil, comedy shall take the form of satire. But, even with this restriction, it must be allowed that Sidney takes a wider view than might appear at a hasty reading; wider, it is probable, than was at all common among the men of his generation. No Shakespeare had yet arisen to touch the baser qualities of men with a gleam of heroism or to humanize the most stoical endurance with a strain of weakness.

And even Shakespeare, in turning from the practice to the theory of his art, could find no words very different from those of Sidney. To him, as to Sidney, the aim of the drama is "to show virtue her own image and scorn her own feature"; though by a saving clause, which Sidney perhaps would hardly have accepted, it is further defined as being to show "the very age and body of the time his form and pressure". Yet it must be remembered that Sidney is loud in praise of so unflinching a portraiture of life, base and noble, as Chaucer's Troilus and Cressida. And on the whole it remains true that the limitations of Sidney are the limitations of his age, while his generosity is his own.

The remainder of the Apologie is necessarily of slighter texture. Apart from the examination of Plato's banishment of the poetsa theme on which Harington also discourses, though with less weight than Sidneyit is concerned mainly with two subjects: an assertion that each form of poetry has its peculiar moral import, and a lament over the decay into which English poetry had fallen in the sixteenth century.

Such a lament sounds strangely to us, accustomed as we are to regard the age of Elizabeth, already half ended when Sidney wrote, as the most fruitful period of our literature. But, when the Apologie was composed, no one of the authors by whose fame the Elizabethan age is now commonly knownSidney himself and Spenser alone exceptedhad begun to write. English poetry was about to wake from the long night that lies between the age of Chaucer and the age of Shakespeare. But it was not yet fully awakened. And the want of a full and free life in creative art goes far to account for the shortcomings of Elizabethan criticism.

Vague the Elizabethan critics undeniably are; they tend to lose themselves either in far-fetched analogies or in generalities that have but a slight bearing upon the distinctive problems of literary appreciation. When not vague, they are apt to fritter their strength on technical details which, important to them, have long lost their significance for the student of literature. But both technicalities and vagueness may be largely traced to the uncertain practice of the poets upon whom, in the first instance, their criticism was based. The work of Surrey and of Sackville was tentative; that of Webbe and Puttenham was necessarily the same. It is the more honour to Sidney that, shackled as he was by conditions from which no man could escape altogether, he should have struck a note at once so deep and so strong as is sounded in the Apologie.

In turning from Sidney to Dryden we pass into a different world. The philosophy, the moral fervour, the prophetic strain of the Elizabethan critic have vanished. Their place is taken by qualities less stirring in themselves, but more akin to those that modern times have been apt to associate with criticism. In fact, whatever qualities we now demand from a critic may be found at least foreshadowed, and commonly much more than foreshadowed, in Dryden. Dryden is master of comparative criticism: he has something of the historical method; he is unrivalled in the art of seizing the distinctive qualities of his author and of setting them before us with the lightest touch. His very style, so pointed yet so easy, is enough in itself to mark the gulf that lies between the age of Elizabeth and the age of the Restoration.

All the Elizabethan critics, Sidney himself hardly excepted, bore some trace of the schoolmaster. Dryden was the first to meet his readers entirely as an equal, and talk to them as a friend with friends. It is Dryden, and not Sainte-Beuve, who is the true father of the literary causerie; and he still remains its unequalled master. There may be other methods of striking the right note in literary criticism. Lamb showed that there may be; so did Mr. Pater. But few indeed are the critics who have known how to attune the mind of the reader to a subject, which beyond all others cries out for harmonious treatment, so skilfully as Dryden.

That the first great critic should come with the Restoration, was only to be expected. The age of Elizabeth was essentially a creative age. The imagination of men was too busy to leave room for self-scrutiny. Their thoughts took shape so rapidly that there was no time to think about the manner of their coming. Not indeed that there is, as has sometimes been urged, any inherent strife between the creative and the critical spirit. A great poet, we can learn from Goethe and Coleridge, may also be a great critic. More than that: without some touch of poetry in himself, no man can hope to do more than hack-work as a critic of others.

Yet it may safely be said that, if no critical tradition exists in a nation, it is not an age of passionate creation, such as was that of Marlowe and Shakespeare, that will found it. With all their alertness, with all their wide outlook, with all their zeal for classical models, the men of that time were too much of children, too much beneath the spell of their own genius, to be critics. Compare them with the great writers of other ages; and we feel instinctively that, in spite of their surroundings, they have far more of vital kindred with Homer or the creators of the mediaval epic, than with the Greek dramatistsAschylus exceptedor with Dante or with Goethe. The "freshness of the early world" is still upon them; neither they nor their contemporaries were born to the task of weighing and pondering, which is the birthright of the critic.

It was far otherwise with the men of the Restoration. The creative impulse of a century had at length spent its force. For the first time since Wyatt and Surrey, England deserted the great themes of literature, the heroic passions of Tamburlaine and Faustus, of Lear and Othello, for the trivial round of social portraiture and didactic discourse; for Essays on Satire and on Translated Verse, for the Tea-Table of the Spectator, for dreary exercises on the Pleasures of the Imagination and the Art of Preserving Health. A new era had opened. It was the day of small things. Yet it would be wrong to regard the new movement as merely negative. Had that been all, it would be impossible to account for the passionate enthusiasm it aroused in those who came beneath its spell; an enthusiasm which lived long after the movement itself was spent, and whichexcept in so far as it led to absurd comparisons with the Elizabethanswas abundantly justified by the genius of Butler and Dryden, of Congreve and Swift and Pope.

Negative, on one side, the ideal of Restoration and Augustan poetry undoubtedly was. It was a reaction against the "unchartered freedom", the real or fancied extravagances, of the Elizabethan poets. But, on the higher side, it was no less positive, though doubtless far less noble, than the ideal it displaced. The great writers of the eighty years following the Restoration were consumed by a passion for observationo-bservation of the men and things that lay immediately around them. They may have seen but little; but what they did see, they grasped with surprising force and clearness. They may not have gone far beneath the surface; but, so far as they went, their work was a model of acuteness and precision. This was the secret of their power. To this may be traced their victory in the various tasks that they undertook.

Hence, on the one hand, their success in painting the manners of their own daya task from which, with some notable exceptions, the greatest of the Elizabethans had been apt to shrink, as from something alien to their genius; and, on the other hand, the range and keenness of their satire. Hence, finally, the originality of their work in criticism, and their new departure in philosophy. The energies of these men were diverse: but all sprang from the same rootfrom their invincible resolve to see and understand their world; to probe life, as they knew it, to the bottom.

Thus the new turn given to criticism by Dryden was part of a far- reaching intellectual movement; a movement no less positive and self- contained than, in another aspect, it was negative and reactionary. And it is only when taken as part of that movement, as side by side with the philosophy of Locke and the satire of Swift or Pope, that its true meaning can be understood. Nor is it the least important or the least attractive of Dryden's qualities, as a critic, that both the positive and the negative elements of the prevailing tendencyboth the determination to understand and the wish to bring all things under ruleshould make themselves felt so strongly and, on the whole, so harmoniously in his Essays.

No man could have felt more keenly the shortcomings of the Elizabethan writers. No man could have set greater store by that "art of writing easily" which was the chief pride of the Restoration poets. Yet no man has ever felt a juster admiration for the great writers of the opposite school; and no man has expressed his reverence for them in more glowing words. The highest eulogy that has yet been passed on Milton, the most discriminating but at the same time the most generous tribute that has ever been offered to Shakespeareboth these are to be found in Dryden. And they are to be found in company with a perception, at once reasoned and instinctive, of what criticism means, that was altogether new to English literature.

The finest and most characteristic of Dryden's critical writingsbut it is unfortunately also the longestis without doubt the Essay of Dramatic Poesy. The subject was one peculiarly well suited to Dryden's genius. It touched a burning question of the day, and it opened the door for a discussion of the deeper principles of the drama. The Essay itself forms part of a long controversy between Dryden and his brother-in-law, Sir Robert Howard. The dispute was opened by Dryden's preface to his tragi-comedy, The Rival Ladies, published probably, as it was certainly first acted, in 1664; and in the beginning Dryden, then first rising into fame as a dramatist, confines himself to pleading the cause of rhyme against blank verse in dramatic writing.. But, from the general drift of the argument, it seems probable that Dryden was speaking of the drama in general.

At a later stage of the dispute, however, he distinguishes between tragedy and comedy, and allows that the arguments in favour of rhyme apply only to the formera curious inversion of the truth, as it would appear to the modern mind.Ib., pp. 561, 566. Howardwho, it may reasonably be guessed, had had some brushes with Dryden over their joint tragedy, The Indian

Queenat once took up the cudgels. He had written rhymed plays himself, it is true; the four plays, to which his attack on rhyme was prefixed, were such; but he saw a chance of paying off old scores against his brother-in-law, and he could not resist it. Dryden began his reply at once; but three years passed before it was published.

And the world has no reason to regret his tardiness. There are few writings of which we can say with greater certainty, as Dryden himself said of a more questionable achievement, 'T is not the hasty product of a day, But the well-ripened fruit of wise delay. The very form of the Essay bears witness to the spirit in which it is written. It is cast as a dialogue, "related"as Dryden truly says"without passion or interest, and leaving the reader to decide in favour of which part he shall judge most reasonable". The balance between opposing views is held as evenly as may be.

It is a search for truth, carried out in the "rude and undigested manner" of a friendly conversation. Roughly speaking, the subjects of the Essay are two. The first, and the more slightly treated, is the quarrel of rhyme against blank verse. The second is the far more important question, How far is the dramatist bound by conventional restrictions? The formera revival under a new form of a dispute already waged by the Elizabethansleads Dryden to sift the claims of the "heroic drama"; and his treatment of it has the special charm belonging to an author's defence of his artistic hearth and home. The latter is a theme which, under some shape or other, will be with us wherever the stage itself has a place in our life.

This is not the place to discuss at length the origin or the historical justification of the Heroic Drama. There is perhaps no form of art that so clearly marks the transition from the Elizabethan age to that of the Restoration. Transitional it must certainly be called; for, in all vital points, it stands curiously apart from the other forms of Restoration literature. It has nothing either of the negative or the positive qualities, nothing of the close observation and nothing of the measure and self-restraint, that all feel to be the distinctive marks of the Restoration temper. On the other hand the heroic drama, of which Dryden's Conquest of Granada and Tyrannic Love may be taken as fair samples, has obvious affinities with the more questionable side of the Elizabethan stage. It may be defined as wanting in all the virtues and as exaggerating all the vices of the Elizabethan dramatists.

Whatever was most wild in the wildest of the Elizabethan playsthe involved plots, the extravagant incidents, the swelling metaphors and similesall this reappears in the heroic drama. And it reappears without any of the dramatic force or of the splendid poetry which are seldom entirely absent from the work of the Elizabethan and Jacobean dramatists. The term "heroic drama" is, in fact, a fraud. The plays of Dryden and his school are at best but moc-heroic; and they are essentially undramatic. The truth is that these plays take something of the same place in the history of the English drama that is held by the verse of Donne and Cowley in the history of the English lyric. The extravagant incidents correspond to the far-fetched conceits which, unjustly enough, made the name of Donne a by-word with the critics of the last century.

The metaphors and similes are as abundant and overcharged, though assuredly not so rich in imagination, as those of the "metaphysical" poets. And Dryden, if we may accept the admission of Bayes, "loved argument in verse"; a confession that Donne and Cowley would heartily have echoed. The exaggerations of the heroic drama are the exaggerations of the metaphysical poets transferred from the study to the stage; with the extravagance deepened, as was natural, by the glare of their new surroundings. And, just as the extravagance of the "metaphysicians" led to the reaction that for a hundred years stifled the lyric note in English song, so the extravagance of the heroic drama gave the death-blow to English tragedy.

Against this parallel the objection may be raised that it takes no reckoning of the enormous gulf that, when all is said, separates even the weakest of the Elizabethan plays from the rant and fustian of Dryden: a gulf wider, it must be admitted, than that which parts the metaphysical poets from the "singing birds" of the Elizabethan era. And, so far as we have yet gone, the objection undoubtedly has force. It is only to be met if we can find some connecting link; if we can point to some author who, on the one hand, retains something of the dramatic instinct, the grace and flexibility of the Elizabethans; and, on the other hand, anticipates the metallic ring, the declamation and the theatrical conventions of Dryden.

Such an author is to be found in Shirley; in Shirley, as he became in his later years; at the time, for instance, when he wrote The Cardinal (1641). The Cardinal is, in many respects, a powerful play. It is unmistakably written under the influence of Webster; and of Webster at his most sombre and his bestthe Webster of the Duchess of Malfi. But it is no less unmistakably wanting in the subtle strength, the dramatic grip and profound poetry, of its model. The villainy of the Cardinal is mere mechanism beside the satanic, yet horribly human, iniquity of Ferdinand and Bosolo. And, at least in one scene, Shirley sinksit is true, in the person of a subordinate characterto a foul-mouthed vulgarity which recalls the shameless bombast of the heroes and heroines of Dryden.

Yet, with all his shortcomings, Shirley preserves in the main the great tradition of the Elizabethans. A further step downwards, a more deadly stage in the history of decadence, is marked by Sir William Davenant. That arch-impostor, as is well known, had the effrontery to call himself the "son of Shakespeare": a phrase which the unwary have taken in the physical sense, but which was undoubtedly intended to mark his literary kinship with the Elizabethans in general and with the greatest of Elizabethan dramatists in particular.

So far as dates go, indeed, the work of Davenant may be admitted to fall within what we loosely call the Elizabethan period; or, more strictly, within the last stage of the period that began with Elizabeth and continued throughout the reigns of her two successors. His first tragedy, Albovine, King of the Lombards, was brought out in 1629; and his earlier work was therefore contemporary with that of Massinger and Ford. But much beyond this his relation to the Elizabethans can hardly claim to go. Charity may allow him some faint and occasional traces of the dramatic power which is their peculiar glory; and this is perhaps more strongly marked in his earliest play than in any of its successors. What strikes us most forcibly, howeverand that, even in his more youthful workis the obvious anticipation of much that we associate only with the Restoration period. The historical plot, the metallic ring of the verse,the fustian and the bombast we have here every mark, save one, of what afterwards came to be known as the heroic drama. The rhymed couplet alone is wanting.

And that was added by Davenant himself at a later stage of his career. It was in The Siege of Rhodes, of which the first part was published in 1656, that the heroic couplet, after an interval of about sixty years, made its first reappearance on the English stage. It was garnished, no doubt, with much of what then passed for Pindaric lyric; it was eked out with music. But the fashion was set; and within ten years the heroic couplet and the heroic drama had swept everything before them. The above dates are enough to disprove the common belief that the heroic drama, rhymed couplet and all, was imported from France. Albovine, as we have seen, has every mark of the heroic drama, except the couplet; and Albovine was written seven years before the first masterpiece of Corneille, one year before his first attempt at tragedy.

A superficial likeness to the drama of Corneille and, subsequently, of Racine may doubtless have given wings to the popularity of the new style both with Davenant and his admirers. But the heroic drama is, in truth, a native growth: for good or for evil, to England alone must be given the credit of its birth. Dryden, no doubt, more than once claims French descent for the literary form with which his fame was then bound up. In a well-known prologue he describes his tragic-comedy, The Maiden Queen, as a mingled chime Of Jonson's humour and Corneille's rhyme.

But the fact is that of Corneille there is no more trace in Dryden's tragedy than there is of Jonson in his comedy; that is, just none at all. The heroic temper, which was at once the essence of Corneille's plays and true to the very soul of the man, was mere affectation and mise-en-scene with Dryden. The heroes of Corneille reflect that nobility of spirit which never entirely forsook France till the days of the Regency; those of Dryden give utterance to nothing better than the insolent swagger of the Restoration.

To the peculiar spirit of the heroic dramato its strength as well as to its weaknessno metrical form could have been more closely adapted than the heroic couplet. It was neither flexible nor delicate; but in the hands of Dryden, even more than in those of Davenant, it became an incomparably vigorous and effective weapon of declamation. As the most unmistakable and the most glaring mark of the new method it was naturally placed in the forefront of the battle waged by Dryden in defence of the heroic drama. It seems, indeed, to have struck him as the strongest advantage possessed by the Restoration drama over the Elizabethan, and as that which alone was wanting to place the Elizabethan drama far ahead both of the Greek and of the French.

The claims of rhyme to Dryden's regard would seem to have been twofold. On the one hand, he thought that it served to "bound and circumscribe" the luxuriance of the poet's fancy. On the other hand, it went to "heighten" the purely dramatic element and to "move that admiration which is the delight of serious plays" and to which "a bare imitation" will not suffice. Both grounds of defence will seem to the modern reader questionable enough. Howard at once laid his finger upon the weak spot of the first. "It is", he said, "no argument for the matter in hand. For the dispute is not what way a man may write best in; but which is most proper for the subject he writes upon. And, if this were let pass, the argument is yet unsolved in itself; for he that wants judgment in the liberty of his fancy may as well shew the want of it in its confinement." Besides, he adds in effect on the next page, so far from "confining the fancy" rhyme is apt to lead to turgid and stilted writing.

The second argument stands on higher ground. It amounts to a plea for the need of idealization; and, so far, may serve to remind us that the extravagances of the heroic drama had their stronger, as well as their weaker, side. No one, however, will now be willing to admit that the cause of dramatic idealization is indeed bound up with the heroic couplet; and a moment's thought will show the fallacy of Dryden's assumption that it is. In the first place, he takes for granted that, the further the language of the drama is removed from that of actual life, the nearer the spirit of it will approach to the ideal. An unwarrantable assumption, if there ever was one; and an assumption, as will be seen, that contains the seeds of the whole eighteenth-century theory of poetic diction. In the second placebut this is, in truth, only the deeper aspect of the former pleaDryden comes perilously near to an acceptance of the doctrine that idealization in a work of art depends purely on the outward form and has little or nothing to do with the conception or the spirit.

The bond between form and matter would, according to this view, be purely arbitrary. By a mere turn of the hand, by the substitution of rhyme for proseor for blank verse, which is on more than "measured" or harmonious prosethe baldest presentment of life could be converted into a dramatic poem. From the grosser forms of this fallacy Dryden's fine sense was enough to save him. Indeed, in the remarks on Jonson's comedies that immediately follow, he expressly rejects them; and seldom does he show a more nicely balanced judgment than in what he there says on the limits of imitation in the field of art. But in the passage before usin his assertion that "the converse must be heightened with all the arts and ornaments of poetry"it is hard to resist a vision of the dramatist first writing his dialogue in bald and skimble-skamble prose, and then wringing his brains to adorn it "with all the arts" of the dramatic gradus.

Here again we have the seeds of the fatal theory which dominated the criticism and perverted the art of the eighteenth century; the theory which, finding in outward form the only distinction between prose and poetry, was logically led to look for the special themes of poetic art in the dissecting-room or the pulpit, and was driven to mark the difference by an outrageous diction that could only be called poetry on the principle that it certainly was not prose; the theory which at length received its death-blow from the joint attack of Wordsworth and Coleridge.

It remains only to note the practical issue of the battle of the metres. In the drama the triumph of the heroic couplet was for the moment complete; but it was short-lived. By 1675, the date of Aurungzebe, Dryden proclaimed himself already about to "weary of his long-loved mistress, Rhyme"; and his subsequent plays were all written in blank verse or prose. But the desertion of "his mistress" brought him little luck; and the rest of his tragedies show a marked falling off in that splendid vigour which went far to redeem even the grossest absurdities of his heroic plays.

A more sensitive, though a weaker, genius joined him in the rejection of rhyme; and the example of Otwaywhose two crucial plays belong to 1680 and 1682did perhaps more than that of Dryden himself, more even than the assaults of The Rehearsal, to discredit the heroic drama. With the appearance of Venice Preserved, rhyme ceased to play any part in English tragedy. But at the same time, it must be noted, tragedy itself began to drop from the place which for the last century it had held in English life. From that day to this no acting tragedy, worth serious attention, has been written for the English stage.

The reaction against rhyme was not confined to the drama. The epic, indeedor what in those days passed for suchcan hardly be said to have come within its scope. In the Essay of Dramatic Poesy Drydenand this is one of the few judgments in which Howard heartily agrees with himhad denounced rhyme as "too low for a poem"; by which, as the context shows, is meant an epic. This was written the very year in which Paradise Lost, with its laconic sneer at rhyme as a device "to set off wretched matter and lame metre", was given to the world. That, however, did not prevent Dryden from asking, and obtaining, leave to "tag its verses" into an opera; nor did it deter Blackmoreand, at a much later time, Wilkie from reverting to the metre that Milton had scorned to touch. It is not till the present century that blank verse can be said to have fairly taken seisin of the epic; one of the many services that English poetry owes to the genius of Keats.

In the more nondescript kinds of poetry, however, the revolt against rhyme spread faster than in the epic. In descriptive and didactic poetry, if anywhere, rhyme might reasonably claim to hold its place. There is much to be said for the opinion that, in such subjects, rhyme is necessary to fix the wandering attention of the reader. Yet, for all that, the great efforts of the reflective muse during the next century were, with hardly an exception, in blank verse.

It is enough to recall the Seasons of Thomson, the discourses of Akenside and Armstrong, and the Night Thoughts of the arch-moralist Young. In the case of Youngas later in that of Cowperthis is the more remarkable, because his Satires show him to have had complete command of the mechanism of the heroic couplet. That he should have deliberately chosen the rival metre is proofa proof which even the exquisite work of Goldsmith is not sufficient to gainsaythat, by the middle of the eighteenth century the heroic couplet had been virtually driven from every field of poetry, save that of satire. We may now turn to the second of the two themes with which Dryden is mainly occupied in the Essay of Dramatic Poesy. What are the conventional restrictions that surround the dramatist, and how far are they of binding force?

That the drama is by nature a conventionmore than this, a convention accepted largely with a view to the need of idealizationthe men of Dryden's day were in no danger of forgetting. The peril with them was all the other way. The fashion of that age was to treat the arbitrary usages of the classical theatre as though they were binding for all time. Thus, of the four men who take part in the dialogue of the Essay, three are emphatically agreed in bowing down before the three unities as laws of nature.

Dryden himself (Neander) is alone in questioning their divinity: a memorable proof of his critical independence; but one in which, as he maliciously points out, he was supported by the greatest of living dramatists. Corneille could not be suspected of any personal motive for undertaking the defence of dramatic license. Yet he closed his Discourse of the Three Unities with the admission that he had "learnt by experience how much the French stage was constrained and bound up by the observance of these rules, and how many beauties it had sacrificed". When the two leading masters of the 'Classical Drama', the French and the English, joined hands to cast doubt upon the sacred unities, its opponents might well feel easy as to the ultimate issue of the dispute.

Dryden was not the man to bound his argument by any technical question, even when it touched a point so fundamental as the unities. Nothing is more remarkable in the Essay, as indeed in all his critical work, than the wide range which he gives to the discussion. And never has the case againstwe can hardly add, forthe French drama been stated more pointedly than by him. His main charge, as was to be expected, is against its monotony, and, in close connection with that, against its neglect of action and its preference for declamation. Having defined the drama as "a just and lively image of human nature, in its actions, passions and traverses of fortune", he proceeds to test the claims of the French stage by that standard.

Its characters, he finds, are wanting in variety and nature. Its range of passion and humour is lamentably narrow. Its declamations "tire us with their length; so that, instead of grieving for their imaginary heroes, we are concerned for our own trouble, as we are in the tedious visits of bad company; we are in pain till they are gone". The best tragedies of the FrenchCinna and Pompey"are not so properly to be called Plays as long discourses of Reason of State". Upon their avoidance of action he is hardly less severe. "If we are to be blamed for showing too much of the action"one is involuntarily reminded of the closing scene of Tyrannic Love and of the gibes in The Rehearsal"the French are as faulty for discovering too little of it ".

Given the definition with which he startsbut it is a definition that no Frenchman of the seventeenth or eighteenth century would have admittedit is hard to see how Dryden could have reached a substantially different result. Nor, if comparisons of this sort are to be made at all, is there muchso far, at least, as Shakespeare is concernedto find fault with in the verdict with which he closes. Yet it is impossible not to regret that Dryden should have failed to recognize the finer spirit and essence of French tragedy, as conceived by Corneille: the strong-tempered heroism of soul, the keen sense of honour, the consuming fire of religion, to which it gives utterance. The truth is that Dryden stood at once too near, and too far from, the ideals of Corneille to appreciate them altogether at their just value. Too near because he instinctively associated them with the heroic drama, which at the bottom of his heart he knew to be no better than an organized trick, done daily with a view to "elevate and surprise". Too far, because, in spite of his own candid and generous temper, it was well-nigh impossible for the Laureate of the Restoration to comprehend the highly strung nature of a man like Corneille, and his intense realization of the ideal.

But, if Dryden is blind to the essential qualities of Corneille, he is at least keenly alive to those of Shakespeare. It is a memorable thing that the most splendid tribute ever offered to the prince of Elizabethans should have come from the leading spirit of the Restoration. It has often been quoted, but it will bear quoting once again.

"Shakespeare was the man who, of all modern and perhaps ancient poets, had the largest and most comprehensive soul. All the images of nature were still present to him; and he drew them not laboriously, but luckily. When he describes anything, you more than see it, you feel it too. Those who accuse him to have wanted learning give him the great commendation. He was naturally learned. He needed not the spectacles of books to read nature; he looked inwards and found her there. I cannot say he is everywhere alike. Were he so, I should do him injury to compare him with the greatest of mankind. He is many times flat, insipid; his comic wit degenerating into clenches, his serious swelling into bombast. But he is always great when some great occasion is presented to him. No man can say, he ever had a fit subject for his wit, and did not then raise himself as high above the rest of poets, Quantum lenta solent inter viburna cupressi."

The same keenness of appreciation is found in Dryden's estimate of other writers who might have seemed to lie beyond the field of his immédiate vision. Of Milton he is recorded to have said: "He cuts us all out, and the ancients too".On Chaucer he is yet more explicit. "As he is the father of English poetry, so I hold him in the same degree of veneration as the Grecians held Homer, or the Romans Virgil. He is a perpetual fountain of good sense; learned in all sciences, and therefore speaks properly on all subjects.

As he knew what to say, so he knows also when to leave off, a continence which is practised by few writers, and scarcely by any of the ancients, excepting Virgil and Horace... Chaucer followed nature everywhere, but was never so bold to go beyond her." This points to what was undoubtedly the most shining quality of Dryden, as a critic: his absolute freedom from preconceived notions, his readiness to "follow nature" and to welcome nature in whatever form she might appear. That was the more remarkable because it ran directly counter both to the general spirit of the period to which he belonged and to the prevailing practice of the critics who surrounded him. The spirit of the Restoration age was critical in the invidious, no less than in the nobler, sense of the word. It was an age of narrow ideals and of little ability to look beyond them. In particular, it was an age of carping and of fault-finding; an age within measurable distance of the pedantic system perfected in France by Boileau, and warmly adopted by a long line of English critics from Roscoromon and Buckinghamshire to the Monthly Reviewers and to Johnson. Such writers might always have "nature" on their lips; but it was nature seen through the windows of the lecture room or down the vista of a street.

With Dryden it was not so. With him we never fail to get an unbiassed judgment; the judgment of one who did not crave for nature "to advantage dressed", but trusted to the instinctive freshness of a mind, one of the most alert and open that ever gave themselves to literature. It is this that puts an impassable barrier between Dryden and the men of his own day, or for a century to come. It is this that gives him a place among the great critics of modern literature, and makes the passage from him to the schoolmen of the next century so dreary a descent. Dryden's openness of mind was his own secret. The comparative method was, in some measure, the common property of his generation. This, in fact, was the chief conquest of the Restoration and Augustan critics. It is the mark that serves to distinguish them most clearly from those of the Elizabethan age. Not that the Elizabethans are without comparisons; but that the parallels they saw were commonly of the simplest, not to say of the most childish, cast. Every sentence of Meres' critical effortor, to be rigorously exact, every sentence but oneis built on "as" and "so"; but it reads like a parodya schoolmaster's parodyof Touchstone's improvement on Orlando's verses in praise of Rosalind. Shakespeare is brought into line with Ovid, Elizabeth with Achilles, and Homer with William Warner.

This, no doubt, is an extreme instance; but it is typical of the artless methods dear to the infancy of criticism. In Jonson's Discoveries, such comparisons as there are have indisputable point; but they are few, and, for the most part, they are limited to the minuter matters of style. It is with the Restoration that the comparative method first made its way into English criticism; and that both in its lawful and less lawful use. The distinction must be jealously made; for there are few matters that lend themselves so readily to confusion and misapprehension as this. Between two men, or two forms of art, a comparison may be run either for the sake of placing the one above the head of the other, or for the sake of drawing out the essential differences between the one and the other. The latter method is indispensable to the work of the critic. Without reference, express or implied, to other types of genius or to other ways of treatment it is impossible for criticism to take a single step in definition either of an author, or a movement, or a form of art.

In a vague and haphazard fashion, even the Elizabethans were comparative. Meres was so in his endless stream of classical parallels; Sidney, after a loftier strain, in his defence of harmonious prose as a form of poetry. And it is the highest achievement of modern criticism to have brought science and order into the comparative method, and largely to have widened its scope. In this sense, comparison is criticism; and to compare with increased intelligence, with a clearer consciousness of the end in view, is to reform criticism itself, to make it a keener weapon and more effective for its purpose.

A comparison of qualities, however, is one thing, and a comparison between different degrees of merit is quite another. The former is the essence of criticism; the latter, one of the most futile pastimes that can readily be imagined. That each man should have his own preferences is right enough. It would be a nerveless and unprofitable mind to which such preferences were unknown. More than that, some rough classification, some understanding with oneself as to what authors are to be reckoned supreme masters of their craft, is hardly to be avoided. The mere fact that the critic lays stress on certain writers and dismisses others with scant notice or none at all, implies that in some sense he has formed an estimate of their relative merits.

But to drag this process from the backgroundif we ought not rather to say, from behind the scenesto the very foot-lights, to publish it, to insist upon it, is as irrelevant as it would be for the historian and he, too, must make his own perspectiveto explain why he has recorded some events and left others altogether unnoticed. All this is work for the dark room; it should leave no trace, or as little as may be, upon the finished picture. Criticism has suffered from few things so much as from its incurable habit of granting degrees in poetry with honours. "The highest art", it has been well said, "is the region of equals." It must be admitted that the Restoration critics had an immoderate passion for classing authors according to their supposed rank in the scale of literary desert.

A glance at The Battle of the Booksa faint reflection of the quarrel between the ancients and the modernsis enough to place this beyond dispute. Dryden himself is probably as guilty as any in this matter. His parallel between Juvenal and Horace, his comparison of Homer with Virgil, are largely of the nature of an attempt to show each poet to his proper place, to determine their due order of precedence in the House of Fame. In the early days of criticism this was perhaps to be expected. Men were feeling their way to the principles; and the shortest road might naturally seem to lie through a comparative table of the men. They were right in thinking that the first step was to ascertain what qualities, and what modes of treatment, give lasting pleasure in poetry; and, to do this, they could not but turn to compare the works of individual poets. But they were wrong in supposing that they could learn anything by striking the balance between the merits of one poet, as a sum total, and the merits of another.

The fault was, no doubt, largely in the Restoration critics themselves; and it is a fault which, so long as the competitive instinct holds sway with men, will never be entirely unknown. But its hold on the men of Dryden's day was in great measure due to the influence of the French critics, and to the narrow lines which criticism had taken in France. No one can read Boileau's Art Poetique, no one can compare it with the corresponding Essay of Pope, without feeling that the purely personal element had eaten into the heart of French criticism to a degree which could never have been natural in England, and which, even in the darkest days of English literature, has seldom been approached. But at the same time it will be felt that never has England come nearer to a merely personal treatment of artistic questions than in the century between Dryden and Johnson; and that it was here, rather than in the adoption of any specific form of literaturerather, for instance, than in the growth of the heroic dramathat the influence of France is to be traced.

Side by side, however, with the baser sort of comparisons, we find in the Restoration critics no small use of the kind that profits and delights. Rymer's Remarks on the Tragedies of the Former Age are an instance of the comparative method, in its just sense, as employed by a man of talent. The essays of Dryden abound in passages of this nature, that could only have been written by a man of genius. They may have a touch of the desire to set one form of art, or one particular poet, in array against another. But, when all abatements have been made, they remain unrivalled samples of the manner in which the comparative vein can be worked by a master spirit. To the student of English literature they have a further interestnotably, perhaps, the comparison between Juvenal and Horace and the eulogy of Shakespeareas being among the most striking examples of that change from the Latinized style of the early Stuart writers to the short, pointed sentence commonly associated with French; the change that was inaugurated by Hobbes, but only brought to completion by Dryden. Once again. As Dryden was among the earliest to give the comparative method its due place in English criticism, so he was the first to make systematic use of the historical method. Daniel, indeed, in a remarkable essay belonging to the early years of the century, had employed that method in a vague and partial manner.

He had defended rhyme on the score of its popularity with all ages and all nations. Celts, Slavs, and HunsParthians and Medes and Elamitesare all pressed into the service. That is, perhaps, the first instance in which English criticism can be said to have attempted tracing a literary form through the various stages of its growth. But Daniel wrote without system and without accuracy. It was reserved for Drydenavowedly following in the steps of the French critic Dacierto introduce the order and the fulness of knowledgein Dryden's case, it must be admitted, a knowledge at second handwhich are indispensable to a fruitful use of the historical method. In this sense, tooas in his use of the comparative method, as in the singular grace and aptness of his styleDryden was a pioneer in the field of English criticism.

Over the century that parts Dryden from Johnson it is not well to linger. During that time criticism must be said, on the whole, to have gone back rather than to have advanced. With some reservations to be noticed later, the critics of the eighteenth century are a depressing study. Their conception of the art they professed was barren; their judgments of men and things were lamentably narrow. The more valuable elements traceable in the work of Drydenthe comparative and the historical treatmentdisappear or fall into the background. We are left with little but the futile exaltation of one poet at the expense of his rivals, or the still more futile insistence upon faults, shortcomings, and absurdities. The Dunciad, the most marked critical work of the period, may be defended on the ground that it is the Dunciad; a war waged by genius upon the fool, the pedant, and the fribble. But, none the less, it had a disastrous influence upon English criticism and English taste. It gave sanction to the habit of indiscriminate abuse; it encouraged the purely personal treatment of critical discussions. Its effects may be traced on writers even of such force as Smollett; of such genius and natural kindliness as Goldsmith. But it was on Johnson that Pope's influence made itself most keenly felt.

And The Lives of the Poets, though not written till the movement that gave it birth had spent its force, is the most complete and the most typical record of the tendencies that shaped English literature and gave the law to English taste from the Restoration to the French Revolution: a notable instance of the fact so often observed, and by some raised to the dignity of a general law, that both in philosophy and in art, the work of the critic does not commonly begin till the creative impulse of a given period is exhausted.

What, then, was Johnson's method? and what its practical application? The method is nothing if not magisterial. It takes for granted certain fixed lawswhether the laws formulated by Aristotle, or by Horace, or the French critics, is for the moment beside the questionand passes sentence on every work of art according as it conforms to the critical decalogue or transgresses it. The fault of this method is not, as is sometimes supposed, that it assumes principles in a subject where none are to be sought; but that its principles are built on a miserably narrow and perverted basis. That there are principles of criticism, that the artist's search for beauty must be guided by some idea, is obvious enough.

It can be questioned only by those who are prepared to deny the very possibility of criticism; who would reduce the task both of critic and of artist to a mere record of individual impressions. It need hardly be said that the very men who are most ready to profess such a doctrine with their lips, persistently, and rightly, give the lie to it in their deeds. No creative work, no critical judgment, either is or can be put forward as a mere impression; it is the impression of a trained mindthat is, of a mind which, instinctively or as a conscious process, is guided by principles or ideas.

So far, then, as he may be held to have borne witness to the need of ideas, Johnson was clearly in the right. It was when he came to ask, What is the nature of those ideas, and how does the artist or the critic arrive at them? that he began to go astray. Throughout he assumes that the principles of artand that, not only in their general bearing (proportion, harmony, and the like), but in their minuter details-are fixed and invariable. To him they form a kind of case-law, which is to be extracted by the learned from the works of a certain number of "correct writers", ancient and modern; and which, once established, is binding for all time both on the critic and on those he summons to his bar.

In effect, this was to declare that beauty can be conceived in no other way than as it presented itself, say, to Virgil or to Pope. It was to lay the dead hand of the past upon the present and the future. More than this. The models that lent themselves to be models, after the kind desired by Johnson, were inevitably just those it was most cramping and least inspiring to follow. They were the men who themselves wrote, to some degree, by rule; in whom "correctness" was stronger than inspiration; who, however admirable in their own achievement, were lacking in the nobler and subtler qualities of the poet. They were not the Greeks; not even, at first hand, the Latins; though the names both of Greek and Latin were often on Johnson's lips. They were rather the Latins as filtered through the English poets of the preceding century; the Latins in so far as they had appealed to the writers of the "Augustan age", but no further; the Latins, as masters of satire, of declamation, and of the lighter kinds of verse. It was Latin poetry without Lucretius and Catullus, without the odes of Horace, without the higher strain of the genius of Virgil. In other words, it was poetry as conceived by Boileau or Addison-or Mr. Smith.

Yet again. In the hands of Johnsonand it was a necessary consequence of his critical methodpoetry becomes more and more a mere matter of mechanism. Once admit that the greatness of a poet depends upon his success in following certain models, and it is but a short stepif indeed it be a stepfurther to say that he must attempt no task that has not been set him by the example of his forerunners. It is doubtless true that Johnson did not, in so many words, commit himself to this absurdity. But it is equally true that any poet, who overstepped the bounds laid down by previous writers, was likely to meet with but little mercy at his hands.

Milton, Cowley, Grayfor all had the audacity to take an untrodden path in poetry-one after another are dragged up for execution. It is clear that by example, if not by precept, Johnson was prepared to "make poetry a mere mechanic art"; and Cowper was right in saying that it had become so with Pope's successors. Indeed Johnson himself, in closing his estimate of Pope, seems half regretfully to anticipate Cowper's verdict. "By perusing the works of Dryden, he discovered the most perfect fabrick of English verse, and habituated himself to that only which he found the best.

New sentiments and new images others may produce; but to attempt any further improvement of versification will be dangerous. Art and diligence have now done their best, and what shall be added will be the effort of tedious toil and needless curiosity". But Johnson failed to see that his own view of poetry led inevitably to this lame and impotent conclusion.

To adopt Johnson's method is, in truth, to misconceive the whole nature of poetry and of poetic imagination. The ideas that have shaped the work of one poet may act as guide and spur, but can never be a rulefar less a lawto the imagination of another. The idea, as it comes to an artist, is not a law imposing itself from without; it is a seed of life and energy springing from within. This, however, was a truth entirely hidden from the eyes of Johnson and the Augustan critics. To assert it both by word and deed, both as critics and as poets, was the task of Coleridge, and of those who joined hands with Coleridge, in the succeeding generation. Apart from the undying beauty of their work as artists, this was the memorable service they rendered to poetry in England.

It remains to illustrate the method of Johnson by its practical application. As has already been said, Johnson is nothing if not a hanging judge; and it is just where originality is most striking that his sentences are the most severe. If there was one writer who might have been expected to win his favour, it was Pope; and if there is any work that bears witness to the originality of Pope's genius, it is the imitations of Horace. These are dismissed in a disparaging sentence.

There is no adequate recognition of Congreve's brilliance as a dramatist; none of Swift's amazing powers as a satirist. Yet all these were men who lived more or less within the range of ideas and tendencies by which Johnson's own mind was moulded and inspired. The case is still worse when we turn to writers of a different school. Take the poets from the Restoration to the closing years of the American war; and it is not too much to say that, with the exception of Thomsonsaved perhaps by his "glossy, unfeeling diction"there is not one of them who overstepped the bounds marked out for literary effort by the prevailing taste of the Augustan age, in its narrowest sense, without paying the price for his temerity in the sneers or reprobation of Johnson.

Collins, it is true, escapes more lightly than the rest; but that is probably due to the affection and pity of his critic. Yet even Collins, perhaps the most truly poetic spirit of the century between Milton and Burns, is blamed for a "diction often harsh, unskillfully laboured, and injudiciously selected"; for "lines commonly of slow motion"; for "poetry that may sometimes extort praise, when it gives little pleasureThe poems of Grayan exception must be made, to Johnson's honour, in favour of the Elegy are slaughtered in detail; the man himself is given dog's burial with the compendious epitaph: "A dull fellow, sir; dull in company, dull in his closet, dull everywhere".

But most astonishing of all, as is well known, is the treatment bestowed on Milton. Of all Milton's works, Paradise Lost seems to have been the only one that Johnson genuinely admired. That he praises with as little of reservation as was in the nature of so stern a critic. On Paradise Regained he is more guarded; on Samson, more guarded yet. But it is in speaking of the earlier poems that Johnson shows his hand most plainly. Comus "is a drama in the epic style, inelegantly splendid and tediously instructive". As for the sonnets, "they deserve not any particular criticism. For of the best it can only be said that they are not bad; and perhaps only the eighth and twenty-first are truly entitled to this slender commendation.... These little pieces may be dismissed without much anxiety".

It would be hardly worth while to record these ill-tempered judgments if they were not the natural outcome of a method which held unquestioned sway over English taste for a full centuryin France for nearly twoand which, during that time, if we except Gray and his friends, was not seriously disputed by a single man of mark. The one author in whose favour the rules of "correct writing" were commonly set aside was Shakespeare; and perhaps there is no testimony to his greatness so convincing as the unwilling homage it extorted from the contemporaries of Pope, of Johnson, and of Hume. Johnson's own notes and introductions to the separate plays are at times trifling enough; but his general preface is a solid and manly piece of work. It contrasts strangely not only with the verdicts given above, but with his jeers at Chevy Chase One more instance, and we may leave this depressing study in critical perversity.

Among the great writers of Johnson's day there was none who showed a truer originality than Fielding; no man who broke more markedly with the literary superstitions of the time; none who took his own road with more sturdiness and self-reliance. This was enough for Johnson, who persistently depreciated both the man and his work. Something of this should doubtless be set down to disapproval of the free speech and readiness to allow for human frailty, which could not but give offence to a moralist so unbending as Johnson. But that will hardly account for the assertion that "Harry Fielding knew nothing but the outer shell of life"; still less for the petulant ruling that he "was a barren rascal".

The truth isand Johnson felt it instinctivelythat the novel, as conceived by Fieldingthe novel that gloried in painting all sides of life, and above all in drawing out the humour of its "lower spheres"dealt a fatal blow not only at the pompous canons which the Rambler was pleased to call "the indispensable laws of Aristotelian criticism", but also at the view which found "human life to be a state where much is to be endured and little to be enjoyed". It would be hard to say whether Johnson found more in Fielding to affront him, as pessimist or as critic.

And it would be equally hard to say in which of the two characters lay the greater barrier to literary insight. Even Richardsonno less revolutionary, though in a different way, than Fieldingwas only saved so as by fire; by the undying hatred which he shared with Johnson for his terrible rival. It was rather as moralist than as artist, rather for "the sentiment" than for the tragic force of his work, that Richardson seems to have won his way to Johnson's heart.

Is not the evidence conclusive? Is it a harsh judgment to say that no critic so narrow, so mechanical, so hostile to originality as Johnson has ever achieved the dictatorship of English letters? The supremacy of Johnson would have been impossible, had not the way been smoothed for it by a long succession of critics like-minded with himself. Such a succession may be traced from Swift to Addison, from Addison to Pope, andwith marked reservationsfrom Pope to Goldsmith. It would be unjust to charge all, or indeed any, of these with the narrowness of view betrayed in Johnson's verdicts on individual writers.

To arrive at this perfection of sourness was a work of time; and the nature of Addison and Goldsmith at least was too genial to allow of any approach to it. But, with all their difference of temperament, the method of the earlier critics is hardly to be distinguished from that of Johnson. There is the same orderliness of treatmentfirst the fable, then the characters, lastly the sentiment and the diction; the same persistency in applying general rules to a matter which, above all others, is a law to itself; the same invincible faith in "the indispensable laws of Aristotelian criticism". It is this that, in spite of its readiness to admire, makes Addison's criticism of Paradise Lost so dreary a study; and this that, in an evil hour, prompted

Goldsmith to treat the soliloquy of Hamlet as though it were a schoolboy's exercise in rhetoric and logic. And yet it is with Goldsmith that we come to the first dawn of better things. The carping strain and the stiffness of method, that we cannot overlook in him, were the note of his generation. The openness to new ideas, the sense of nature, the fruitful use of the historical method, are entirely his own. There had been nothing like them in our literature since Dryden.

In criticism, as in creative work, Goldsmith marks the transition from the old order to the new. Perhaps the clearest indication of this is to be found in his constant appeal to nature. In itself, as we have seen, this may mean much or little. "Nature" is a vague word; it was the battle-cry of Wordsworth, but it was also the battle-cry of Boileau.

And, at first sight, it might seem to be used by Goldsmith in the narrower rather than in the wider sense. "It is the business of art", he writes, "to imitate nature, but not with a servile pencil; and to choose those attitudes and dispositions only which are beautiful and engaging." But a glance at the context will show that what Goldsmith had in mind was not "nature to advantage dressed", not nature with any adornments added by man; but nature stripped of all that to man has degrading associations; nature, to adopt the words used by Wordsworth on a kindred subject, "purified from all lasting or rational causes of dislike or disgust". It may well be that Goldsmith gave undue weight to this reservation. It may well be that he did not throw himself on nature with the unwavering constancy of Wordsworth.

But, none the less, we have hereand we have it worked out in detail the germ of the principle which, in bolder hands, gave England the Lyrical Ballads and the Essays of Lamb. In an essay not commonly reprinted, Goldsmith, laying his finger on the one weak spot in the genius of Gray, gives the poet the memorable adviceto "study the people". And throughout his own critical work, as in his novel, his comedies, and his poems, there is an abiding sense that, without this, there is no salvation for poetry. That in itself is enough to fix an impassable barrier between Goldsmith and the official criticism of his day. The other main service rendered by Goldsmith was his return to the historical method. It is true that his knowledge is no more at first hand, and is set out with still less system than that of Dryden a century before. But it is also true that he has a far keener sense of the strength which art may draw from history than his great forerunner.

Dryden confines himself to the history of certain forms of art; Goldsmith includes the history of nations also in his view. With Dryden the past is little more than an antiquarian study; with Goldsmith it is a living fountain of inspiration for the present. The art of the pastthe poetry, say, of Teutonic or Celtic antiquityis to him an undying record of the days when man still walked hand in hand with nature. The history of the past is at once a storehouse of stirring themes ready to the hand of the artist, and the surest safeguard against both flatness and exaggeration in his work.: It offers, moreover, the truest schooling of the heart, and insensibly "enlists the passions on the side of humanity". "Poetry", Byron said, "is the feeling of a former world, and future"; and to the first half of the statement Goldsmith would have heartily subscribed.

For the historical method in his hands is but another aspect of the counsel he gave to Gray: "Study the people". It is an anticipationvague, no doubt, but still unmistakableof the spirit which, both in France and England, gave birth to the romantic movement a generation or two later. That zeal for the literature of the past was in the air when Goldsmith wrote is proved by works so different as those of Gray and Percy, of Chatterton and MacPherson, of Mallet and Warton.But it may be doubted whether any one of them, Gray excepted, saw the true bearing of the movement more clearly than Goldsmith, or did more to open fresh springs of thought and beauty for the poetry of the next age, if not of his own. It would be unpardonable to turn from the writers of the eighteenth century with no notice of a book which, seldom now read, is nevertheless perhaps the most solid piece of work that modern Europe had as yet to show in any branch of literary criticism. This is Burke's treatise On the Sublime and the Beautiful.

Few will now be prepared to accept the material basis

which Burke finds for the ideas of the imagination. But none can deny the skill with which he works out his theory, nor the easy mastery with which each part is fitted into its place. The speculative power of the book and the light it throws on the deeper springs of the imagination are alike memorable.

The first is not unworthy of the Reflections or the Appeal from the New to the Old Whigs; the second shows that fruitful study of the Bible and the poets, English and classical, to which his later writings and speeches bear witness on every page. If the originality and depth of Burke's treatise is to be justly measured, it should be set side by side with those papers of Addison which Akenside expanded in his dismal Pleasures of the Imagination. The performance of Addison, grateful though one must be to him for attempting it, is thin and lifeless. That of Burke is massive and full of suggestion.

At every turn it betrays the hand of the craftsman who works with his eye upon his tools. The speculative side of criticism has never been a popular study with Englishmen, and it is no accident that one of the few attempts to deal seriously with it should have been made at the only time when philosophy was a living power among us, and when the desire to get behind the outward shows of things was keener than it has ever been before or since. But for Burke's treatise, a wide gap would have been left both in the philosophy and the criticism of the eighteenth century; and it is to be wished that later times had done more to work the vein which he so skilfully explored.

As it is, the writers both of France and Germanyabove all, Hegel in his Aesthetikhave laboured with incomparably more effect than his own countrymen, Mr. Ruskin excepted, upon the foundations that he laid. IV. Johnson's Lives of the Poets was the last word of the school which the Restoration had enthroned; the final verdict of the supreme court which gave the law to English letters from the accession of Anne to the French Revolution.

Save in the splenetic outbursts of Byronand they are not to be taken too seriouslythe indispensable laws of Aristotelian criticism fell silent at Johnson's death. A time of anarchy followed; anarchy plus the policeman's truncheon of the Edinburgh and the Quarterly. The ill-fame of these Reviews, as they were in their pride of youth, is now so great that doubts may sometimes suggest themselves whether it can possibly be deserved. No one who feels such doubts can do better than turn to the earlier numbers; he will be forced to the conclusion that, whatever their services as the journeymen of letters and of party politics, few critics could have been so incompetent to judge of genius as the men who enlisted under the standard of Jeffrey or of Gifford.

There is not, doubtless, in either Review the same iron wall of reasoned prejudice that has been noted in Johnson, but there is a plentiful lack of the clear vision and the openness to new impressions which are the first necessity of the critic. What Carlyle says of Jeffrey and the Edinburgh may be taken as the substantial truth also about Gifford and the Quarterly, and it is the most pregnant judgment that has yet been passed upon them. "Jeffrey may be said to have begun the rash, reckless style of criticising everything in heaven and earth by appeal to Moliere's maid: 'Do you like it?' 'Don't you like it?' a style which, in hands more and more inferior to that sound-hearted old lady and him, has since grown gradually to such immeasurable length among us; and he himself is one of the first that suffers by it. If praise and blame are to be perfected, not in the mouth of Moliere's maid only but in that of mischievous, precocious babes and sucklings, you will arrive at singular judgments by degrees."

Carlyle has much here to say of Jeffrey's "recklessness", his defiance of all rules, his appeal to the chance taste of the man in the crowd. He has much also to say of his acuteness, and the unrivalled authority of his decrees. But he is discreetly silent on their severity and short-sightedness.Yet this is the unpardonable sin of both Reviews: that mediocrity was applauded, but that, whenever a man of genius came before them, the chances were ten to one that he would be held up to ridicule and contempt. The very first number of the Edinburgh lays this down as an article of faith. Taking post on the recent appearance of Thalaba, the reviewer opens fire by a laboured parallel between poetry and religion. With an alteration of names it might have been written by a member of the English Church Union, or of the Holy Inquisition. "The standards of poetry have been fixed long ago by certain inspired writers, whose authority it is no longer lawful to call in question. Many profess to be entirely devoted to poetry, who have no good works to produce in support of their pretensions. The Catholic poetical Church too... has given birth to an infinite variety of heresies and errors, the followers of which have hated and persecuted each other as heartily as other bigots."

Then, turning to business, the writer proceeds to apply his creed to Southey and all his works, not forgetting the works also of his friends. "The author belongs to a sect of poets that has established itself in this country within these ten or twelve years"it would be hard to say for whose benefit in particular this date was taken"and is looked upon as one of its chief champions and apostles". "The doctrines of this sect"the Reviewer continues, with an eye upon the Alien Act"are of German origin, or borrowed from the great apostle of Geneva". Rousseau is then "named" for expulsion, together with a miscellaneous selection of his following: Schiller and Kotzebue (the next number includes Kant under the anathema), Quarles and Donne, Ambrose Phillips and Cowperperhaps the most motley crew that was ever brought together for excommunication.

It is not, however, till the end of the essay that the true root of bitterness between the critic and his victims is suffered fully to appear. "A splenetic and idle discontent with the existing institutions of society seems to be at the bottom of all their serious and peculiar sentiments." In other words, the Edinburgh takes up the work of the Anti-Jacobin; with no very good grace Jeffrey affects to sit in the seat of Canning and of Frere. So much for the "principles" of the new venture; principles, it will be seen, which appear to rest rather upon a hatred of innovation in general than upon any reasoned code, such as that of Johnson or the "Aristotelian laws", in particular. On that point, it must be clearly realized, Carlyle was in the right. It is that which marks the essential difference of the

Reviewerswe can hardly say their advanceas against Johnson. We may now turn to watch the Reviewers, knife in hand, at the dissecting-table. For the twenty-five years that followed the foundation of the Edinburgh, England was more full of literary genius than it had been at any time since the age of Elizabeth. And it is not too much to say that during that period there was not one of the men, now accepted as among the chief glories of English literature, who did not fall under the lash of one, or both, of the Reviews. The leading cases will suffice.

And first, the famous attacknot altogether undeserved, it must be allowedof the Edinburgh upon Byron. "The poetry of this young lord belongs to the class which neither gods nor men are said to permit", and so on for two or three pages of rather vulgar and heartless merriment at the young lord's expense. The answer to the sneer, as all the world knows, was English Bards and Scotch Reviewers. The author of the article had reason to be proud of his feat. Never before did pertness succeed in striking such unexpected fire from genius. And it is only fair to say that the Review took its beating like a gentleman. A few years later, and the Edinburgh was among the warmest champions of the "English Bard". It was reserved for Southey, a pillar of the Quarterly, to rank him as the "Goliath" of the "Satanic school". Let us now turn to the Quarterly upon Keats. Endymion, in spite of the noble self-criticism of its preface, is denounced as "Cockney poetry" a stupid and pointless vulgarismand is branded as clothing "the most incongruous ideas in the most uncouth language".

The author is dismissed with the following amenities: "Being bitten by Leigh Hunt's insane criticism, he more than rivals the insanity of his poetry"; and we are half-surprised not to find him told, as he was by Blackwood, to "go back to the shop, Mr. John; back to the plasters, pills, and ointment-boxes". With this insolence it is satisfactory to contrast the verdict of the Edinburgh: "We have been exceedingly struck with the genius these poemsEndymion, Lamia, Isabella, The Eve of St. Agnes, &c.display, and the spirit of poetry which breathes through all their extravagance.... They are at least as full of genius as absurdity." Of Hyperion the Reviewer says:

"An original character and distinct individuality is bestowed upon the poet's mythological persons.... We cannot advise its completion. For, though there are passages of some force and grandeur, it is sufficiently obvious that the subject is too far removed from all the sources of human interest to be successfully treated by any modern author". A blundering criticism, which, however, may be pardoned in virtue of the discernment, not to say the generosity, of the foregoing estimate. It would have been well had the Edinburgh always written in this vein. But Wordsworth was a sure stumbling-block to the sagacity of his critics, and he certainly never failed to call forth the insolence and flippancy of Jeffrey. Two articles upon him remain as monuments to the incompetence of the Edinburgh; the first prompted by the Poems of 1807, the second by the Excursion.

The former pronounces sentence roundly at the very start: "Mr. Wordsworth's diction has nowhere any pretence to elegance or dignity, and he has scarcely ever condescended to give the grace of correctness or dignity to his versification". From this sweeping condemnation four poemsBrougham Castle, and the sonnets on Venice, Milton, and Bonaparteare generously excepted. But, as though astonished at his own moderation, the reviewer quickly proceeds to deal slaughter among the rest. Of the closing lines of Resolution and Independence he writes: "We defy Mr. Wordsworth's bitterest enemy to produce anything at all parallel to this from any collection of English poetry, or even from the specimens of his friend, Mr. Southey". Of the stanzas to the sons of Burns, "never was anything more miserable". Alice Fell is "trash"; Yarrow Unvisited, "tedious and affected". The lines from the Ode to Duty.

"Thou dost preserve the stars from wrong, And the most ancient heavens through thee are fresh and strong," are "utterly without meaning". The poem on the Cuckoo is "absurd". The Ode on Immortality is "the most illegible and unintelligible part of the whole publication". "We venture to hope that there is now an end of this folly." But the hope is doomed to disappointment. The publication of the Excursion a few years later finds the reviewer still equal to his task. "This will never do", he begins in a fury; "the case of Mr. Wordsworth is now manifestly hopeless. We give him up as altogether incurable and beyond the power of criticism." The story of Margaret, indeed, though "it abounds, of course, with mawkish sentiment and details of preposterous minuteness, has considerable pathos".

But the other passage which one would have thought must have gone home to every heartthat which describes the communing of the wanderer with nature is singled out for ridicule; while the whole poem is judged to display "a puerile ambition of singularity, grafted on an unlucky predilection for truisms". It would be idle to maintain that in some of these slashing verdicts criticisms they cannot be calledthe reviewer does not fairly hit the mark. But these are chance strokes; and they are dealt, as the whole attack is conceived, in the worst style of the professional swash- buckler. Yet, low as is the deep they sound, a lower deep is opened by the Quarterly in its article on Shelley; an article which bears unmistakable marks of having been written under the inspiration, if not by the hand, of Southey. It is impossible to know anything about Southey without feeling that, both in character and in intellect, he had many of the qualities that go to make an enlightened critic. But his fine nature was warped by a strain of bigotry; and he had what, even in a man who otherwise gave conclusive proof of sincerity and whole-heartedness, must be set down as a strong touch of the Pharisee.

After every allowance has been made, no feeling other than indignation is possible at the tone which he thought fit to adopt towards Shelley. He opens the assault, and it is well that he does so, by an acknowledgment that the versification of the Revolt of Islam, the corpus delicti at that moment under the scalpel, is "smooth and harmonious", and that the poem is "not without beautiful passages, free from errors of taste". But the "voice of warning", as he himself would too generously have called it, is not long in making itself heard. "Mr. Shelley, with perfect deliberation and the steadiest perseverance, perverts all the gifts of his nature, and does all the injury, both public and private, which his faculties enable him to perpetrate....He draws largely on the rich stores of another mountain poet, to whose religious mind it must be matter of perpetual sorrow to see the philosophy, which comes pure and holy from his pen, degraded and perverted by this miserable crew of atheists and pantheists."

So far, perhaps, the writer may claim not to have outstepped the traditional limits of theological hatred. For what follows there is not even that poor excuse. "If we might withdraw the veil of his private life and tell what we now know about him, it would be indeed a disgusting picture that we should exhibit, but it would be an unanswerable comment on our text...Mr. Shelley is too young, too ignorant, too inexperienced, and too vicious to undertake the task of reforming any world but the little world within his own breast."For the credit of both Reviews it must be said that it would be difficult to find another instance of so foul a blow as this: Non ragioniam di lui, ma guarda e passa. Apart from their truculence, the early numbers of the Edinburgh and Quarterly are memorable for two reasons in the history of English literature. They mark the downfall of the absolute standard assumed by Johnson and others to hold good in criticism. And they led the way, slowly indeed but surely, to the formation of a general interest in literature, which, sooner or later, could not but be fatal to their own haphazard dogmatism. By their very nature they were an appeal to the people; and, like other appeals of the kind, they ended in a revolution.

Of the men who fixed the lines on which this revolution was to run, four stand out taller from the shoulders upwards than their fellows. These are Coleridge, Lamb, Hazlitt, and Carlyle. The critical work of all four belongs to the first thirty years or so of the present century; and of the four it is probable that Carlyle, by nature certainly the least critical, had the greatest influence in changing the current of critical ideas. Space forbids any attempt to treat their work in detail. All that can be done is to indicate what were the shortcomings of English criticism as it came into their hands, and how far and in what manner they modified its methods and its aims. Till the beginning of the present century, criticism in England had remained a very simple thing. When judgment had once been passed, for good or evil, on an individual work or an individual writer, the critic was apt to suppose that nothing further could reasonably be expected of him. The comparative method, foreshadowed but only foreshadowed by Dryden, had not been carried perceptibly further by Dryden's successors. The historical method was still more clearly in its infancy. The connection between the two, the unity of purpose which alone gives significance to either, was hardly as yet suspected. It may be saidan English critic of the eighteenth century would undoubtedly have saidthat these, after all, are but methods; better, possibly, than other methods; but still no more than means to an end the eternal end of criticism, which is to appraise and to classify.

The view is disputable enough. It leaves out of sight all that criticismthe criticism of literature and arthas done to throw light upon the dark places of human thought and history, upon the growth and subtle transformations of spiritual belief, upon the power of reason and imagination to mould the shape of outward institutions. All these things are included in the scope of the historical and comparative methods; and all of them stand entirely apart from the need to judge or classify the works of individual poets.

But, for the moment, such wider considerations may be put aside, and the objection weighed on its own merits. It must then be answered that, without comparison and without the appeal to history, even to judge and classify reasonably would be impossible; and hence that, however much we narrow the scope of criticism, these two methodsor rather, two aspects of the same methodmust still find place within its range. For, failing them, the critic in search of a standardand without some standard or criterion there can be no such thing as criticismis left with but two possible alternatives. He must either appeal to some absolute standardthe rules drawn from the "classical writers", in a sense wider or narrower, as the case may be; or he must decide everything by his own impression of the moment, eked out by the "appeal to Moliere's maid". The latter is the negation of all criticism. The former, spite of itself, is the historical method, but the historical method applied in an utterly arbitrary and irrational way. The former was the method of Johnson; the latter, of the Edinburgh and the Quarterly. Each in turn, as we have seen, had ludicrously broken down.

In the light of recent inventions, it might have been expected that some attempt would be made to limit the task of the critic to a mere record of his individual impressions. This, in fact, would only have been to avow, and to give the theory of what the Edinburgh and the Quarterly had already reduced to practice. But the truth is that the men of that day were not strong in such fine-spun speculations. It was a refinement from which even Lamb, who loved a paradox as well as any man, would have shrunk with playful indignation. It was in another direction that Coleridge and his contemporaries sought escape from the discredit with which criticism was threatened.

This was by changing the issue on which the discussion was to be fought. In its most general form, the problem of criticism amounts to this: What is the nature of the standard to be employed in literary judgments? Hithertoat least to the Reviewersthe question may be said to have presented itself in the following shape: Is the standard to be sought within or without the mind of the critic? Is it by his own impression, or by the code handed down from previous critics, that in the last resort the critic should be guided? In the hands of Coleridge and others, this was replaced by the question: Is the touchstone of excellence to be found within the work of the poet, or outside of it?

Are we to judge of a given work merely by asking: Is it clearly conceived and consistently carried out? Or are we bound to consider the further question: Is the original conception just, and capable of artistic treatment; and is the workmanship true to the vital principles of poetry? The change is significant. It makes the poet, not the critic, master of the situation. It implies that the critic is no longer to give the law to the poet; but that, in some sense more or less complete, he must begin, if not by putting himself in the place of the individual writer as he was when at work on the individual poem, at least by taking upon himselfby making his own, as far as may bewhat he may conceive to be the essential temperament of the poet.

This, indeed, is one of the first things to strike us in passing from the old criticism to the new. The Edinburgh and Quarterly plunge straight into the business of the moment. From the first instantwith "This will never do"the Reviewer poses as the critic, or rather as the accuser. Not so Coleridge and Hazlitt. Like the Edinburgh and Quarterly, they undertake to discourse on individual poets.

Unlike them, each opens his enquiry with the previous question-a question that seems to have found no lodgment in the mind of the ReviewersWhat is poetry? Further than this. Hazlitt, in a passage of incomparably greater force than any recorded utterance of Coleridge, makes it his task to trace poetry to the deepest and most universal springs of human nature; asserts boldly that it is poetry which, in the strictest sense, is "the life of all of us"; and calls on each one of us to assert his birthright by enjoying it. It is in virtue of the poet latent in him, that the plain man has the power to become a critic. Starting then from the question as just stated: Is it within the mind of the individual poet, or without it, that the standard of judgment should be sought?neither Coleridge nor Hazlitt could have any doubt as to the answer.

It is not, they would tell us, in the individual work but in the nature of poetryof poetry as written large in the common instincts of all men no less than in the particular achievement of exceptional artiststhat the test of poetic beauty must be discovered. The opposite view, doubtless, finds some countenance in the precepts, if not the example, of Goethe. But, when pressed to extremes, it is neither more nor less than the impressionist conception of criticism transferred to the creative faculty; and, like its counterpart, is liable to the objection that the impression of one poet, so long as it is sincerely rendered, is as good as the impression of another. It is the abdication of art, as the other is the abdication of criticism.

Yet Hazlitt alsofor, leaving Coleridge, we may now confine ourselves to himis open to attack. His fine critical powers were marred by the strain of bitterness in his nature. And the result is that his judgment on many poets, and notably the poets of his own day, too often sounds like an intelligent version of the Edinburgh or the Quarterly. Or, to speak more accurately, he betrays some tendency to return to principles which, though assuredly applied in a more generous spirit, are at bottom hardly to be distinguished from the principles of Johnson. He too has his "indispensable laws", or something very like them. He too has his bills of exclusion and his list of proscriptions. The poetry of earth, he more than suspects, is for ever dead; after Milton, no claimant is admitted to anything more substantial than a courtesy title. This, no doubt, was in part due to his morose temper; but it was partly also the result of the imperfect method with which he started.

The fault of his conceptionand it was that which determined his methodis to be too absolute. It allows too much room to poetry in the abstract; too little to the ever-varying temperament of the individual poet. And even that is perhaps too favourable a statement of the case. His idea of poetry may in part be drawnand its strength is to have been partly drawndirect from life and nature. But it is also taken, as from the nature of the case it must be with all of us, from the works of particular poets. And, in spite of his appeal to Dante and the Bible, it is clear that, in framing it, he was guided too exclusively by his loving study of the earlier English writers, from Chaucer to Milton.

The model, so framed, is laid with heavy hand upon all other writers, who naturally fare ill in the comparison. Is it possible to account otherwise for his disparagement of Moliere, or his grudging praise of Wordsworth and of Coleridge? It was here that Carlyle came in to redress the balance. From interests, in their origin perhaps less purely literary than have moved any man who has exercised a profound influence on literature, Carlyle was led to quicken the sense of poetic beauty, and by consequence to widen the scope of criticism, more than any writer of his day. He may have sought German literature more for its matter than for its artistic beautyhere, too, he brought a new, if in some ways a dangerous, element into criticismbut neither he nor his readers could study it, least of all could they study the work of Goethe, without awakening to a whole world of imagination and beauty, to which England had hitherto been dead. With all its shortcomings, the discovery of German literature was a greater revelation than any made to Europe since the classical Renaissance.

The shockfor it was nothing lesscame at a singularly happy moment. The blow, given by Carlyle as critic, was closely followed up by the French Romantiques, as creative artists. Nothing could well have been more alien to English taste, as understood by the Edinburgh and Quarterly, than the early works, or indeed any works, of Hugo and those who owned him for chiefif it were not the works of Goethe and the countrymen of Goethe. Different as these were from each other, they held common ground in uniting the most opposite prejudices of Englishmen against them. The sarcasms of Thackeray on the French writers speak to this no less eloquently than the fluent flippancies of De Quincey upon the Germans.Yet, in the one case as in the otherthanks, in no small measure, to Matthew Arnold and Mr. Swinburnegenius, in the long run, carried the day.

And the same history has been repeated, as the literatures of Russia and of Scandinavia have each in turn been brought within our ken. These discoveries have all fallen within little more than half a century since Carlyle, by the irony of fate, reviewed Richter and the State of German Literature in the pages of the Edinburgh. And their result has been to modify the standards of taste and criticism in a thousand ways. They have opened our eyes to aspects of poetry that we should never otherwise have suspected, and unveiled to us fields of thought, as well as methods of artistic treatment which, save by our own fault, must both have widened and deepened our conception of poetry. That is the true meaning of the historical method. The more we broaden our vision, the less is our danger of confounding poetry, which is the divine genius of the whole world, with the imperfect, if not misshapen idols of the tribe, the market-place and the cave. Of this conquest Carlyle must in justice be reckoned as the pioneer. For many years he stood almost single-handed as the champion of German thought and German art against the scorn or neglect of his countrymen. But he knew that he was right, and was fully conscious whither the path he had chosen was to lead. Aware that much in the work of Goethe would seem "faulty" to many, he forestalls the objection at the outset.

"To see rightly into this matter, to determine with any infallibility whether what we call a fault is in very deed a fault, we must previously have settled two points, neither of which may be so readily settled. First, we must have made plain to ourselves what the poet's aim really and truly was, how the task he had to do stood before his own eye, and how far, with such means as it afforded him, he has fulfilled it. Secondly, we must have decided whether and how far this aim, this task of his accordednot with us and our individual crotchets, and the crotchets of our little senate where we give or take the lawbut with human nature and the nature of things at large; with the universal principles of poetic beauty, not as they stand written in our text-books, but in the hearts and imaginations of all men. Does the answer in either case come out unfavourable; was there an inconsistency between the means and the end, a discordance between the end and the truth, there is a fault; was there not, there is no fault."

Nothing could ring clearer than this. No man could draw the line more accurately between the tendency to dispense with principles and the tendency to stereotype them, which are the twin dangers of the critic. But it is specially important to note Carlyle's relation, in this matter, to Hazlitt He insists with as much force as Hazlitt upon the need of basing all poetry on "human nature and the nature of things at large"; upon the fact that its principles are written "in the hearts and imaginations of all men". But, unlike Hazlitt, he bids us also consider what the aim of the individual poet was, and how far he has taken the most fitting means to reach it. In other words, he allows, as Hazlitt did not allow, for the many-sidedness of poetry, and the infinite variety of poetic genius.

And, just because he does so, he is able to give a deeper meaning to "nature" and the universal principles of imagination than Hazlitt, with all his critical and reflective brilliance, was in a position to do. Hazlitt is too apt to confine "nature" to the nature of Englishmen in general and, in his weaker moments, of Hazlitt in particular.

Carlyle makes an honest attempt to bound it only by the universal instincts of man, and the "everlasting reason" of the world. Thus, in Carlyle's conception, "it is the essence of the poet to be new"; it is his mission "to wrench us from our old fixtures"; for it is only by so doing that he can show us some aspect of nature or of man's heart that was hidden from us before. The originality of the poet, the impossibility of binding him by the example of his forerunners, is the necessary consequence of the infinity of truth. That Carlyle saw this, and saw it so clearly, is no doubt partly due to a cause, of which more must be said directly; to his craving for ideas. But it was in part owing to his hearty acceptance of the historical method. Both as critic and as historian, he knewat that time, no man so wellthat each nation has its own genius; and justly pronounced the conduct of that nation which "isolates itself from foreign influence, regards its own modes as so many laws of nature, and rejects all that is different as unworthy even of examination", to be "pedantry".

This was the first, and perhaps the most fruitful consequence that he drew from the application of historical ideas to literature. They enlarged his field of comparison; and, by so doing, they gave both width and precision to his definition of criticism.

But there is anotherand a more usual, if a narrowersense of the historical method; and here, too, Carlyle was a pioneer. He was among the first in our country to grasp the importance of studying the literature of a nation, as a whole, and from its earliest monuments, its mythological and heroic legends, downwards to the present. The year 1831a turning-point in the mental history of Carlyle, for it was also the year in which Sartor Resartus took shape "among the mountain solitudes"was largely devoted to Essays on the history of

German literature, of which one, that on the Nibelungenlied, is specially memorable. And some ten years later (1840) he again took up the theme in the first of his lectures on Heroes, which still remains the most enlightening, because the most poetic, account of the primitive Norse faith, or rather successive layers of faith, in our language. But what mainly concerns us here is that Carlyle, in this matter as in others, had clearly realized and as clearly defines the goal which the student, in this case the student of literary history, should set before his eyes.

"A History... of any national Poetry would form, taken in its complete sense, one of the most arduous enterprises any writer could engage in. Poetry, were it the rudest, so it be sincere, is the attempt which man makes to render his existence harmonious, the utmost he can do for that end; it springs, therefore, from his whole feelings, opinions, activity, and takes its character from these. It may be called the music of his whole manner of being; and, historically considered, is the test how far Music, or Freedom, existed therein; how the feeling of Love, of Beauty, and Dignity, could be elicited from that peculiar situation of his, and from the views he there had of Life and Nature, of the Universe, internal and external.

Hence, in any measure to understand the Poetry, to estimate its worth and historical meaning, we ask, as a quite fundamental inquiry: What that situation was? Thus the History of a nation's Poetry is the essence of its History, political, economic, scientific, religious. With all these the complete Historian of a national Poetry will be familiar; the national physiognomy, in its finest traits and through its successive stages of growth, will be dear to him: he will discern the grand spiritual Tendency of each period, what was the highest Aim and Enthusiasm of mankind in each, and how one epoch naturally evolved itself from the other. He has to record the highest Aim of a nation, in its successive directions and developments; for by this the Poetry of the nation modulates itself; this is the Poetry of the nation."

Never has the task of the literary historian been more accurately defined than in this passage; and never do we feel so bitterly the gulf between the ideal and the actual performance, at which more than one man of talent has since tried his hand, as when we read it. It strikes perhaps the first note of Carlyle's lifelong war against "Dryasdust". But it contains at least two other points on which it is well for us to pause. The first is the inseparable bond which Carlyle saw to exist between the poetry of a nation and its history; the connection which inevitably follows from the fact that both one and the other are the expression of its character.

This is a vein of thought that was first struck by Vico and by Montesquieu; but it was left for the German philosophers, in particular Fichte and Hegel, to see its full significance; and Carlyle was the earliest writer in this country to make it his own. It is manifest that the connection between the literature and the history of a nation may be taken from either side. We may illustrate its literature from its history, or its history from its literature. It is on the necessity of the former study that Carlyle dwells in the above.

And in the light of later exaggerations, notably those of Taine, it is well to remember, what Carlyle himself would have been the last man to forget, that no man of genius is the creature of his time or his surroundings; and, consequently, that when we have mastered all the circumstances, in Carlyle's phrase the whole "situation", of the poet, we are still only at the beginning of our task. We have still to learn what his genius made out of its surroundings, and what the eye of the poet discovered in the world of traditional belief; in other words, what it was that made him a poet, what it was that he saw and to which all the rest were blind. We have studied the soil; we have yet to study the tree that grew from it and overshadows it.

In reversing the relation, in reading history by the light of literature, the danger is not so great. The man of genius may, and does, see deeper than his contemporaries; but, for that very reason, he is a surer guide to the tendencies of his time than they. He is above and beyond his time; but, just in so far as he is so, he sees over it and through it. As Shakespeare defined it, his "end, both at the first and now, was and is... to show the very age and body of the time his form and pressure". Some allowance must doubtless be made for the individuality of the poet; for the qualities in which he stands aloof from his time, and in which, therefore, he must not be taken to reflect it. But to make such allowance is a task not beyond the skill of the practised critic; and many instances suggest themselves in which it has, more or less successfully, been done. Witness not a few passages in Michelet's Histoire de France, and some to be found in the various works of Ranke.Witness, again, Hegel's illustration of the Greek conception of the family from the Antigone and the Oedipus of Sophocles; or, if we may pass to a somewhat different field, his "construction" of the French Revolution from the religious and metaphysical ideas of Rousseau.

So far as it employs literature to give the key to the outward history of a nation or to the growth of its spiritual faith, it is clear that the historical method ceases to be, in the strict sense of the word, a literary instrument. It implies certainly that a literary judgment has been passed; but, once passed, that judgment is used for ends that lie altogether apart from the interests of literature. But it is idle to consider that literature loses caste by lending itself to such a purpose. It would be wiser to say that it gains by anything that may add to its fruitfulness and instructiveness.

In any case, and whether it pleases us or no, this is one of the things that the historical method has done for literature; and neither Carlyle, nor any other thinker of the century, would have been minded to disavow it. This brings us to the second point that calls for remark in the foregoing quotation from Carlyle. Throughout he assumes that the matter of the poet is no less important than his manner. And here again he dwells on an aspect of literature that previous, and later, critics have tended to throw into the shade.

That Carlyle should have been led to assert, and even at times to exaggerate, the claims of thought in imaginative work was inevitable; and that, not only from his temperament, but from those principles of his teaching that we have already noticed. If the poetry of a nation be indeed the expression of its spiritual aims, then it is clear that among those aims must be numbered its craving to make the world intelligible to itself, and to comprehend the working of God both within man and around him. Not that Carlyle shows any disposition to limit "thought" to its more abstract forms; on the contrary, it is on the sense of "music, love, and beauty" that he specially insists. What he does demand is that these shall be not merely outward adornments, but the instinctive utterance of a deeper harmony within; that they shall be such as not merely to "furnish a languid mind with fantastic shows and indolent emotions, but to incorporate the everlasting reason of man in forms visible to his sense, and suitable to it". The "reason" is no less necessary to poetry than its sensible form; and whether its utterance be direct or indirect, that is a matter for the genius of the individual poet to decide. Gott und Welt, we may be sure Carlyle would have said, is poetry as legitimate as Der Erlkonig or the songs of Mignon.

In this connection he more than once appeals to the doctrine of Fichte, one of the few writers whom he was willing to recognize as his teachers. "According to Fichte, there is a 'divine idea' pervading the visible universe; which visible universe is indeed but its symbol and sensible manifestation, having in itself no meaning, or even true existence independent of it. To the mass of men this divine idea of the world lies hidden; yet to discern it, to seize it, and live wholly in it, is the condition of all genuine virtue, knowledge, freedom; and the end, therefore, of all spiritual effort in every age.

Literary men are the appointed interpreters of this divine idea; a perpetual priesthood, we might say, standing forth, generation after generation, as the dispensers and living types of God's everlasting wisdom, to show it in their writings and actions, in such particular form as their own particular times require it in. For each age, by the law of its nature, is different from every other age, and demands a different representation of the divine idea, the essence of which is the same in all; so that the literary man of one century is only by mediation and reinterpretation applicable to the wants of another."

The particular form of Fichte's teaching may still sound

unfamiliar enough. But in substance it has had the deepest influence on the aims and methods of criticism; and, so far as England is concerned, this is mainly due to the genius of Carlyle. Compare the criticism of the last century with that of the present, and we at once see the change that has come over the temper and instincts of Englishmen in this matter.

When Johnson, or the reviewers of the next generation, quittedas they seldom did quitthe ground of external form and regularity and logical coherence, it was only to ask: Is this work, this poem or this novel, in conformity with the traditional conventions of respectability, is it such as can be put into the hands of boys and girls? To them this was the one ground on which the matter of literature, as apart from the beggarly elements of its form, could come under the cognizance of the critic. And this narrowness, a narrowness which belonged at least in equal measure to the official criticism of the French, naturally begot a reaction almost as narrow as itself. The cry of "art for art's sake", a cry raised in France at the moment when Carlyle was beginning his work in England, must be regarded as a protest against the moralizing bigotry of the classical school no less than against its antiquated formalities.

The men who raised it were themselves not free from the charge of formalism; but the forms they worshipped were at least those inspired by the spontaneous genius of the artist, not the mechanical rules inherited from the traditions of the past. Nor, whatever may be the case with those who have taken it up in our own day, must the cry be pressed too rigorously against the men of 1830.

The very man, on whom it was commonly fathered, was known to disavow it; and certainly in his own works, in their burning humanity and their "passion for reforming the world", was the first to set it at defiance. The moralist and the formalist still make their voice heard, and will always do so. But since Carlyle wrote, it is certain that a wider, a more fruitful, view of criticism has gained ground among us. And, if it be asked where lies the precise difference between such a view and that which satisfied the critics of an earlier day, the answer must be, that we are no longer contented to rest upon the outward form of a work of art, still less upon its conventional morality. We demand to learn what is the idea, of which the outward form is the harmonious utterance; and which, just because the form is individual, must itself too have more or less of originality and power. We are resolved to know what is the artist's peculiar fashion of conceiving life, what is his insight, that which he has to teach us of God and man and nature. "Poetry", said Wordsworth, "is the breath and finer spirit of all knowledge; it is the impassioned expression which is in the countenance of all Science." And Wordsworth is echoed by Shelley. But it is again to Carlyle that we must turn for the explicit application of these ideas to criticism:

"Criticism has assumed a new form...; it proceeds on other principles, and proposes to itself a higher aim. The grand question is not now a question concerning the qualities of diction, the coherence of metaphors, the fitness of sentiments, the general logical truth, in a work of art, as it was some half-century ago among most critics; neither is it a question mainly of a psychological sort, to be answered by discovering and delineating the peculiar nature of the poet from his poetry, as is usual with the best of our own critics at present: but it isnot indeed exclusively, but inclusively of those two other questionsproperly and ultimately a question on the essence and peculiar life of the poetry itself. The first of these questions, as we see it answered, for instance, in the criticisms of Johnson and Kames, relates, strictly speaking, to the garment of poetry: the second, indeed, to its body and material existence, a much higher point; but only the last to its soul and spiritual existence, by which alone can the body... be informed with significance and rational life.

The problem is not now to determine by what mechanism Addison composed sentences and struck out similitudes; but by what far finer and more mysterious mechanism Shakespeare organized his dramas, and gave life and individuality to his Ariel and his Hamlet? Wherein lies that life; how have they attained that shape and individuality? Whence comes that empyrean fire, which irradiates their whole being, and pierces, at least in starry gleams, like a diviner thing, into all hearts? Are these dramas of his not verisimilar only, but true; nay, truer than reality itself, since the essence of unmixed reality is bodied forth in them under more expressive symbols? What is this unity of theirs; and can our deeper inspection discern it to be indivisible, and existing by necessity, because each work springs, as it were, from the general elements of all thought, and grows up therefrom into form and expansion by its own growth?

Not only who was the poet, and how did he compose; but what and how was the poem, and why was it a poem and not rhymed eloquence, creation and not figured passion? These are the questions for the critic." And, a few pages later: "As an instance we might refer to Goethe's criticism of Hamlet.... This truly is what may be called the poetry of criticism: for it is in some sort also a creative art; aiming, at least, to reproduce under a different shape the existing product of the poet; painting to the intellect what already lay painted to the heart and the imagination."

Instances of criticism, conceived in this spirit, are unhappily still rare. But some of Coleridge's on Shakespeare, and some of Lamb's on the Plays of the Elizabethan Dramatistsin particular The Duchess of Malfi and The Broken Heartmay fairly be ranked among them. So, and with still less of hesitation, may Mr. Ruskin's rendering of the Last Judgment of Tintoret, and Mr. Pater's studies on Lionardo, Michaelangelo, and Giorgione. Of these, Mr. Pater's achievement is probably the most memorable; for it is an attempt, and an attempt of surprising power and subtlety, to reproduce not merely the effect of a single poem or picture, but the imaginative atmosphere, the spiritual individuality, of the artist. In a sense still higher than would be true even of the work done by Lamb and Ruskin, it deserves the praise justly given by Carlyle to the masterpiece of Goethe; it is "the very poetry of criticism".

We have now reviewed the whole circle traversed by criticism during the present century, and are in a position to define its limits and extent. We have seen that a change of method was at once the cause and indication of a change in spirit and in aim. The narrow range of the eighteenth century was enlarged on the one hand by the study of new literatures, and on the other hand by that appeal to history, and that idea of development which has so profoundly modified every field of thought and knowledge.

In that lay the change of method. And this, in itself, was enough to suggest a wider tolerance, a greater readiness to make allowance for differences of taste, whether as between nation and nation or as between period and period, than had been possible for men whose view was practically limited to Latin literature and to such modern literatures as were professedly moulded upon the Latin. With such diversity of material, the absolute standard, absurd enough in any case, became altogether impossible to maintain. It was replaced by the conception of a common instinct for beauty, modified in each nation by the special circumstances of its temperament and history.

But even this does not cover the whole extent of the revolution in critical ideas. Side by side with a more tolerantand, it may be added, a keenerjudgment of artistic form, came a clearer sense of the inseparable connection between form and matter, and the impossibility of comprehending the form, if it be taken apart from the matter, of a work of art. This, too, was in part the natural effect of the historical method, one result of which was to establish a closer correspondence between the thought of a nation and its art than had hitherto been suspected. But it was in part also a consequence of the intellectual and spiritual revolution of which Rousseau was the herald and which, during fifty years, found in German philosophy at once its strongest inspiration and its most articulate expression.

Men were no longer satisfied to explain to themselves what Carlyle calls the "garment" and the "body" of art; they set themselves to pierce through these to the soul and spirit within. They instinctively felt that the art which lives is the art that gives man something to live by; and that, just because its form is more significant than other of man's utterances, it must have a deeper significance also in substance and in purport. Of this purport Criticism of lifethe phrase suggested by one who was at once a poet and a criticis doubtless an unhappy, because a pedantic definition; and it is rather creation of life, than the criticism of it, that art has to offer. But it must be life in all its fulness and variety; as thought, no less than as action; as energy, no less than as beauty As power, as love, as influencing soul.

This is the mission of art; and to unfold its working in the art of all times and of all nations, to set it forth by intuition, by patient reason, by every means at his command, is the function of the critic. To have seen this, and to have marked out the way for its performance, is not the least among the services rendered by Carlyle to his own generation and to ours. Later critics can hardly be said to have yet filled out the design that he laid. They have certainly not gone beyond it.

SIR PHILIP SIDNEY.

(1554-1586.)

Chapter 14

An Apologie for Poetrie

The Apologie was probably written about 1580; Gosson's pamphlet, which clearly suggested it, having appeared in 1579. Nothing need here be added to what has been said in the Introduction. When the right virtuous Edward Wotton and I were at the emperor's court together, we gave ourselves to learn horsemanship of John Pietro Pugliano: one that with great commendation had the place of an esquire in his stable. And he, according to the fertileness of the Italian wit, did not only afford us the demonstration of his practice, but sought to enrich our minds with the contemplations therein, which he thought most precious. But with none I remember mine ears were at any time more laden, than when (either angered with slow payment, or moved with our learner-like admiration) he exercised his speech in the praise of his faculty.

He said, soldiers were the noblest estate of mankind, and horsemen, the noblest of soldiers. He said, they were the masters of war, and ornaments of peace: speedy goers, and strong abiders, triumphers both in camps and courts. Nay, to so unbelieved a point he proceeded, as that no earthly thing bred such wonder to a prince, as to be a good horseman. Skill of government was but a pedanteria in comparison: then would he add certain praises, by telling what a peerless beast a horse was. The only serviceable courtier without flattery, the beast of most beauty, faithfulness, courage, and such more, that, if I had not been a piece of a logician before I came to him, I think he would have persuaded me to have wished myself a horse.

But thus much at least with his no few words he drove

into me, that self-love is better than any gilding to make that seem gorgeous, wherein ourselves are parties. Wherein, if Pugliano his strong affection and weak arguments will not satisfy you, I will give you a nearer example of myself, who (I know not by what mischance) in these my not old years and idlest times, having slipped into the title of a poet, am provoked to say something unto you in the defence of that my unelected vocation; which if I handle with more good will than good reasons, bear with me, sith the scholar is to be pardoned that followeth the steps of his master.

And yet I must say that, as I have just cause to make a pitiful defence of poor poetry, which from almost the highest estimation of learning is fallen to be the laughing-stock of children, so have I need to bring some more available proofs: sith the former is by no man barred of his deserved credit, the silly latter hath had even the names of philosophers used to the defacing of it, with great danger of civil war among the muses. And first, truly to all them that professing learning inveigh against poetry may justly be objected, that they go very near to ungratefulness, to seek to deface that which, in the noblest nations and languages that are known, hath been the first light-giver to ignorance, and first nurse, whose milk by little and little enabled them to feed afterwards of tougher knowledges: and will they now play the hedgehog that, being received into the den, drove out his host? or rather the vipers, that with their birth kill their parents?

Let learned Greece in any of her manifold sciences, be able to show me one book, before Musaeus, Homer, and Hesiodus, all three nothing else but poets. Nay, let any history be brought, that can say any writers were there before them, if they were not men of the same skill, as Orpheus, Linus, and some other are named: who having been the first of that country, that made pens deliverers of their knowledge to their posterity, may justly challenge to be called their fathers in learning: for not only in time they had this priority (although in itself antiquity be venerable) but went before them, as causes to draw with their charming sweetness the wild untamed wits to an admiration of knowledge. So as Amphion was said to move stone with his poetry, to build Thebes. And Orpheus to be listened to by beasts indeed, stony and beastly people. So among the Romans were Livius Andronicus, and Ennius. So in the Italian language, the first that made it aspire to be a treasure-house of science were the poets Dante, Boccace, and Petrarch. So in our English were Gower and Chaucer.

After whom, encouraged and delighted with their excellent foregoing, others have followed, to beautify our mother tongue, as well in the same kind as in other arts. This did so notably show itself, that the philosophers of Greece durst not a long time appear to the world but under the masks of poets. So Thales, Empedocles, and Parmenides sang their natural philosophy in verses: so did Pythagoras and Phocylides their moral counsels: so did Tyrtaus in war matters, and Solon in matters of policy: or rather, they being poets, did exercise their delightful vein in those points of highest knowledge, which before them lay hid to the world.

For that wise Solon was directly a poet, it is manifest, having written in verse the notable fable of the Atlantic Island, which was continued by Plato. And truly, even Plato, whosoever well considereth, shall find, that in the body of his work, though the inside and strength were philosophy, the skin as it were and beauty depended most of poetry: for all standeth upon dialogues, wherein he feigneth many honest burgesses of Athens to speak of such matters, that if they had been set on the rack, they would never have confessed them. Besides, his poetical describing the circumstances of their meetings, as the well ordering of a banquet, the delicacy of a walk, with interlacing mere tales, as Gyges' ring, and others, which who knows not to be the flowers of poetry, did never walk into Apollo's garden.

And even historiographers (although their lips sound of things done, and verity be written in their foreheads) have been glad to borrow both fashion, and perchance weight, of poets. So Herodotus entitled his history by the name of the nine Muses: and both he, and all the rest that followed him, either stole or usurped of poetry their passionate describing of passions, the many particularities of battles, which no man could affirm: or if that be denied me, long orations put in the mouths of great kings and captains, which it is certain they never pronounced. So that truly, neither philosopher nor historiographer could at the first have entered into the gates of popular judgments, if they had not taken a great passport of poetry, which, in all nations at this day where learning flourisheth not, is plain to be seen: in all which they have some feeling of poetry.

In Turkey, besides their law-giving divines, they have no other writers but poets. In our neighbour country Ireland, where truly learning goeth very bare, yet are their poets held in a devout reverence. Even among the most barbarous and simple Indians where no writing is, yet have they their poets, who make and sing songs which they call areytos, both of their ancestors' deeds, and praises of their Gods. A sufficient probability, that, if ever learning come among them, it must be by having their hard dull wits softened and sharpened with the sweet delights of poetry.

For until they find a pleasure in the exercises of the mind, great promises of much knowledge will little persuade them, that know not the fruits of knowledge. In Wales, the true remnant of the ancient Britons, as there are good authorities to show the long time they had poets, which they called bards: so through all the conquests of Romans, Saxons, Danes, and Normans, some of whom did seek to ruin all memory of learning from among them, yet do their poets, even to this day, last; so as it is not more notable in soon beginning than in long continuing. But since the authors of most of our sciences were the Romans, and before them the Greeks, let us a little stand upon their authorities, but even so far as to see what names they have given unto this now scorned skill.

Among the Romans a poet was called vates, which is as much as a diviner, fore-seer, or prophet, as by his conjoined words vaticinium and vaticinari is manifest: so heavenly a title did that excellent people bestow upon this heart-ravishing knowledge. And so far were they carried into the admiration thereof, that they thought in the chanceable hitting upon any such verses great foretokens of their following fortunes were placed. Whereupon grew the word of Sortes Virgilianae, when, by sudden opening Virgil's book, they lighted upon any verse of his making, whereof the histories of the emperors' lives are full: as of Albinus the governor of our island, who in his childhood met with this verse Arma amens capio nee sat rationis in armis: and in his age performed it; which although it were a very vain and godless superstition, as also it was to think that spirits were commanded by such verses (whereupon this word charms, derived of Carmina, cometh), so yet serveth it to show the great reverence those wits were held in. And altogether not without ground, since both the oracles of Delphos and Sibylla's prophecies were wholly delivered in verses. For that same exquisite observing of number and measure in words, and that high-flying liberty of conceit proper to the Poet, did seem to have some divine force in it.

And may not I presume a little further, to show the reasonableness of this word vates? And say that the holy David's Psalms are a divine poem? If I do, I shall not do it without the testimony of great learned men, both ancient and modern: but even the name Psalms will speak for me; which being interpreted is nothing but songs. Then that it is fully written in metre, as all learned Hebricians agree, although the rules be not yet fully found.

Lastly and principally, his handling his prophecy, which is merely poetical. For what else is the awaking his musical instruments? The often and free changing of persons? His notable prosopopeias, when he maketh you, as it were, see God coming in His majesty? His telling of the beasts' joyfulness, and hills leaping, but a heavenly poesy: wherein almost he showeth himself a passionate lover of that unspeakable and everlasting beauty to be seen by the eyes of the mind, only cleared by faith? But truly now having named him, I fear me I seem to profane that holy name, applying it to poetry, which is among us thrown down to so ridiculous an estimation: but they that with quiet judgments will look a little deeper into it, shall find the end and working of it such as, being rightly applied, deserveth not to be scourged out of the Church of

God. But now, let us see how the Greeks named it, and how they deemed of it. The Greeks called him a poet, which name hath, as the most excellent, gone through other languages. It cometh of this word poiein, which is, to make: wherein I know not, whether by luck or wisdom, we Englishmen have met with the Greeks, in calling him a maker: which name, how high and incomparable a title it is, I had rather were known by marking the scope of other sciences, than by my partial allegation.

There is no art delivered to mankind, that hath not the works of nature for his principal object, without which they could not consist, and on which they so depend, as they become actors and players, as it were, of what nature will have set forth. So doth the astronomer look upon the stars, and by that he seeth, setteth down what order nature hath taken therein. So do the geometrician, and arithmetician, in their diverse sorts of quantities. So doth the musician, in times, tell you which by nature agree, which not.

The natural philosopher thereon hath his name, and the moral philosopher standeth upon the natural virtues, vices, and passions of man; and follow nature (saith he) therein, and thou shalt not err. The lawyer saith what men have determined. The historian what men have done. The grammarian speaketh only of the rules of speech; and the rhetorician, and logician, considering what in nature will soonest prove and persuade, thereon give artificial rules, which still are compassed within the circle of a question, according to the proposed matter.

The physician weigheth the nature of a man's body, and the nature of things helpful, or hurtful unto it. And the metaphysic, though it be in the second and abstract notions, and therefore be counted supernatural, yet doth he indeed build upon the depth of nature: only the poet, disdaining to be tied to any such subjection, lifted up with the vigour of his own invention, doth grow in effect another nature, in making things either better than nature bringeth forth, or quite anew forms such as never were in nature, as the heroes, demigods, cyclops, chimeras, furies, and such like: so as he goeth hand in hand with nature, not inclosed within the narrow warrant of her gifts, but freely ranging only within the zodiac of his own wit. Nature never set forth the earth in so rich tapestry, as divers poets have done, neither with pleasant rivers, fruitful trees, sweet-smelling flowers: nor whatsoever else may make the too much loved earth more lovely. Her world is brazen, the poets only deliver a golden: but let those things alone and go to man, for whom as the other things are, so it seemeth in him her uttermost cunning is employed, and know whether she have brought forth so true a lover as Theagenes, so constant a friend as Pylades, so valiant a man as Orlando, so right a prince as Xenophon's Cyrus: so excellent a man every way, as Virgil's Aneas.

Neither let this be jestingly conceived, because the works of the one be essential, the other, in imitation or fiction; for any understanding knoweth the skill of the artificer standeth in that idea or fore-conceit of the work, and not in the work itself. And that the poet hath that idea, is manifest, by delivering them forth in such excellency as he hath imagined them. Which delivering forth also is not wholly imaginative, as we are wont to say by them that build castles in the air: but so far substantially it worketh, not only to make a Cyrus, which had been but a particular excellency, as Nature might have done, but to bestow a Cyrus upon the world, to make many Cyruses, if they will learn aright, why and how that maker made him. Neither let it be deemed too saucy a comparison to balance the highest point of man's wit with the efficacy of Nature: but rather give right honour to the heavenly Maker of that maker: who, having made man to his own likeness, set him beyond and over all the works of that second nature, which in nothing he showeth so much as in poetry: when, with the force of a divine breath, he bringeth things forth far surpassing her doings, with no small argument to the incredulous of that first accursed fall of Adam; sith our erected wit maketh us know what perfection is, and yet our infected will keepeth us from reaching unto it.

But these arguments will by few be understood, and by fewer granted. Thus much (I hope) will be given me, that the Greeks, with some probability of reason, gave him the name above all names of learning. Now let us go to a more ordinary opening of him, that the truth may be more palpable: and so I hope, though we get not so unmatched a praise as the etymology of his names will grant, yet his very description, which no man will deny, shall not justly be barred from a principal commendation.

Poesy, therefore, is an art of imitation, for so Aristotle termeth it in his word Mimesis, that is to say, a representing, counterfeiting, or figuring forth: to speak metaphorically, a speaking picture: with this end, to teach and delight; of this have been three several kinds. The chief both in antiquity and excellency, were they that did imitate the inconceivable excellencies of God. Such were David in his Psalms, Solomon in his Song of Songs, in his Ecclesiastes, and Proverbs: Moses and Deborah, in their hymns, and the writer of Job; which, beside other, the learned Emanuel Tremilius and Franciscus Junius do entitle the poetical part of Scripture. Against these none will speak that hath the Holy Ghost in due holy reverence. In this kind, though in a full wrong divinity, were Orpheus, Amphion, Homer in his hymns, and many other, both Greeks and Romans: and this poesy must be used by whosoever will follow St. James his counsel, in singing psalms when they are merry: and I know is used with the fruit of comfort by some, when, in sorrowful pangs of their death-bringing sins, they find the consolation of the never-leaving goodness. The second kind, is of them that deal with matters philosophical; either moral, as Tyrtaus, Phocylides, and Cato: or natural, as Lucretius and Virgil's Georgics; or astronomical, as Manilius, and Pontanus; or historical, as Lucan; which who mislike, the fault is in their judgments quite out of taste, and not in the sweet food of sweetly-uttered knowledge.

But because this second sort is wrapped within the fold of the proposed subject, and takes not the course of his own invention, whether they properly be poets or no, let grammarians dispute; and go to the third, indeed right poets, of whom chiefly this question ariseth; betwixt whom and these second is such a kind of difference, as betwixt the meaner sort of painters (who counterfeit only such faces as are set before them) and the more excellent; who, having no law but wit, bestow that in colours upon you which is fittest for the eye to see; as the constant, though lamenting look of Lucretia, when she punished in herself another's fault. Wherein he painteth not Lucretia whom he never saw, but painteth the outward beauty of such a virtue: for these third be they which most properly do imitate to teach and delight; and, to imitate, borrow nothing of what is, hath been, or shall be: but range, only reined with learned discretion, into the divine consideration of what may be, and should be. These be they that, as the first and most noble sort may justly be termed Vates, so these are waited on in the excellentest languages and best understandings, with the fore-described name of poets: for these indeed do merely make to imitate: and imitate both to delight and teach: and delight to move men to take that goodness in hand, which without delight they would fly as from a stranger: and teach, to make them know that goodness whereunto they are moved, which being the noblest scope to which ever any learning was directed, yet want there not idle tongues to bark at them.

These be subdivided into sundry more special denominations. The most notable be the heroic, lyric, tragic, comic, satiric, iambic, elegiac, pastoral, and certain others. Some of these being termed according to the matter they deal with, some by the sorts of verses they liked best to write in, for indeed the greatest part of poets have apparelled their poetical inventions in that numbrous kind of writing which is called verse: indeed but apparelled, verse being but an ornament and no cause to poetry: sith there have been many most excellent poets that never versified, and now swarm many versifiers that need never answer to the name of poets. For Xenophon, who did imitate so excellently, as to give us effigiem justi imperii the portraiture of a just empire under the name of Cyrus (as Cicero says of him), made therein an absolute heroical poem.

So did Heliodorus in his sugared invention of that picture of love in Theagenes and Chariclea, and yet both these wrote in prose: which I speak to show, that it is not rhyming and versing that maketh a poet, no more than a long gown maketh an advocate: who, though he pleaded in armour, should be an advocate and no soldier. But it is that feigning notable images of virtues, vices, or what else, with that delightful teaching which must be the right describing note to know a poet by: although, indeed, the senate of poets hath chosen verse as their fittest raiment, meaning, as in matter they passed all in all, so in manner to go beyond them: not speaking (table-talk fashion, or like men in a dream) words as they chanceably fall from the mouth, but peyzing each syllable of each word by just proportion according to the dignity of the subject. Now, therefore, it shall not be amiss first to weigh this latter sort of poetry by his works, and then by his parts; and if in neither of these anatomies he be condemnable, I hope we shall obtain a more favourable sentence.

This purifying of wit, this enriching of memory, enabling of judgment, and enlarging of conceit, which commonly we call learning, under what name soever it come forth, or to what immediate end soever it be directed, the final end is, to lead and draw us to as high a perfection, as our degenerate souls made worse by their clayey lodgings, can be capable of. This, according to the inclination of the man, bred many formed impressions; for some that thought this felicity principally to be gotten by knowledge, and no knowledge to be so high and heavenly as acquaintance with the stars, gave themselves to astronomy; others, persuading themselves to be demigods if they knew the causes of things, became natural and supernatural philosophers; some an admirable delight drew to music; and some the certainty of demonstration, to the mathematics. But all, one and other, having this scope to know, and by knowledge to lift up the mind from the dungeon of the body, to the enjoying his own divine essence.

But when by the balance of experience it was found, that the astronomer looking to the stars might fall into a ditch, that the inquiring philosopher might be blind in himself, and the mathematician might draw forth a straight line with a crooked heart: then lo, did proof the overruler of opinions make manifest that all these are but serving sciences, which, as they have each a private end in themselves, so yet are they all directed to the highest end of the mistress knowledge, by the Greeks called Arkitektonike, which stands (as I think) in the knowledge of a man's self, in the ethic and politic consideration, with the end of well-doing, and not of well-knowing only; even as the saddler's next end is to make a good saddle: but his farther end, to serve a nobler faculty, which is horsemanship: so the horseman's to soldiery, and the soldier not only to have the skill, but to perform the practice of a soldier: so that the ending end of all earthly learning, being virtuous action, those skills that most serve to bring forth that, have a most just title to be princes over all the rest.

Wherein if we can show the poet's nobleness, by setting him before his other competitors, among whom as principal challengers step forth the moral philosophers, whom methinketh I see coming towards me with a sullen gravity, as though they could not abide vice by daylight, rudely clothed for to witness outwardly their contempt of outward things, with books in their hands against glory, whereto they set their names, sophistically speaking against subtlety, and angry with any man in whom they see the foul fault of anger; these men casting largess as they go, of definitions, divisions, and distinctions, with a scornful interrogative, do soberly ask, whether it be possible to find any path, so ready to lead a man to virtue, as that which teacheth what virtue is? and teacheth it not only by delivering forth his very being, his causes, and effects: but also, by making known his enemy vice, which must be destroyed, and his cumbersome servant passion, which must be mastered, by showing the generalities that contain it, and the specialities that are derived from it: lastly, by plain setting down, how it extendeth itself out of the limits of a man's own little world, to the government of families and maintaining of public societies.

The historian scarcely giveth leisure to the moralist, to say so much, but that he, laden with old mouse-eaten records, authorizing himself (for the most part) upon other histories, whose greatest authorities are built upon the notable foundation of hearsay, having much ado to accord differing writers, and to pick truth out of partiality, better acquainted with a thousand years ago than with the present age, and yet better knowing how this world goeth than how his own wit runneth, curious for antiquities and inquisitive of novelties, a wonder to young folks, and a tyrant in table-talk, denieth in a great chafe that any man, for teaching of virtue and virtuous actions, is comparable to him. I am Lux vitae, Temporum Magistra, Vita memoriae, Nuncia vetustatis, and c.

The philosopher (saith he) teacheth a disputative virtue, but I do an active: his virtue is excellent in the dangerless academy of Plato, but mine showeth forth her honourable face in the battles of Marathon, Pharsalia, Poitiers, and Agincourt. He teacheth virtue by certain abstract considerations, but I only bid you follow the footing of them that have gone before you. Old-aged experience goeth beyond the fine- witted philosopher, but I give the experience of many ages. Lastly, if he make the songbook, I put the learner's hand to the lute; and if he be the guide, I am the light. Then would he allege you innumerable examples, conferring story by story, how much the wisest senators and princes have been directed by the credit of history, as Brutus, Alphonsus of Aragon, and who not, if need be? At length the long line of their disputation maketh a point in this, that the one giveth the precept, and the other the example.

Now, whom shall we find (sith the question standeth for the highest form in the school of learning) to be moderator? Truly, as me seemeth, the poet; and if not a moderator, even the man that ought to carry the title from them both, and much more from all other serving sciences. Therefore compare we the poet with the historian and with the moral philosopher, and, if he go beyond them both, no other human skill can match him. For as for the divine, with all reverence it is ever to be excepted, not only for having his scope as far beyond any of these, as eternity exceedeth a moment, but even for passing each of these in themselves. And for the lawyer, though Jus be the daughter of Justice, and Justice the chief of virtues, yet because he seeketh to make men good, rather Formidine poenae than Virtutis amore or to say righter, doth not endeavour to make men good, but that their evil hurt not others: having no care, so he be a good citizen, how bad a man he be. Therefore, as our wickedness maketh him necessary, and necessity maketh him honourable, so is he not in the deepest truth to stand in rank with these, who all endeavour to take naughtiness away, and plant goodness even in the secretest cabinet of our souls. And these four are all that any way deal in that consideration of men's manners, which being the supreme knowledge, they that best breed it deserve the best commendation.

The philosopher therefore and the historian are they which would win the goal: the one by precept, the other by example. But both not having both, do both halt. For the philosopher, setting down with thorny argument the bare rule, is so hard of utterance, and so misty to be conceived, that one that hath no other guide but him shall wade in him till he be old before he shall find sufficient cause to be honest; for his knowledge standeth so upon the abstract and general, that happy is that man who may understand him, and more happy that can apply what he doth understand. On the other side, the historian wanting the precept is so tied, not to what should be, but to what is, to the particular truth of things, and not to the general reason of things, that his example draweth no necessary consequence, and therefore a less fruitful doctrine.

Now doth the peerless poet perform both: for whatsoever the philosopher saith should be done, he giveth a perfect picture of it in some one, by whom he presupposeth it was done. So as he coupleth the general notion with the particular example. A perfect picture, I say; for he yieldeth to the powers of the mind an image of that whereof the philosopher bestoweth but a wordish description: which doth neither strike, pierce, nor possess the sight of the soul so much as that other doth.

For as in outward things, to a man that had never seen an elephant or a rhinoceros, who should tell him most exquisitely all their shapes, colour, bigness, and particular marks; or of a gorgeous palace, the architecture; with declaring the full beauties, might well make the hearer able to repeat, as it were by rote, all he had heard, yet should never satisfy his inward conceits, with being witness to itself of a true lively knowledge: but the same man, as soon as he might see those beasts well painted, or the house well in model, should straightway grow without need of any description, to a judicial comprehending of them: so no doubt the philosopher with his learned definition, be it of virtue, vices, matters of public policy or private government, replenisheth the memory with many infallible grounds of wisdom: which, notwithstanding, lie dark before the imaginative and judging power, if they be not illuminated or figured forth by the speaking picture of poesy.

Tully taketh much pains and many times not without poetical helps, to make us know the force love of our country hath in us. Let us but hear old Anchises speaking in the midst of Troy's flames, or see Ulysses, in the fulness of all Calypso's delights, bewail his absence from barren and beggarly Ithaca. Anger, the Stoics say, was a short madness; let but Sophocles bring you Ajax on a stage, killing and whipping sheep and oxen, thinking them the army of Greeks, with their chieftains Agamemnon and Menelaus, and tell me if you have not a more familiar insight into anger, than finding in the schoolmen his genus and difference. See whether wisdom and temperance in Ulysses and Diomedes, valour in Achilles, friendship in Nisus and Euryalus, even to an ignorant man, carry not an apparent shining: and contrarily, the remorse of conscience in Odipus, the soon repenting pride of Agamemnon, the self-devouring cruelty in his father Atreus, the violence of ambition in the two Theban brothers, the sour-sweetness of revenge in Medea, and to fall lower, the Terentian Gnatho and our Chaucer's Pandar, so expressed, that we now use their names to signify their trades.

And finally, all virtues, vices, and passions so in their own natural seats laid to the view, that we seem not to hear of them, but clearly to see through them. But even in the most excellent determination of goodness, what philosopher's counsel can so readily detect a prince, as the feigned Cyrus in Xenophon? or a virtuous man in all fortunes, as Aneas in Virgil? or a whole commonwealth, as the way of Sir Thomas More's Utopia? I say the way; because where Sir Thomas More erred, it was the fault of the man and not of the poet; for that way of patterning a commonwealth was most absolute, though he perchance hath not so absolutely performed it: for the question is, whether the feigned image of poesy, or the regular instruction of philosophy, hath the more force in teaching; wherein if the philosophers have more rightly showed themselves philosophers than the poets have obtained to the high top of their profession, as in truth Mediocribus esse poetis, Non Di, non homines, non concessere columna: it is I say again, not the fault of the art, but that by few men that art can be accomplished.

Certainly, even our Saviour Christ could as well have given the moral commonplaces of uncharitableness and humbleness, as the divine narration of Dives and Lazarus: or of disobedience and mercy, as that heavenly discourse of the lost child and the gracious Father; but that his through-searching wisdom knew the estate of Dives burning in hell, and of Lazarus being in Abraham's bosom, would more constantly (as it were) inhabit both the memory and judgment. Truly, for myself, meseems I see before my eyes the lost child's disdainful prodigality, turned to envy a swine's dinner: which by the learned divines are thought not historical acts, but instructing parables.

For conclusion, I say the philosopher teacheth, but he teacheth obscurely, so as the learned only can understand him: that is to say, he teacheth them that are already taught, but the poet is the food for the tenderest stomachs, the poet is indeed the right popular philosopher, whereof Asop's tales give good proof: whose pretty allegories, stealing under the formal tales of beasts, make many, more beastly than beasts, begin to hear the sound of virtue from these dumb speakers.

But now may it be alleged that, if this imagining of matters be so fit for the imagination, then must the historian needs surpass, who bringeth you images of true matters, such as indeed were done, and not such as fantastically or falsely may be suggested to have been done. Truly Aristotle himself in his discourse of poesy, plainly determineth this question, saying that poetry is philosophoteron and spoudaioteron, that is to say, it is more philosophical, and more studiously serious, than history. His reason is, because poesy dealeth with katholou, that is to say, with the universal consideration; and the history with kathekaston, the particular; now saith he, the universal weighs what is fit to be said or done, either in likelihood or necessity (which the poesy considereth in his imposed names), and the particular only marks, whether Alcibiades did, or suffered, this or that. Thus far Aristotle: which reason of his (as all his) is most full of reason.

For indeed, if the question were whether it were better to have a particular act truly or falsely set down, there is no doubt which is to be chosen, no more than whether you had rather have Vespasian's picture right as he was, or at the painter's pleasure nothing resembling. But if the question be for your own use and learning, whether it be better to have it set down as it should be, or as it was: then certainly is more doctrinable the feigned Cyrus of Xenophon than the true Cyrus in Justin: and the feigned Aeneas in Virgil, than the right Aeneas in Dares Phrygius.

As to a lady that desired to fashion her countenance to the best grace, a painter should more benefit her to portrait a most sweet face, writing Canidia upon it, than to paint Canidia as she was, who, Horace sweareth, was foul and ill-favoured. If the poet do his part aright, he will show you in Tantalus, Atreus, and such like, nothing that is not to be shunned. In Cyrus, Aeneas, Ulysses, each thing to be followed; where the historian, bound to tell things as things were, cannot be liberal (without he will be poetical) of a perfect pattern: but as in Alexander or Scipio himself, show doings, some to be liked, some to be misliked.

And then how will you discern what to follow but by your own discretion, which you had without reading Quintus Curtius? And whereas a man may say, though in universal consideration of doctrine the poet prevaileth, yet that the history, in his saying such a thing was done, doth warrant a man more in that he shall follow; the answer is manifest: that if he stand upon that was; as if he should argue, because it rained yesterday, therefore it should rain to-day; then indeed it hath some advantage to a gross conceit: but if he know an example only informs a conjectured likelihood, and so go by reason, the poet doth so far exceed him, as he is to frame his example to that which is most reasonable: be it in warlike, politic, or private matters; where the historian in his bare Was, hath many times that which we call fortune, to overrule the best wisdom. Many times he must tell events, whereof he can yield no cause: or if he do, it must be poetical; for that a feigned example hath as much force to teach, as a true example (for as for to move, it is clear, sith the feigned may be tuned to the highest key of passion), let us take one example, wherein a poet and a historian do concur.

Herodotus and Justin do both testify that Zopyrus, King Darius' faithful servant, seeing his master long resisted by the rebellious Babylonians, feigned himself in extreme disgrace of his king: for verifying of which, he caused his own nose and ears to be cut off: and so flying to the Babylonians, was received: and for his known valour so far credited, that he did find means to deliver them over to Darius. Much like matter doth Livy record of Tarquinius and his son. Xenophon excellently feigneth such another stratagem, performed by Abradates in Cyrus' behalf.

Now would I fain know, if occasion be presented unto you, to serve your prince by such an honest dissimulation, why you do not as well learn it of Xenophon's fiction, as of the others' verity: and truly so much the better, as you shall save your nose by the bargain: for Abradates did not counterfeit so far. So then the best of the historian is subject to the poet; for whatsoever action or faction, whatsoever counsel, policy or war stratagem, the historian is bound to recite, that may the poet (if he list) with his imitation make his own; beautifying it both for further teaching, and more delighting, as it pleaseth him: having all, from Dante his heaven, to his hell, under the authority of his pen. Which if I be asked what poets have done so, as I might well name some, yet say I, and say again, I speak of the art, and not of the artificer.

Now to that which commonly is attributed to the praise of histories, in respect of the notable learning is gotten by marking the success, as though therein a man should see virtue exalted, and vice punished; truly that commendation is peculiar to poetry, and far off from history.

For indeed poetry ever setteth virtue so out in her best colours, making fortune her well-waiting handmaid, that one must needs be enamoured of her. Well may you see Ulysses in a storm and in other hard plights; but they are but exercises of patience and magnanimity, to make them shine the more in the near-following prosperity. And of the contrary part, if evil men come to the stage, they ever go out (as the tragedy writer answered, to one that misliked the show of such persons) so manacled, as they little animate folks to follow them. But the historian, being captived to the truth of a foolish world, is many times a terror from well-doing, and an encouragement to unbridled wickedness.

For see we not valiant Miltiades rot in his fetters? The just Phocion, and the accomplished Socrates, put to death like traitors? The cruel Severus live prosperously? The excellent Severus miserably murdered? Sulla and Marius dying in their beds? Pompey and Cicero slain then, when they would have thought exile a happiness? See we not virtuous Cato driven to kill himself? and rebel Caesar so advanced, that his name yet after 1600 years, lasteth in the highest honour? And mark but even Caesar's own words of the fore-named Sulla, (who in that only did honestly, to put down his dishonest tyranny,) literas nescivit, as if want of learning caused him to do well. He meant it not by poetry, which not content with earthly plagues deviseth new punishments in hell for tyrants: nor yet by philosophy, which teacheth occidendos esse: but no doubt by skill in history: for that indeed can afford your Cypselus, Periander, Phalaris, Dionysius, and I know not how many more of the same kennel, that speed well enough in their abominable unjustice or usurpation.

I conclude therefore that he excelleth history, not only in furnishing the mind with knowledge, but in setting it forward, to that which deserveth to be called and accounted good:

which setting forward, and moving to well-doing, indeed setteth the laurel crown upon the poet as victorious, not only of the historian, but over the philosopher: howsoever in teaching it may be questionable. For suppose it be granted (that which I suppose with great reason may be denied) that the philosopher, in respect of his methodical proceeding, doth teach more perfectly than the poet; yet do I think that no man is so much philophilosophos, as to compare the philosopher, in moving, with the poet.

And that moving is of a higher degree than teaching, it may by this appear: that it is well-nigh the cause and the effect of teaching. For who will be taught, if he be not moved with desire to be taught? and what so much good doth that teaching bring forth (I speak still of moral doctrine) as that it moveth one to do that which it doth teach? for as Aristotle saith, it is not Gnosis but Praxis must be the fruit. And how Praxis cannot be, without being moved to practice, it is no hard matter to consider. The philosopher showeth you the way, he informeth you of the particularities; as well of the tediousness of the way, as of the pleasant lodging you shall have when your journey is ended, as of the many by-turnings that may divert you from your way. But this is to no man but to him that will read him, and read him with attentive studious painfulness.

Which constant desire, whosoever hath in him, hath already passed half the hardness of the way, and therefore is beholding to the philosopher but for the other half. Nay truly, learned men have learnedly thought, that where once reason hath so much overmastered passion, as that the mind hath a free desire to do well, the inward light each mind hath in itself is as good as a philosopher's book; seeing in nature we know it is well to do well, and what is well, and what is evil, although not in the words of art, which philosophers bestow upon us. For out of natural conceit, the philosophers drew it; but to be moved to do that which we know, or to be moved with desire to know, Hoc opus, hic labour est.

Now therein of all sciences (I speak still of human, and according to the human conceits), is our poet the Monarch. For he doth not only show the way, but giveth so sweet a prospect into the way, as will entice any man to enter into it. Nay, he doth as if your journey should lie through a fair vineyard, at the first give you a cluster of grapes: that, full of that taste, you may long to pass further. He beginneth not with obscure definitions, which must blur the margent with interpretations, and load the memory with doubtfulness: but he cometh to you with words sent in delightful proportion, either accompanied with, or prepared for the well enchanting skill of music; and with a tale forsooth he cometh unto you: with a tale which holdeth children from play, and old men from the chimney corner.

And pretending no more, doth intend the winning of the mind from wickedness to virtue: even as the child is often brought to take most wholesome things, by hiding them in such other as have a pleasant taste: which, if one should begin to tell them the nature of Aloes or Rhubarb they should receive, would sooner take their physic at their ears than at their mouth. So it is in men (most of which are childish in the best things, till they be cradled in their graves), glad they will be to hear the tales of Hercules, Achilles, Cyrus, and Aneas; and hearing them, must needs hear the right description of wisdom, valour, and justice; which, if they had been barely, that is to say philosophically, set out, they would swear they be brought to school again. That imitation, whereof poetry is, hath the most conveniency to Nature of all other, insomuch, that as Aristotle saith, those things which in themselves are horrible, as cruel battles, unnatural monsters, are made in poetical imitation delightful. Truly I have known men that, even with reading Amadis de Gaule (which God knoweth wanteth much of a perfect poesy), have found their hearts moved to the exercise of courtesy, liberality, and especially courage.

Who readeth Aneas carrying old Anchises on his back, that wisheth not it were his fortune to perform so excellent an act? Whom do not the words of Turnus move? (the tale of Turnus having planted his image in the imagination) Fugientem hoec terra videbit; Usque adeone mori miserum est? Where the philosophers, as they scorn to delight, so must they be content little to move: saving wrangling, whether virtue be the chief, or the only good: whether the contemplative, or the active life do excel: which Plato and Boethius well knew, and therefore made Mistress Philosophy very often borrow the masking raiment of poesy. For even those hard-hearted evil men, who think virtue a school name, and know no other good but indulgere genio, and therefore despise the austere admonitions of the philosopher, and feel not the inward reason they stand upon, yet will be content to be delighted: which is all the good fellow poet seemeth to promise: and so steal to see the form of goodness (which seen they cannot but love) ere themselves be aware, as if they took a medicine of cherries. Infinite proofs of the strange effects of this poetical invention might be alleged; only two shall serve, which are so often remembered, as I think all men know them.

The one of Menenius Agrippa, who when the whole people of Rome had resolutely divided themselves from the Senate, with apparent show of utter ruin: though he were (for that time) an excellent orator, came not among them upon trust of figurative speeches, or cunning insinuations: and much less, with far-fetched maxims of philosophy, which (especially if they were Platonic, they must have learned geometry before they could well have conceived: but forsooth he behaves himself, like a homely, and familiar poet. He telleth them a tale, that there was a time, when all the parts of the body made a mutinous conspiracy against the belly, which they thought devoured the fruits of each other's labour; they concluded they would let so unprofitable a spender starve. In the end, to be short (for the tale is notorious, and as notorious that it was a tale), with punishing the belly, they plagued themselves.

This, applied by him, wrought such effect in the people, as I never read that ever words brought forth but then, so sudden and so good an alteration; for upon reasonable conditions, a perfect reconcilement ensued. The other is of Nathan the prophet, who when the holy David had so far forsaken God, as to confirm adultery with murder: when he was to do the tenderest office of a friend, in laying his own shame before his eyes, sent by God to call again so chosen a servant: how doth he it but by telling of a man, whose beloved lamb was ungratefully taken from his bosom? the application most divinely true, but the discourse itself feigned: which made David (I speak of the second and instrumental cause), as in a glass, to see his own filthiness, as that heavenly psalm of mercy well testifieth.

By these therefore examples and reasons, I think it may be manifest, that the poet, with that same hand of delight, doth draw the mind more effectually than any other art doth; and so a conclusion not unfitly ensueth: that, as virtue is the most excellent resting-place for all worldly learning to make his end of, so poetry, being the most familiar to teach it, and most princely to move towards it, in the most excellent work is the most excellent workman. But I am content not only to decipher him by his works (although works in commendation or dispraise must ever hold an high authority), but more narrowly will examine his parts: so that (as in a man) though altogether he may carry a presence full of majesty and beauty, perchance in some one defectious piece we may find a blemish: now in his parts, kinds, or species (as you list to term them), it is to be noted, that some poesies have coupled together two or three kinds, as tragical and comical, whereupon is risen the tragi-comical. Some in the like manner have mingled prose and verse, as Sanazzar and Boethius.

Some have mingled matters heroical and pastoral. But that cometh all to one in this question; for if severed they be good, the conjunction cannot be hurtful. Therefore perchance forgetting some, and leaving some as needless to be remembered, it shall not be amiss in a word to cite the special kinds, to see what faults may be found in the right use of them. Is it then the pastoral poem which is misliked? for perchance, where the hedge is lowest, they will soonest leap over. Is the poor pipe disdained, which sometime out of Melibeus's mouth, can show the misery of people under hard lords, or ravening soldiers? And again, by Tityrus, what blessedness is derived to them that lie lowest from the goodness of them that sit highest? Sometimes, under the pretty tales of wolves and sheep, it can include the whole considerations of wrong-doing and patience.

Sometimes show, that contention for trifles can get but a trifling victory. Where perchance a man may see that even Alexander and Darius, when they strave who should be cock of this world's dunghill, the benefit they got, was that the after-livers may say, Hac memini et victum frustra contendere Thyrsin; Ex illo Corydon, Corydon est tempore nobis.

Or is it the lamenting Elegiac, which in a kind heart would move rather pity than blame, who bewails with the great philosopher Heraclitus the weakness of mankind, and the wretchedness of the world: who surely is to be praised, either for compassionate accompanying just causes of lamentation, or for rightly painting out how weak be the passions of woefulness. Is it the bitter, but wholesome Iambic which rubs the galled mind, in making shame the trumpet of villany, with bold and open crying out against naughtiness; or the satirist, who Omne vafer vitium ridenti tangit amico? Who sportingly never leaveth, until he make a man laugh at folly, and at length ashamed, to laugh at himself: which he cannot avoid, without avoiding the folly. Who while Circum pracordia ludit, giveth us to feel, how many headaches a passionate life bringeth us to. How when all is done, Est Ulubris, animus si nos non deficit aquus. No perchance it is the comic, whom naughty play-makers and stage- keepers have justly made odious. To the argument of abuse, I will answer after.

Only thus much now is to be said, that the comedy is an imitation of the common errors of our life, which he representeth in the most ridiculous and scornful sort that may be. So as it is impossible that any beholder can be content to be such a one. Now, as in geometry, the oblique must be known as well as the right: and in arithmetic, the odd as well as the even, so in the actions of our life, who seeth not the filthiness of evil, wanteth a great foil to perceive the beauty of virtue. This doth the comedy handle so in our private and domestical matters, as with hearing it we get as it were an experience, what is to be looked for of a niggardly Demea: of a crafty Davus: of a flattering Gnatho: of a vainglorious Thraso: and not only to know what effects are to be expected, but to know who be such, by the signifying badge given them by the comedian. And little reason hath any man to say that men learn evil by seeing it so set out: sith, as I said before, there is no man living but, by the force truth hath in nature, no sooner seeth these men play their parts, but wisheth them in Pistrinum: although perchance the sack of his own faults lie so behind his back, that he seeth not himself dance the same measure: whereto yet nothing can more open his eyes, than to find his own actions contemptibly set forth. So that the right use of comedy will (I think) by nobody be blamed, and much less of the high and excellent tragedy, that openeth the greatest wounds, and showeth forth the vicers that are covered with tissue: that maketh kings fear to be tyrants, and tyrants manifest their tyrannical humours: that, with stirring the effects of admiration and commiseration, teacheth the uncertainty of this world, and upon how weak foundations golden roofs are builded. That maketh us know,

Qui sceptra scevus duro imperio regit,
Timet timentes, metus in auctorem redit.

But how much it can move, Plutarch yieldeth a notable testimony, of the abominable tyrant, Alexander Pheraus; from whose eyes, a tragedy well made and represented drew abundance of tears: who, without all pity, had murdered infinite numbers, and some of his own blood. So as he, that was not ashamed to make matters for tragedies, yet could not resist the sweet violence of a tragedy.

And if it wrought no further good in him, it was, that he in despite of himself withdrew himself from hearkening to that, which might mollify his hardened heart. But it is not the tragedy they do mislike: for it were too absurd to cast out so excellent a representation of whatsoever is most worthy to be learned. Is it the lyric that most displeaseth, who with his tuned lyre, and well accorded voice, giveth praise, the reward of virtue, to virtuous acts? who gives moral precepts and natural problems, who sometimes raiseth up his voice to the height of the heavens, in singing the lauds of the immortal God. Certainly I must confess my own barbarousness, I never heard the old song of Percy and Douglas, that I found not my heart moved more than with a trumpet: and yet is it sung but by some blind crouder, with no rougher voice than rude style: which being so evil apparelled in the dust and cobwebs of that uncivil age, what would it work trimmed in the gorgeous eloquence of Pindar? In Hungary I have seen it the manner at all feasts and other such meetings, to have songs of their ancestors' valour; which that right soldier-like nation think the chiefest kindlers of brave courage. The incomparable Lacedemonians did not only carry that kind of music ever with them to the field, but even at home, as such songs were made, so were they all content to be the singers of them, when the lusty men were to tell what they did, the old men what they had done, and the young men what they would do.

And where a man may say that Pindar many times praiseth highly victories of small moment, matters rather of sport than virtue: as it may be answered, it was the fault of the poet, and not of the poetry; so indeed, the chief fault was in the time and custom of the Greeks, who set those toys at so high a price, that Philip of Macedon reckoned a horse-race won at Olympus, among his three fearful felicities. But as the inimitable Pindar often did, so is that kind most capable and most fit to awake the thoughts from the sleep of idleness, to embrace honourable enterprises.

There rests the heroical, whose very name (I think) should daunt all backbiters; for by what conceit can a tongue be directed to speak evil of that which draweth with it no less champions than Achilles, Cyrus, Aneas, Turnus, Tydeus, and Rinaldo? who doth not only teach and move to a truth, but teacheth and moveth to the most high and excellent truth? who maketh magnanimity and justice shine, throughout all misty fearfulness and foggy desires? who, if the saying of Plato and Tully be true, that who could see Virtue, would be wonderfully ravished with the love of her beauty, this man sets her out to make her more lovely in her holiday apparel, to the eye of any that will deign, not to disdain, until they understand.

But if anything be already said in the defence of sweet poetry, all concurreth to the maintaining the heroical, which is not only a kind, but the best, and most accomplished kind of poetry. For as the image of each action stirreth and instructeth the mind, so the lofty image of such worthies most inflameth the mind with desire to be worthy, and informs with counsel how to be worthy. Only let Aneas be worn in the tablet of your memory, how he governeth himself in the ruin of his country, in the preserving his old father, and carrying away his religious ceremonies: in obeying the god's commandment to leave Dido, though not only all passionate kindness, but even the humane consideration of virtuous gratefulness, would have craved other of him. How in storms, how in sports, how in war, how in peace, how a fugitive, how victorious, how besieged, how besieging, how to strangers, how to allies, how to his enemies, how to his own: lastly, how in his inward self, and how in his outward government. And I think, in a mind not prejudiced with a prejudicating humour, he will be found in excellency fruitful: yea, even as Horace saith:

Melius Chrysippo et Crantore. But truly I imagine, it falleth out with these poet-whippers, as with some good women, who often are sick, but in faith they cannot tell where. So the name of poetry is odious to them; but neither his cause, nor effects, neither the sum that contains him, nor the particularities descending from him, give any fast handle to their carping dispraise.

Sith then poetry is of all human learning the most ancient, and of most fatherly antiquity, as from whence other learnings have taken their beginnings: sith it is so universal, that no learned nation doth despise it, nor no barbarous nation is without it: sith both Roman and Greek gave divine names unto it, the one of prophesying, the other of making: and that indeed that name of making is fit for him; considering, that whereas other arts retain themselves within their subject, and receive, as it were, their being from it, the poet only bringeth his own stuff, and doth not learn a conceit out of a matter, but maketh matter for a conceit: sith neither his description, nor his end, containeth any evil, the thing described cannot be evil: sith his effects be so good as to teach goodness and to delight the learners: sith therein (namely, in moral doctrine, the chief of all knowledges), he doth not only far pass the historian, but for instructing is well- nigh comparable to the philosopher: and for moving, leaves him behind him: sith the Holy Scripture (wherein there is no uncleanness) hath whole parts in it poetical: and that even our Saviour Christ vouchsafed to use the flowers of it: sith all his kinds are not only in their united forms, but in their severed dissections fully commendable, I think (and think I think rightly), the laurel crown, appointed for triumphing captains, doth worthily (of all other learnings) honour the poet's triumph. But because we have ears as well as tongues, and that the lightest reasons that may be, will seem to weigh greatly, if nothing be put in the counter-balance: let us hear, and as well as we can ponder, what objections may be made against this art, which may be worthy, either of yielding or answering.

First truly I note, not only in these mysomousoi poet-haters, but in all that kind of people, who seek a praise by dispraising others, that they do prodigally spend a great many wandering words, in quips, and scoffs; carping and taunting at each thing, which, by stirring the spleen, may stay the brain from a through beholding the worthiness of the subject. Those kind of objections, as they are full of very idle easiness, sith there is nothing of so sacred a majesty, but that an itching tongue may rub itself upon it: so deserve they no other answer, but instead of laughing at the jest, to laugh at the jester. We know a playing wit can praise the discretion of an ass; the comfortableness of being in debt, and the jolly commodity of being sick of the plague. So of the contrary side, if we will turn Ovid's verse: Ut lateat virtus proximitate mali, that good lie hid in nearness of the evil: Agrippa will be as merry in showingthe vanity of science, as Erasmus was in commending of folly.

Neither shall any man or matter escape some touch of these smiling railers. But for Erasmus and Agrippa, they had another foundation than the superficial part would promise. Marry, these other pleasant fault-finders, who will correct the verb, before they understand the noun, and confute others' knowledge before they confirm their own: I would have them only remember, that scoffing cometh not of wisdom. So as the best title in true English they get with their merriments is to be called good fools: for so have our grave forefathers ever termed that humorous kind of jesters: but that which giveth greatest scope to their scorning humours is rhyming and versing. It is already said (and as I think, truly said) it is not rhyming and versing that maketh poesy. One may be a poet without versing, and a versifier without poetry. But yet, presuppose it were inseparable (as indeed it seemeth Scaliger judgeth) truly it were an inseparable commendation. For if oratio next to ratio, speech next to reason, be the greatest gift bestowed upon mortality: that cannot be praiseless, which doth most polish that blessing of speech, which considers each word, not only (as a man may say) by his forcible quality, but by his best measured quantity, carrying even in themselves, a harmony: without (perchance) number, measure, order, proportion, be in our time grown odious. But lay aside the just praise it hath, by being the only fit speech for music (music, I say, the most divine striker of the senses): thus much is undoubtedly true, that if reading be foolish, without remembering, memory being the only treasurer of knowledge, those words which are fittest for memory, are likewise most convenient for knowledge.

Now, that verse far exceedeth prose in the knitting up of the memory, the reason is manifest. The words (besides their delight, which hath a great affinity to memory), being so set, as one word cannot be lost, but the whole work fails: which accuseth itself, calleth the remembrance back to itself, and so most strongly confirmeth it. Besides, one word so as it were begetting another, as be it in rhyme or measured verse, by the former a man shall have a near guess to the follower. Lastly, even they that have taught the art of memory have showed nothing so apt for it, as a certain room divided into many places well and thoroughly known. Now, that hath the verse in effect perfectly: every word having his natural seat, which seat must needs make the words remembered. But what needeth more in a thing so known to all men? Who is it that ever was a scholar, that doth not carry away some verses of Virgil, Horace, or Cato, which in his youth he learned, and even to his old age serve him for hourly lessons? But the fitness it hath for memory is notably proved by all delivery of arts: wherein for the most part, from grammar to logic, mathematic, physic, and the rest, the rules chiefly necessary to be borne away are compiled in verses. So that, verse being in itself sweet and orderly, and being best for memory, the only handle of knowledge, it must be in jest that any man can speak against it. Now then go we to the most important imputations laid to the poor poets; for aught I can yet learn, they are these: first, that there being many other more fruitful knowledges, a man might better spend his time in them, than in this. Secondly, that it is the mother of lies.

Thirdly, that it is the nurse of abuse, infecting us with many pestilent desires: with a siren's sweetness, drawing the mind to the serpent's tail of sinful fancy. And herein especially, comedies give the largest field to err, as Chaucer saith: how both in other nations and in ours, before poets did soften us, we were full of courage, given to martial exercises; the pillars of man-like liberty, and not lulled asleep in shady idleness with poets' pastimes. And lastly, and chiefly, they cry out with an open mouth, as if they outshot Robin Hood, that Plato banished them out of his commonwealth. Truly, this is much, if there be much truth in it. First to the first: that a man might better spend his time, is a reason indeed: but it doth (as they say) but petere principium. For if it be as I affirm, that no learning is so good as that which teacheth and moveth to virtue; and that none can both teach and move thereto so much as poetry: then is the conclusion manifest, that ink and paper cannot be to a more profitable purpose employed.

And certainly, though a man should grant their first assumption, it should follow (methinks) very unwillingly, that good is not good, because better is better. But I still and utterly deny that there is sprung out of earth a more fruitful knowledge. To the second, therefore, that they should be the principal liars; I answer paradoxically, but truly I think, truly; that of all writers under the sun, the poet is the least liar: and though he would, as a poet can scarcely be a liar, the astronomer, with his cousin the geometrician, can hardly escape, when they take upon them to measure the height of the stars. How often, think you, do the physicians lie, when they aver things good for sicknesses, which afterwards send Charon a great number of souls drowned in a potion before they come to his ferry? And no less of the rest, which take upon them to affirm. Now, for the poet, he nothing affirms, and therefore never lieth. For, as I take it, to lie is to affirm that to be true which is false.

So as the other artists, and especially the historian, affirming many things, can in the cloudy knowledge of mankind hardly escape from many lies. But the poet (as I said before) never affirmeth. The poet never maketh any circles about your imagination, to conjure you to believe for true what he writes. He citeth not authorities of other histories, but even for his entry calleth the sweet Muses to inspire into him a good invention: in truth, not labouring to tell you what is or is not, but what should or should not be: and therefore, though he recount things not true, yet because he telleth them not for true, he lieth not, without we will say that Nathan lied in his speech, before alleged, to David. Which as a wicked man durst scarce say, so think I, none so simple would say, that Asop lied in the tales of his beasts: for who thinks that Asop wrote it for actually true, were well worthy to have his name chronicled among the beasts he writeth of.

What child is there, that coming to a play, and seeing Thebes written in great letters upon an old door, doth believe that it is Thebes? If then a man can arrive, at that child's age, to know that the poet's persons and doings are but pictures what should be, and not stories what have been, they will never give the lie to things not affirmatively, but allegorically and figuratively, written. And therefore as in history, looking for truth, they go away full fraught with falsehood: so in poesy, looking for fiction, they shall use the narration but as an imaginative groundplot of a profitable invention. But hereto is replied that the poets give names to men they write of, which argueth a conceit of an actual truth, and so, not being true, proves a falsehood. And doth the lawyer lie, then, when under the names of John a stile and John a noakes, he puts his case?

But that is easily answered. Their naming of men is but to make their picture the more lively, and not to build any history: painting men, they cannot leave men nameless. We see we cannot play at chess, but that we must give names to our chessmen; and yet methinks he were a very partial champion of truth that would say we lied for giving a piece of wood the reverend title of a bishop. The poet nameth Cyrus or Aneas no other way than to show what men of their fames, fortunes, and estates should do.

Their third is, how much it abuseth men's wit, training it to wanton sinfulness and lustful love; for indeed that is the principal, if not the only abuse I can hear alleged. They say the comedies rather teach than reprehend amorous conceits. They say the lyric is larded with passionate sonnets. The elegiac weeps the want of his mistress. And that even to the heroical, Cupid hath ambitiously climbed.

Alas, Love! I would thou couldst as well defend thyself as thou canst offend others. I would those on whom thou dost attend could either put thee away or yield good reason why they keep thee. But grant love of beauty to be a beastly fault, although it be very hard, sith only man and no beast hath that gift, to discern beauty. Grant that lovely name of love to deserve all hateful reproaches: although even some of my masters the philosophers spent a good deal of their lamp-oil in setting forth the excellency of it. Grant, I say, whatsoever they will have granted; that not only love, but lust, but vanity, but (if they list) scurrility, possesseth many leaves of the poet's books: yet think I, when this is granted, they will find their sentence may with good manners put the last words foremost; and not say that poetry abuseth man's wit, but that man's wit abuseth poetry.

For I will not deny but that man's wit may make poesy (which should be eikastike, which some learned have defined, figuring forth good things) to be fantastic: which doth contrariwise infect the fancy with unworthy objects. As the painter, that should give to the eye either some excellent perspective or some fine picture fit for building or fortification, or containing in it some notable example, as Abraham sacrificing his son Isaac, Judith killing Holofernes, David fighting with Goliath, may leave those and please an ill-pleased eye with wanton shows of better hidden matters. But what, shall the abuse of a thing make the right use odious? Nay, truly, though I yield that poesy may not only be abused, but that, being abused by the reason of his sweet charming force, it can do more hurt than any other army of words: yet shall it be so far from concluding that the abuse should give reproach to the abused, that contrariwise it is a good reason that whatsoever being abused, doth most harm, being rightly used (and upon the right use each thing conceiveth his title) doth most good. Do we not see the skill of physic (the best rampire to our often- assaulted bodies), being abused, teach poison the most violent destroyer?

Doth not knowledge of law, whose end is to even and right all things, being abused, grow the crooked fosterer of horrible injuries? Doth not (to go to the highest) God's word, abused, breed heresy? and His name abused, become blasphemy? Truly a needle cannot do much hurt, and as truly (with leave of ladies be it spoken) it cannot do much good. With a sword thou mayest kill thy father, and with a sword thou mayest defend thy prince and country. So that, as in their calling poets the fathers of lies they say nothing: so in this their argument of abuse they prove the commendation.

They allege herewith that, before poets began to be in price, our nation hath set their hearts' delight upon action and not upon imagination: rather doing things worthy to be written than writing things fit to be done. What that before time was, I think scarcely Sphinx can tell: sith no memory is so ancient that hath the precedence of poetry. And certain it is that, in our plainest homeliness, yet never was the Albion nation without poetry. Marry, this argument, though it be levelled against poetry, yet is it indeed a chain-shot against all learning, or bookishness, as they commonly term it. Of such mind were certain Goths, of whom it is written that, having in the spoils of a famous city taken a fair library, one hangman (belike fit to execute the fruits of their wits) who had murdered a great number of bodies, would have set fire on it.

"No", said another very gravely, "take heed what you do, for while they are busy about these toys, we shall with more leisure conquer their countries." This indeed is the ordinary doctrine of ignorance, and many words sometimes I have heard spent in it; but because this reason is generally against all learning, as well as poetry; or rather, all learning but poetry: because it were too large a digression to handle, or at least too superfluous: (sith it is manifest that all government of action is to be gotten by knowledge, and knowledge best by gathering many knowledges, which is, reading), I only with Horace, to him that is of that opinion, Jubeo stultum esse libenter: for as for poetry itself, it is the freest from this objection. For poetry is the companion of the camps.

I dare undertake, Orlando Furioso or honest King Arthur will never displease a soldier; but the quiddity of ens and prima materia will hardly agree with a corslet; and therefore, as I said in the beginning, even Turks and Tartars are delighted with poets. Homer, a Greek, flourished before Greece flourished. And if to a slight conjecture a conjecture may be opposed, truly it may seem that, as by him their learned men took almost their first light of knowledge, so their active men received their first motions of courage. Only Alexander's example may serve, who by Plutarch is accounted of such virtue that fortune was not his guide but his footstool; whose acts speak for him, though Plutarch did not: indeed, the Phoenix of warlike princes. This Alexander left his schoolmaster, living Aristotle, behind him, but took dead Homer with him; he put the philosopher Calisthenes to death for his seeming philosophical, indeed mutinous stubbornness. But the chief thing he ever was heard to wish for was that Homer had been alive.

He well found he received more bravery of mind by the pattern of Achilles than by hearing the definition of fortitude; and therefore, if Cato misliked Fulvius for carrying Ennius with him to the field, it may be answered that, if Cato misliked it, the noble Fulvius liked it, or else he had not done it. For it was not the excellent Cato Uticensis (whose authority I would much more have reverenced), but it was the former: in truth, a bitter punisher of faults, but else a man that had never well sacrificed to the Graces. He misliked and cried out upon all Greek learning, and yet, being 80 years old, began to learn it. Belike, fearing that Pluto understood not Latin. Indeed, the Roman laws allowed no person to be carried to the wars but he that was in the soldiers' roll; and therefore, though Cato misliked his unmustered person, he misliked not his work. And if he had, Scipio Nasica, judged by common consent the best Roman, loved him. Both the other Scipio brothers, who had by their virtues no less surnames than of Asia and Affrick, so loved him that they caused his body to be buried in their sepulchre. So as Cato, his authority being but against his person, and that answered with so far greater than himself, is herein of no validity.

But now, indeed, my burden is great; now Plato his name is laid upon me, whom I must confess, of all philosophers, I have ever esteemed most worthy of reverence, and with great reason, sith of all philosophers he is the most poetical. Yet if he will defile the fountain, out of which his flowing streams have proceeded, let us boldly examine with what reasons he did it. First, truly, a man might maliciously object that Plato, being a philosopher, was a natural enemy of poets; for, indeed, after the philosophers had picked out of the sweet mysteries of poetry the right discerning true points of knowledge, they forthwith putting it in method, and making a school-art of that which the poets did only teach by a divine delightfulness, beginning to spurn at their guides like ungrateful 'prentices, were not content to set up shops for themselves, but sought by all means to discredit their masters.

Which by the force of delight being barred them, the less they could overthrow them, the more they hated them. For, indeed, they found for Homer seven cities strove who should have him for their citizen: where many cities banished philosophers, as not fit members to live among them. For only repeating certain of Euripides' verses, many Athenians had their lives saved of the Syracusians: when the Athenians themselves thought many philosophers unworthy to live.

Certain poets, as Simonides and Pindarus had so prevailed with Hiero the first, that of a tyrant they made him a just king, where Plato could do so little with Dionysius, that he himself, of a philosopher, was made a slave.

But who should do thus, I confess, should requite the objections made against poets, with like cavillation against philosophers; as likewise one should do, that should bid one read Phaedrus or Symposium in Plato, or the discourse of love in Plutarch, and see whether any poet do authorize abominable filthiness, as they do. Again, a man might ask out of what commonwealth Plato did banish them? in sooth, thence where he himself alloweth community of women: so as, belike, this banishment grew not for effeminate wantonness, sith little should poetical sonnets be hurtful, when a man might have what woman he listed.

But I honour philosophical instructions, and bless the wits which bred them: so as they be not abused, which is likewise stretched to poetry. St. Paul himself, who yet (for the credit of poets) allegeth twice two poets, and one of them by the name of a prophet, setteth a watch-word upon philosophy, indeed upon the abuse. So doth Plato, upon the abuse, not upon poetry. Plato found fault, that the poets of his time filled the world with wrong opinions of the gods, making light tales of that unspotted essence; and therefore, would not have the youth depraved with such opinions. Herein may much be said, let this suffice: the poets did not induce such opinions, but did imitate those opinions already induced. For all the Greek stories can well testify, that the very religion of that time stood upon many and many-fashioned gods, not taught so by the poets, but followed, according to their nature of imitation.

Who list, may read in Plutarch, the discourses of Isis, and Osiris, of the cause why oracles ceased, of the divine providence: and see, whether the theology of that nation stood not upon such dreams, which the poets superstitiously observed, and truly, (sith they had not the light of Christ,) did much better in it than the philosophers, who, shaking off superstition, brought in atheism. Plato therefore, (whose authority I had much rather justly construe, than unjustly resist,) meant not in general of poets, in those words of which Julius Scaliger saith qua auctoritate barbari quidam atque hispidi abuti velint, ad poetas e republica exigendos: but only meant, to drive out those wrong opinions of the Deity (whereof now, without further law, Christianity hath taken away all the hurtful belief) perchance (as he thought) nourished by the then esteemed poets. And a man need go no further than to Plato himself, to know his meaning: who in his dialogue called Ion, giveth high, and rightly divine commendation to poetry.

So as Plato, banishing the abuse, not the thing, not banishing it but giving due honour unto it, shall be our patron, and not our adversary. For indeed I had much rather (sith truly I may do it) show their mistaking of Plato, (under whose lion's skin they would make an ass-like braying against poesy,) than go about to overthrow his authority, whom the wiser a man is, the more just cause he shall find to have in admiration: especially, sith he attributeth unto poesy more than myself do; namely to be a very inspiring of a divine force, far above man's wit; as in the aforenamed dialogue is apparent.

Of the other side, who would show the honours have been by the best sort of judgments granted them, a whole sea of examples would present themselves. Alexanders, Caesars, Scipios, all favourers of poets. Lalius, called the Roman Socrates, himself a poet: so as part of Heautontimorumenos in Terence was supposed to be made by him. And even the Greek Socrates, whom Apollo confirmed to be the only wise man, is said to have spent part of his old time in putting Asop's fables into verses. And therefore, full evil should it become his scholar Plato to put such words in his master's mouth against poets. But what need more?

Aristotle writes the Art of Poesy: and why if it should not be written? Plutarch teacheth the use to be gathered of them, and how if they should not be read? And who reads Plutarch's either history or philosophy, shall find he trimmeth both their garments with guards of poesy. But I list not to defend poesy, with the help of her underling, historiography. Let it suffice, that it is a fit soil for praise to dwell upon: and what dispraise may set upon it is either easily overcome, or transformed into just commendation. So that, sith the excellencies of it may be so easily and so justly confirmed, and the low-creeping objections, so soon trodden down; it not being an art of lies, but of true doctrine: not of effeminateness, but of notable stirring of courage: not of abusing man's wit, but of strengthening man's wit: not banished, but honoured by Plato: let us rather plant more laurels, for to engarland our poets' heads, (which honour of being laureat, as besides them, only triumphant captains wear, is a sufficient authority, to show the price they ought to be had in,) than suffer the ill-favouring breath of such wrong-speakers, once to blow upon the clear springs of poesy.

But sith I have run so long a career in this matter, methinks, before I give my pen a full stop, it shall be but a little more lost time, to inquire, why England, (the mother of excellent minds,) should be grown so hard a step-mother to poets, who certainly in wit ought to pass all other: sith all only proceedeth from their wit, being indeed makers of themselves, not takers of others. How can I but exclaim, Musa mihi causas memora, quo numine laso, sweet poesy, that hath anciently had kings, emperors, senators, great captains, such as, besides a thousand others, David, Adrian, Sophocles, Germanicus, not only to favour poets, but to be poets; and of our nearer times, can present for her patrons, a Robert, king of Sicily, the great king Francis of France, King James of Scotland; such cardinals as Bembus, and Bibiena; such famous preachers and teachers, as Beza and Melancthon; so learned philosophers, as Fracastorius and Scaliger; so great orators, as Pontanus and Muretus; so piercing wits as George Buchanan; so grave counsellors, as besides many, but before all, that Hospital of France: than whom (I think) that realme never brought forth a more accomplished judgment: more firmly builded upon virtue; I say these, with numbers of others, not only to read others' poesies, but to poetise for others' reading: that poesy thus embraced in all other places, should only find, in our time, a hard welcome in England, I think the very earth lamenteth it, and therefore decketh our soil with fewer laurels than it was accustomed; for heretofore, poets have in England also flourished; and which is to be noted, even in those times, when the trumpet of Mars did sound loudest.

And now, that an over-faint quietness should seem to strew the house for poets, they are almost in as good reputation as the mountebanks at Venice. Truly even that, as of the one side it giveth great praise to poesy, which like Venus (but to better purpose) hath rather be troubled in the net with Mars, than enjoy the homely quiet of Vulcan: so serves it for a piece of a reason, why they are less grateful to idle England, which now can scarce endure the pain of a pen. Upon this necessarily followeth, that base men with servile wits undertake it: who think it enough, if they can be rewarded of the printer. And so as Epaminondas is said, with the honour of his virtue, to have made an office, by his exercising it, which before was contemptible, to become highly respected: so these, no more but setting their names to it, by their own disgracefulness, disgrace the most graceful poesy.

For now, as if all the Muses were got with child, to bring forth bastard poets, without any commission, they do post over the banks of Helicon, till they make the readers more weary than post-horses: while in the mean time, they Queis meliore luto finxit procordia Titan, are better content, to suppress the outflowing of their wit, than by publishing them to be accounted knights of the same order. But I, that before ever I durst aspire unto the dignity am admitted into the company of the paper-blurrers, do find the very true cause of our wanting estimation, is want of desert: taking upon us to be poets, in despite of Pallas. Now, wherein we want desert were a thank-worthy labour to express: but if I knew, I should have mended myself. But I, as I never desired the title, so have neglected the means to come by it. Only overmastered by some thoughts, I yielded an inky tribute unto them.

Marry, they that delight in poesy itself should seek to know what they do, and how they do; and especially, look themselves in an unflattering glass of reason, if they be inclinable unto it. For poesy must not be drawn by the ears, it must be gently led, or rather, it must lead.

Which was partly the cause, that made the ancient-learned

affirm, it was a divine gift, and no human skill: sith all other knowledges lie ready for any that hath strength of wit: a poet no industry can make, if his own genius be not carried unto it: and therefore is it an old proverb, orator fit; poeta nascitur. Yet confess I always, that as the fertilest ground must be manured, so must the highest-flying wit have a Dadalus to guide him. That Dadalus, they say, both in this and in other, hath three wings, to bear itself up into the air of due commendation: that is, art, imitation, and exercise. But these, neither artificial rules, nor imitative patterns, we much cumber ourselves withal. Exercise indeed we do, but that, very fore-backwardly: for where we should exercise to know, we exercise as having known: and so is our brain delivered of much matter, which never was begotten by knowledge.

For, there being two principal parts, matter to be expressed by words, and words to express the matter, in neither, we use art, or imitation, rightly. Our matter is quodlibet indeed, though wrongly performing Ovid's verse, Quicquid conabar dicere versus erat: never marshalling it into an assured rank, that almost the readers cannot tell where to find themselves. Chaucer undoubtedly did excellently in his Troilus and Cresseid; of whom, truly I know not whether to marvel more, either that he in that misty time, could see so clearly, or that we in this clear age walk so stumblingly after him. Yet had he great wants, fit to be forgiven, in so reverent antiquity. I account the Mirror of Magistrates meetly furnished of beautiful parts; and in the Earl of Surrey's Lyrics, many things tasting of a noble birth, and worthy of a noble mind. The Shepherd's Calendar hath much poetry in his eclogues: indeed worthy the reading, if I be not deceived.

That same framing of his style to an old rustic language I dare not allow, sith neither Theocritus in Greek, Virgil in Latin, nor Sannazar in Italian, did affect it. Besides these, do I not remember to have seen but few (to speak boldly) printed, that have poetical sinews in them: for proof whereof, let but most of the verses be put in prose, and then ask the meaning; and it will be found that one verse did but beget another, without ordering at the first, what should be at the last: which becomes a confused mass of words, with a tingling sound of rhyme, barely accompanied with reason.

Our tragedies and comedies, (not without cause cried out against,) observing rules neither of honest civility nor of skilful poetry, excepting Gorboduc, (again, I say, of those that I have seen,) which notwithstanding as it is full of stately speeches, and well-sounding phrases, climbing to the height of Seneca his style, and as full of notable morality, which it doth most delightfully teach, and so obtain the very end of poesy: yet in truth it is very defectious in the circumstances; which grieveth me, because it might not remain as an exact model of all tragedies. For it is faulty both in place and time, the two necessary companions of all corporal actions.

For where the stage should always represent but one place, and the uttermost time presupposed in it should be, both by Aristotle's precept and common reason, but one day: there is both many days, and many places, inartificially imagined. But if it be so in Gorboduc, how much more in all the rest? where you shall have Asia of the one side, and Africa of the other, and so many other under-kingdoms, that the player, when he cometh in, must ever begin with telling where he is: or else, the tale will not be conceived. Now ye shall have three ladies walk to gather flowers, and then we must believe the stage to be a garden. By and by, we hear news of shipwreck in the same place, and then we are to blame, if we accept it not for a rock. Upon the back of that, comes out a hideous monster, with fire and smoke, and then the miserable beholders are bound to take it for a cave.

While in the meantime, two armies fly in, represented with four swords and bucklers, and then what hard heart will not receive it for a pitched field? Now, of time they are much more liberal, for ordinary it is that two young princes fall in love. After many traverses, she is got with child, delivered of a fair boy, he is lost, groweth a man, falls in love, and is ready to get another child, and all this in two hours' space: which how absurd it is in sense, even sense may imagine, and art hath taught, and all ancient examples justified: and at this day the ordinary players in Italy will not err in. Yet will some bring in an example of Eunuchus in Terence, that containeth matter of two days, yet far short of twenty years.

True it is, and so was it to be played in two days, and so fitted to the time it set forth. And though Plautus hath in one place done amiss, let us hit with him, and not miss with him. But they will say, how then shall we set forth a story, which containeth both many places, and many times? And do they not know that a tragedy is tied to the laws of poesy, and not of history? not bound to follow the story, but having liberty, either to feign a quite new matter, or to frame the history to the most tragical convenience.

Again, many things may be told, which cannot be showed, if they know the difference betwixt reporting and representing. As for example, I may speak (though I am here) of Peru, and in speech digress from that, to the description of Calicut: but in action, I cannot represent it without Pacolet's horse: and so was the manner the ancients took, by some nuncius to recount things done in former time, or other place. Lastly, if they will represent a history, they must not (as Horace saith) begin ab ovo: but they must come to the principal point of that one action, which they will represent. By example this will be best expressed. I have a story of young Polydorus, delivered for safety's sake, with great riches, by his father Priamus to Polymnestor, king of Thrace, in the Trojan war time: he after some years, hearing the overthrow of Priamus, for to make the treasure his own, murdereth the child: the body is taken up by Hecuba: she the same day findeth a slight to be revenged most cruelly of the tyrant: where now would one of our tragedy writers begin, but with the delivery of the child? Then should he sail over into Thrace, and so spend I know not how many years, and travel numbers of places.

But where doth Euripides? Even with the finding of the body, leaving the rest to be told by the spirit of Polydorus. This need no further to be enlarged, the dullest wit may conceive it. But besides these gross absurdities, how all their plays be neither right tragedies, nor right comedies: mingling kings and clowns, not because the matter so carrieth it, but thrust in clowns by head and shoulders, to play a part in majestical matters, with neither decency nor discretion. So as neither the admiration and commiseration, nor the right sportfulness, is by their mongrel tragi-comedy obtained.

I know Apuleius did somewhat so, but that is a thing recounted with space of time, not represented in one moment: and I know, the ancients have one or two examples of tragi-comedies, as Plautus hath Amphitryo: but if we mark them well, we shall find, that they never, or very daintily, match hornpipes and funerals. So falleth it out, that having indeed no right comedy, in that comical part of our tragedy, we have nothing but scurrility, unworthy of any chaste ears: or some extreme show of doltishness, indeed fit to lift up a loud laughter, and nothing else: where the whole tract of a comedy should be full of delight, as the tragedy should be still maintained in a well-raised admiration. But our comedians think there is no delight without laughter, which is very wrong; for though laughter may come with delight, yet cometh it not of delight, as though delight should be the cause of laughter; but well may one thing breed both together: nay, rather in themselves, they have as it were a kind of contrariety: for delight we scarcely do, but in things that have a convenience to ourselves, or to the general nature: laughter almost ever cometh of things most disproportioned to ourselves and nature. Delight hath a joy in it, either permanent, or present. Laughter hath only a scornful tickling.

For example, we are ravished with delight to see a fair woman, and yet are far from being moved to laughter. We laugh at deformed creatures, wherein certainly we cannot delight. We delight in good chances, we laugh at mischances; we delight to hear the happiness of our friends, or country; at which he were worthy to be laughed at, that would laugh; we shall contrarily laugh sometimes, to find a matter quite mistaken, and go down the hill against the bias, in the mouth of some such men, as for the respect of them one shall be heartily sorry, yet he cannot choose but laugh; and so is rather pained, than delighted, with laughter. Yet deny I not, but that they may go well together; for as in Alexander's picture well set out we delight without laughter, and in twenty mad antics we laugh without delight: so in Hercules, painted with his great beard, and furious countenance, in woman's attire, spinning at Omphale's commandment, it breedeth both delight and laughter. For the representing of so strange a power in love, procureth delight: and the scornfulness of the action stirreth laughter. But I speak to this purpose, that all the end of the comical part be not upon such scornful matters as stir laughter only: but mixed with it, that delightful teaching which is the end of poesy.

And the great fault even in that point of laughter, and forbidden plainly by Aristotle, is that they stir laughter in sinful things; which are rather execrable than ridiculous: or in miserable, which are rather to be pitied than scorned. For what is it to make folks gape at a wretched beggar, or a beggarly clown? or, against law of hospitality, to jest at strangers, because they speak not English so well as we do? what do we learn, sith it is certain Nil habet infelix paupertas durius in se, Quam quod ridiculos homines facit: but rather a busy-loving courtier; a heartless threatening Thraso; a self-wise-seeming schoolmaster; an awry-transformed traveller? These if we saw walk in stage names, which we play naturally, therein were delightful laughter, and teaching delightfulness: as in the other, the tragedies of Buchanan do justly bring forth a divine admiration. But I have lavished out too many words of this play-matter. I do it because, as they are excelling parts of poesy, so is there none so much used in England, and none can be more pitifully abused.

Which like an unmannerly daughter, showing a bad education, causeth her mother poesy's honesty to be called in question. Other sorts of poetry almost have we none, but that lyrical kind of songs and sonnets: which Lord, if he gave us so good minds, how well it might be employed, and with how heavenly fruit, both private and public, in singing the praises of the immortal beauty, the immortal goodness of that God, who giveth us hands to write, and wits to conceive, of which we might well want words, but never matter, of which we could turn our eyes to nothing, but we should ever have new budding occasions. But truly many of such writings, as come under the banner of un-resistible love, if I were a mistress, would never persuade me they were in love: so coldly they apply fiery speeches, as men that had rather read lovers' writings, and so caught up certain swelling phrases, which hang together, like a man which once told me, the wind was at north, west, and by south, because he would be sure to name winds enough, than that in truth they feel those passions, which easily (as I think) may be betrayed by that same forcibleness, or energeia (as the Greeks call it) of the writer. But let this be a sufficient, though short note, that we miss the right use of the material point of poesy.

Now, for the outside of it, which is words, or (as I may term it) diction, it is even well worse. So is that honey-flowing matron eloquence apparelled, or rather disguised, in a courtezan-like painted affectation: one time with so far-fetched words, they may seem monsters, but must seem strangers to any poor Englishman; another time, with coursing of a letter, as if they were bound to follow the method of a dictionary: another time, with figures and flowers, extremely winter-starved. But I would this fault were only peculiar to versifiers, and had not as large possession among prose-printers; and (which is to be marvelled) among many scholars; and (which is to be pitied) among some preachers. Truly I could wish, if at least I might be so bold to wish in a thing beyond the reach of my capacity, the diligent imitators of Tully and Demosthenes (most worthy to be imitated) did not so much keep Nizolian paper-books of their figures and phrases, as by attentive translation (as it were) devour them whole, and make them wholly theirs: for now they cast sugar and spice upon every dish that is served to the table; like those Indians, not content to wear earrings at the fit and natural place of the ears, but they will thrust jewels through their nose and lips because they will be sure to be fine.

Tully, when he was to drive out Catiline, as it were with a thunderbolt of eloquence, often used that figure of repetition, Vivit? Vivit; immo in Senatum venit, &c. Indeed, inflamed with a well-grounded rage, he would have his words (as it were) double out of his mouth: and so do that artificially, which we see men do in choler naturally. And we, having noted the grace of those words, hale them in sometime to a familiar epistle, when it were to too much choler to be choleric. Now for similitudes, in certain printed discourses, I think all herbarists, all stories of beasts, fowls, and fishes, are rifled up, that they come in multitudes, to wait upon any of our conceits: which certainly is as absurd a surfeit to the ears as is possible: for the force of a similitude, not being to prove anything to a contrary disputer, but only to explain to a willing hearer, when that is done, the rest is a most tedious prattling: rather over-swaying the memory from the purpose whereto they were applied, than any whit informing the judgment, already either satisfied, or by similitudes not to be satisfied.

For my part, I do not doubt, when Antonius and Crassus, the great forefathers of Cicero in eloquence, the one (as Cicero testifieth of them) pretended not to know art, the other, not to set by it: because with a plain sensibleness they might win credit of popular ears; which credit is the nearest step to persuasion: which persuasion is the chief mark of oratory; I do not doubt (I say) but that they used these tracks very sparingly, which who doth generally use, any man may see doth dance to his own music: and so be noted by the audience more careful to speak curiously, than to speak truly.

Undoubtedly (at least to my opinion undoubtedly), I have found in divers smally learned courtiers a more sound style, than in some professors of learning: of which I can guess no other cause, but that the courtier, following that which by practice he findeth fittest to nature, therein (though he know it not) doth according to art, though not by art: where the other, using art to show art, and not to hide art (as in these cases he should do), flyeth from nature, and indeed abuseth art. But what? methinks I deserve to be pounded, for straying from poetry to oratory: but both have such an affinity in this wordish consideration, that I think this digression will make my meaning receive the fuller understanding: which is not to take upon me to teach poets how they should do, but only finding myself sick among the rest, to show some one or two spots of the common infection, grown among the most part of writers: that, acknowledging ourselves somewhat awry, we may bend to the right use both of matter and manner; whereto our language giveth us great occasion, being indeed capable of any excellent exercising of it. I know, some will say it is a mingled language. And why not so much the better, taking the best of both the other? Another will say it wanteth grammar. Nay, truly, it hath that praise, that it wanteth not grammar; for grammar it might have, but it needs it not; being so easy of itself, and so void of those cumbersome differences of cases, genders, moods, and tenses, which I think was a piece of the Tower of Babylon's curse, that a man should be put to school to learn his mother-tongue. But for the uttering sweetly and properly the conceits of the mind, which is the end of speech, that hath it equally with any other tongue in the world: and is particularly happy, in compositions of two or three words together, near the Greek, far beyond the Latin: which is one of the greatest beauties can be in a language.

Now, of versifying there are two sorts, the one ancient, the other modern: the ancient marked the quantity of each syllable, and according to that framed his verse: the modern, observing only number (with some regard of the accent), the chief life of it standeth in that like sounding of the words, which we call rhyme. Whether of these be the most excellent, would bear many speeches. The ancient (no doubt) more fit for music, both words and tune observing quantity, and more fit lively to express divers passions, by the low and lofty sound of the well-weighed syllable.

The latter likewise, with his rhyme, striketh a certain music to the ear: and in fine, sith it doth delight, though by another way, it obtains the same purpose: there being in either sweetness, and wanting in neither majesty. Truly the English, before any other vulgar language I know, is fit for both sorts: for, for the ancient, the Italian is so full of vowels, that it must ever be cumbered with elisions. The Dutch, so of the other side with consonants, that they cannot yield the sweet sliding fit for a verse. The French, in his whole language, hath not one word, that hath his accent in the last syllable saving two, called

Antepenultima, and little more hath the Spanish: and therefore, very gracelessly may they use Dactyls. The English is subject to none of these defects.

Now, for the rhyme, though we do not observe quantity, yet we observe the accent very precisely: which other languages either cannot do, or will not do so absolutely. That Caesura, or breathing place in the midst of the verse, neither Italian nor Spanish have; the French, and we, never almost fail of. Lastly, even the very rhyme itself, the Italian cannot put in the last syllable, by the French named the masculine rhyme, but still in the next to the last, which the French call the female, or the next before that, which the Italians termed Sdrucciola. The example of the former, is Buono, Suono; of the Sdrucciola, Femina, Semina. The French, on the other side, hath both the male, as Bon, Son, and the female, as Plaise, Taise.

But the Sdrucciola he hath not: where English hath all three, as Due, True, Father, Rather, Motion, Potion with much more which might be said, but that I find already, the triflingness of this discourse is much too much enlarged. So that sith the ever-praiseworthy poesy is full of virtue-breeding delightfulness, and void of no gift, that ought to be in the noble name of learning: sith the blames laid against it are either false, or feeble: sith the cause why it is not esteemed in England, is the fault of poet-apes, not poets: sith lastly, our tongue is most fit to honour poesy, and to be honoured by poesy, I conjure you all, that have had the evil luck to read this ink-wasting toy of mine, even in the name of the nine Muses, no more to scorn the sacred mysteries of poesy: no more to laugh at the name of poets, as though they were next inheritors to fools: no more to jest at the reverend title of a rhymer: but to believe with Aristotle, that they were the ancient treasurers of the Grecians' Divinity. To believe with Bembus, that they were first bringers in of all civility.

To believe with Scaliger, that no philosopher's precepts can sooner make you an honest man, than the reading of Virgil. To believe with Clauserus, the translator of Cornutus, that it pleased the heavenly Deity, by Hesiod and Homer, under the veil of fables, to give us all knowledge, logic, rhetoric, philosophy, natural and moral, and Quid non? To believe with me, that there are many mysteries contained in poetry, which of purpose were written darkly, lest by profane wits it should be abused. To believe with Landin, that they are so beloved of the Gods, that whatsoever they write proceeds of a divine fury. Lastly, to believe themselves, when they tell you they will make you immortal, by their verses. Thus doing, your name shall flourish in the printers' shops; thus doing, you shall be of kin to many a poetical preface; thus doing, you shall be most fair, most rich, most wise, most all, you shall dwell upon superlatives. Thus doing, though you be libertino patre natus, you shall suddenly grow Herculis proles: Si quid mea carmina possunt. Thus doing, your soul shall be placed with Dante's Beatrix, or Virgil's Anchises.

But if (fie of such a but) you be born so near the dull making Cataphract of Nilus, that you cannot hear the planet-like music of poetry, if you have so earth-creeping a mind, that it cannot lift itself up, to look to the sky of poetry: or rather, by a certain rustical disdain, will become such a mome, as to be a momus of poetry: then, though I will not wish unto you the ass's ears of Midas, nor to be driven by a poet's verses (as Bubonax was) to hang himself, nor to be rhymed to death, as is said to be done in Ireland: yet thus much curse I must send you, in the behalf of all poets, that, while you live, you live in love, and never get favour, for lacking skill of a sonnet: and when you die, your memory die from the earth, for want of an epitaph.

JOHN DRYDEN.
(1631-1700)

Chapter 15

Preface to the Fables

The following Preface belongs to the last few months of Dryden's life (1700), and introduces the collection, mainly of translations and adaptations, to which he gave the title of Fables Apart from Alexander's Feast (written in 1697), the most notable pieces in this collection were the versions of Chaucer's Knightes Tale and Nonne Prestes Tale, and of three stories to be found in Boccaccio Sigismunda and Guiscardo, Cymon and Iphigenia, Theodore and Honoria. The Preface is memorable for its critical judgments on Homer, Virgil, and Ovid, still more memorable for its glowing praise of Chaucer.

It closes as it was fitting that the last work of Dryden should close, with an apology, full of manliness and dignity, for the licentiousness of his comedies. For his short-comings in this matter he had lately been attacked by Collier, and in his reply he more than wins back any esteem that he may have lost by his transgression.

It is with a poet, as with a man who designs to build, and is very exact, as he supposes, in casting up the cost beforehand; but, generally speaking, he is mistaken in his account, and reckons short in the expense he first intended. He alters his mind as the work proceeds, and will have this or that convenience more, of which he had not thought when he began. So has it happened to me. I have built a house, where I intended but a lodge; yet with better success than a certain nobleman, who, beginning with a dog-kennel, never lived to finish the palace he had contrived.

From translating the first of Homer's Iliads (which I intended as an essay to the whole work) I proceeded to the translation of the twelfth book of Ovid's Metamorphoses, because it contains, among other things, the causes, the beginning, and ending, of the Trojan war. Here I ought in reason to have stopped; but the speeches of Ajax and Ulysses lying next in my way, I could not baulk them. When I had compassed them, I was so taken with the former part of the fifteenth book (which is the masterpiece of the whole Metamorphoses), that I enjoined myself the pleasing task of rendering it into English. And now I found, by the number of my verses, that they began to swell into a little volume; which gave me an occasion of looking backward on some beauties of my author, in his former books: there occurred to me the Hunting of the Boar, Cinyras and Myrrha, the good-natured story of Baucis and Philemon, with the rest, which I hope I have translated closely enough, and given them the same turn of verse which they had in the original; and this, I may say without vanity, is not the talent of every poet.

He who has arrived the nearest to it, is the ingenious and learned Sandys, the best versifier of the former age, if I may properly call it by that name, which was the former part of this concluding century. For Spenser and Fairfax both flourished in the reign of Queen Elizabeth; great masters in our language, and who saw much farther into the beauties of our numbers than those who immediately followed them. Milton was the poetical son of Spenser, and Mr. Waller of Fairfax, for we have our lineal descents and clans as well as other families. Spenser more than once insinuates that the soul of Chaucer was transfused into his body, and that he was begotten by him two hundred years after his decease. Milton has acknowledged to me that Spenser was his original, and many besides myself have heard our famous Waller own that he derived the harmony of his numbers from the Godfrey of Bulloigne, which was turned into English by Mr. Fairfax.

But to return. Having done with Ovid for this time, it came into my mind that our old English poet, Chaucer, in many things resembled him, and that with no disadvantage on the side of the modern author, as I shall endeavour to prove when I compare them; and as I am, and always have been, studious to promote the honour of my native country, so I soon resolved to put their merits to the trial, by turning some of the Canterbury Tales into our language, as it is now refined; for by this means, both the poets being set in the same light, and dressed in the same English habit, story to be compared with story, a certain judgment may be made betwixt them by the reader, without obtruding my opinion on him.

Or if I seem partial to my countryman, and predecessor in the laurel, the friends of antiquity are not few; and besides many of the learned, Ovid has almost all the beaux, and the whole fair sex, his declared patrons. Perhaps I have assumed somewhat more to myself than they allow me, because I have adventured to sum up the evidence; but the readers are the jury, and their privilege remains entire, to decide according to the merits of the cause, or, if they please, to bring it to another hearing before some other court.

In the meantime, to follow the thread of my discourse (as thoughts, according to Mr. Hobbes, have always some connection), so from Chaucer I was led to think on Boccace, who was not only his contemporary, but also pursued the same studies; wrote novels in prose, and many works in verse; particularly is said to have invented the octave rhyme, or stanza of eight lines, which ever since has been maintained by the practice of all Italian writers, who are, or at least assume the title of Heroic Poets; he and Chaucer, among other things, had this in common, that they refined their mother tongue; but with this difference, that Dante had began to file their language, at least in verse, before the time of Boccace, who likewise received no little help from his master Petrarch. But the reformation of their prose was wholly owing to Boccace himself, who is yet the standard of purity in the Italian tongue, though many of his phrases are become obsolete, as in process of time it must needs happen.

Chaucer (as you have formerly been told by our learned Mr. Rymer) first adorned and amplified our barren tongue from the Provencal, which was then the most polished of all the modern languages; but this subject has been copiously treated by that great critic, who deserves no little commendation from us, his countrymen. For these reasons of time, and resemblance of genius in Chaucer and Boccace, I resolved to join them in my present work, to which I have added some original papers of my own, which, whether they are equal or inferior to my other poems, an author is the most improper judge, and therefore I leave them wholly to the mercy of the reader.

I will hope the best, that they will not be condemned; but if they should, I have the excuse of an old gentleman, who, mounting on horseback before some ladies, when I was present, got up somewhat heavily, but desired of the fair spectators that they would count four-score-and-eight before they judged him. By the mercy of God, I am already come within twenty years of his number, a cripple in my limbs; but what decays are in my mind, the reader must determine. I think myself as vigorous as ever in the faculties of my soul, excepting only my memory, which is not impaired to any great degree; and if I lose not more of it, I have no great reason to complain. What judgment I had, increases rather than diminishes; and thoughts, such as they are, come crowding in so fast upon me, that my only difficulty is to choose or to reject; to run them into verse, or to give them the other harmony of prose. I have so long studied and practised both, that they are grown into a habit, and become familiar to me.

In short, though I may lawfully plead some part of the old gentleman's excuse, yet I will reserve it till I think I have greater need, and ask no grains of allowance for the faults of this my present work, but those which are given of course to human frailty. I will not trouble my reader with the shortness of time in which I writ it, or the several intervals of sickness: they who think too well of their own performances, are apt to boast in their prefaces how little time their works have cost them, and what other business of more importance interfered; but the reader will be as apt to ask the question, why they allowed not a longer time to make their works more perfect, and why they had so despicable an opinion of their judges, as to thrust their indigested stuff upon them, as if they deserved no better.

With this account of my present undertaking, I conclude the first part of this discourse: in the second part, as at a second sitting, though I alter not the draught, I must touch the same features over again, and change the dead colouring of the whole. In general, I will only say, that I have written nothing which savours of immorality or profaneness; at least, I am not conscious to myself of any such intention.

If there happen to be found an irreverent expression, or a thought too wanton, they are crept into my verses through my inadvertency; if the searchers find any in the cargo, let them be staved or forfeited, like contrabanded goods; at least, let their authors be answerable for them, as being but imported merchandise, and not of my own manufacture. On the other side, I have endeavoured to choose such fables, both ancient and modern, as contain in each of them some instructive moral, which I could prove by induction, but the way is tedious; and they leap foremost into sight, without the reader's trouble of looking after them. I wish I could affirm, with a safe conscience, that I had taken the same care in all my former writings; for it must be owned, that supposing verses are never so beautiful or pleasing, yet if they contain anything which shocks religion, or good manners, they are at best what Horace says of good numbers without good sense: Versus inopes rerum, nugaeque canorae.

Thus far, I hope, I am right in court, without renouncing my other right of self-defence, where I have been wrongfully accused, and my sense wire-drawn into blasphemy or bawdry, as it has often been by a religious lawyer, in a late pleading against the stage; in which he mixes truth with falsehood, and has not forgotten the old rule of calumniating strongly, that something may remain.

I resume the thread of my discourse with the first of my translation, which was the first Iliad of Homer. If it shall please God to give me longer life, and moderate health, my intentions are to translate the whole Ilias; provided still that I meet with those encouragements from the public, which may enable me to proceed in my undertaking with some cheerfulness. And this I dare assure the world beforehand, that I have found, by trial, Homer a more pleasing task than Virgil (though I say not the translation will be less laborious). For the Grecian is more according to my genius than the Latin poet. In the works of the two authors we may read their manners and inclinations, which are wholly different. Virgil was of a quiet, sedate temper; Homer was violent, impetuous, and full of fire.

The chief talent of Virgil was propriety of thoughts, and ornament of words; Homer was rapid in his thoughts, and took all the liberties, both of numbers and of expressions, which his language, and the age in which he lived, allowed him: Homer's invention was more copious, Virgil's more confined; so that if Homer had not led the way, it was not in Virgil to have begun heroic poetry; for nothing can be more evident, than that the Roman poem is but the second part of the Ilias; a continuation of the same story, and the persons already formed; the manners of Aeneas are those of Hector superadded to those which Homer gave him. The Adventures of Ulysses in the Odysseis are imitated in the first six books of Virgil's Aeneis; and though the accidents are not the same (which would have argued him of a servile copying, and total barrenness of invention), yet the seas were the same in which both the heroes wandered; and Dido cannot be denied to be the poetical daughter of Calypso.

The six latter books of Virgil's poem are the four and twenty Iliads contracted; a quarrel occasioned by a lady, a single combat, battles fought, and a town besieged. I say not this in derogation to Virgil, neither do I contradict anything which I have formerly said in his just praise: for his Episodes are almost wholly of his own invention; and the form which he has given to the telling, makes the tale his own, even though the original story had been the same. But this proves, however, that Homer taught Virgil to design; and if invention be the first virtue of an Epic poet, then the Latin poem can only be allowed the second place. Mr. Hobbes, in the preface to his own bald translation of the Ilias (studying poetry as he did mathematics, when it was too late), Mr. Hobbes, I say, begins the praise of Homer where he should have ended it. He tells us that the first beauty of an Epic poem consists in diction, that is, in the choice of words, and harmony of numbers; now the words are the colouring of the work, which in the order of nature is the last to be considered.

The design, the disposition, the manners, and the thoughts are all before it; where any of those are wanting or imperfect, so much wants or is imperfect in the imitation of human life; which is in the very definition of a poem. Words, indeed, like glaring colours, are the first beauties that arise, and strike the sight: but if the draught be false or lame, the figures ill-disposed, the manners obscure or inconsistent, or the thoughts unnatural, then the finest colours are but daubing, and the piece is a beautiful monster at the best. Neither Virgil nor Homer were deficient in any of the former beauties; but in this last, which is expression, the Roman poet is at least equal to the Grecian, as I have said elsewhere; supplying the poverty of his language by his musical ear, and by his diligence. But to return: our two great poets, being so different in their tempers, one choleric and sanguine, the other phlegmatic and melancholic; that which makes them excel in their several ways is, that each of them has followed his own natural inclination, as well in forming the design, as in the execution of it. The very heroes show their authors; Achilles is hot, impatient, revengeful, Impiger, iracundus, inexorabilis, acer, &c. Aeneas patient, considerate, careful of his people, and merciful to his enemies; ever submissive to the will of heaven, quo fata trahunt, retrahuntque, sequamur.

I could please myself with enlarging on this subject, but am forced to defer it to a fitter time. From all I have said I will only draw this inference, that the action of Homer being more full of vigour than that of Virgil, according to the temper of the writer, is of consequence more pleasing to the reader. One warms you by degrees; the other sets you on fire all at once, and never intermits his heat. 'T is the same difference which Longinus makes betwixt the effects of eloquence in Demosthenes and Tully. One persuades, the other commands. You never cool while you read Homer, even not in the second book (a graceful flattery to his countrymen); but he hastens from the ships, and concludes not that book till he has made you an amends by the violent playing of a new machine. From thence he hurries on his action with variety of events, and ends it in less compass than two months. This vehemence of his, I confess, is more suitable to my temper; and therefore I have translated his first book with greater pleasure than any part of Virgil; but it was not a pleasure without pains: the continual agitations of the spirits must needs be a weakening of any constitution, especially in age; and many pauses are required for refreshment betwixt the heats; the Iliad of itself being a third part longer than all Virgil's works together. This is what I thought needful in this place to say of Homer. I proceed to Ovid and Chaucer, considering the former only in relation to the latter. With Ovid ended the golden age of the Roman tongue; from Chaucer the purity of the English tongue began. The manners of the poets were not unlike: both of them were well-bred, well-natured, amorous, and libertine, at least in their writings, it may be also in their lives.

Their studies were the same, philosophy and philology. Both of them were known in astronomy, of which Ovid's books of the Roman feasts, and Chaucer's treatise of the Astrolabe, are sufficient witnesses. But Chaucer was likewise an astrologer, as were Virgil, Horace, Persius, and Manilius. Both writ with wonderful facility and clearness: neither were great inventors; for Ovid only copied the Grecian fables; and most of Chaucer's stories were taken from his Italian contemporaries, or their predecessors. Boccace's Decameron was first published, and from thence our Englishman has borrowed many of his Canterbury tales; yet that of Palamon and Arcite was written in all probability by some Italian wit in a former age, as I shall prove hereafter.

The tale of Grizild was the invention of Petrarch; by him sent to Boccace, from whom it came to Chaucer. Troilus and Cressida was also written by a Lombard author, but much amplified by our English translator, as well as beautified; the genius of our countrymen in general being rather to improve an invention than to invent themselves, as is evident not only in our poetry, but in many of our manufactures.

I find I have anticipated already, and taken up from

Boccace before I come to him; but there is so much less behind; and I am of the temper of most kings, who love to be in debt, are all for present money, no matter how they pay it afterwards; besides, the nature of a preface is rambling, never wholly out of the way, nor in it. This I have learned from the practice of honest Montaigne, and return at my pleasure to Ovid and Chaucer, of whom I have little more to say. Both of them built on the inventions of other men; yet since Chaucer had something of his own, as the Wife of Bath's Tale, The Cock and the Fox, which I have translated, and some others, I may justly give our countryman the precedence in that part, since I can remember nothing of Ovid which was wholly his.

Both of them understood the manners, under which name I comprehend the passions, and, in a larger sense, the descriptions of persons, and their very habits; for an example, I see Baucis and Philemon as perfectly before me, as if some ancient painter had drawn them; and all the pilgrims in the Canterbury Tales, their humours, their features, and the very dress, as distinctly as if I had supped with them at the Tabard in Southwark; yet even there too the figures in Chaucer are much more lively, and set in a better light: which though I have not time to prove, yet I appeal to the reader, and am sure he will clear me from partiality.

The thoughts and words remain to be considered in the comparison of the two poets; and I have saved myself one half of that labour, by owning that Ovid lived when the Roman tongue was in its meridian, Chaucer in the dawning of our language; therefore that part of the comparison stands not on an equal foot, any more than the diction of Ennius and Ovid, or of Chaucer and our present English. The words are given up as a post not to be defended in our poet, because he wanted the modern art of fortifying. The thoughts remain to be considered, and they are to be measured only by their propriety, that is, as they flow more or less naturally from the persons described, on such and such occasions. The vulgar judges, which are nine parts in ten of all nations, who call conceits and jingles wit, who see Ovid full of them, and Chaucer altogether without them, will think me little less than mad, for preferring the Englishman to the Roman; yet, with their leave, I must presume to say, that the things they admire are only glittering trifles, and so far from being witty, that in a serious poem they are nauseous, because they are unnatural. Would any man, who is ready to die for love, describe his passion like Narcissus? Would he think of inopem me copia fecit, and a dozen more of such expressions, poured on the neck of one another, and signifying all the same thing?

If this were wit, was this a time to be witty, when the poor wretch was in the agony of death? This is just John Littlewit in Bartholomew Fair, who had a conceit (as he tells you) left him in his misery; a miserable conceit. On these occasions the poet should endeavour to raise pity; but instead of this, Ovid is tickling you to laugh. Virgil never made use of such machines, when he was moving you to commiserate the death of Dido: he would not destroy what he was building. Chaucer makes Arcite violent in his love, and unjust in the pursuit of it; yet when he came to die, he made him think more reasonably: he repents not of his love, for that had altered his character, but acknowledges the injustice of his proceedings, and resigns Emilia to Palamon. What would Ovid have done on this occasion?

He would certainly have made Arcite witty on his death-bed. He had complained he was farther off from possession by being so near, and a thousand such boyisms, which Chaucer rejected as below the dignity of the subject. They, who think otherwise, would by the same reason prefer Lucan and Ovid to Homer and Virgil, and Martial to all four of them.

As for the turn of words, in which Ovid particularly excels all poets, they are sometimes a fault, and sometimes a beauty, as they are used properly or improperly; but in strong passions always to be shunned, because passions are serious, and will admit no playing. The French have a high value for them; and I confess, they are often what they call delicate, when they are introduced with judgment; but Chaucer writ with more simplicity, and followed nature more closely, than to use them. I have thus far, to the best of my knowledge, been an upright judge betwixt the parties in competition, not meddling with the design nor the disposition of it, because the design was not their own, and in the disposing of it they were equal. It remains that I say somewhat of Chaucer in particular.

In the first place, as he is the father of English poetry, so I hold him in the same degree of veneration as the Grecians held Homer or the Romans Virgil: he is a perpetual fountain of good sense, learned in all sciences, and therefore speaks properly on all subjects; as he knew what to say, so he knows also when to leave off, a continence which is practised by few writers, and scarcely by any of the ancients, excepting Virgil and Horace. One of our late great poets is sunk in his reputation, because he could never forgive any conceit which came in his way, but swept like a drag net great and small.

There was plenty enough, but the dishes were ill-sorted; whole pyramids of sweetmeats for boys and women, but little of solid meat for men: all this proceeded not from any want of knowledge, but of judgment; neither did he want that in discerning the beauties and faults of other poets, but only indulged himself in the luxury of writing, and perhaps knew it was a fault, but hoped the reader would not find it. For this reason, though he must always be thought a great poet, he is no longer esteemed a good writer; and for ten impressions, which his works have had in so many successive years, yet at present a hundred books are scarcely purchased once a twelvemonth; for as my last Lord Rochester said, though somewhat profanely, "Not being of God, he could not stand".

Chaucer followed nature everywhere, but was never so bold to go beyond her; and there is a great difference of being poeta and nimis poeta if we believe Catullus, as much as betwixt a modest behaviour and affectation. The verse of Chaucer, I confess, is not harmonious to us, but it is like the eloquence of one whom Tacitus commends, it was auribus istius temporis accommodata: they who lived with him, and some time after him, thought it musical; and it continues so even in our judgment, if compared with the numbers of Lydgate and Gower, his contemporaries; there is the rude sweetness of a Scotch tune in it, which is natural and pleasing, though not perfect. It is true I cannot go so far as he who published the last edition of him; for he would make us believe the fault is in our ears, and that there were really ten syllables in a verse where we find but nine, but this opinion is not worth confuting, it is so gross and obvious an error that common sense (which is a rule in everything but matters of faith and revelation) must convince the reader that equality of numbers in every verse, which we call Heroic, was either not known, or not always practised in Chaucer's age. It were an easy matter to produce some thousands of his verses, which are lame for want of half a foot, and sometimes a whole one, and which no pronunciation can make otherwise. We can only say that he lived in the infancy of our poetry, and that nothing is brought to perfection at the first.

We must be children before we grow men. There was an Ennius, and in process of time a Lucilius and a Lucretius, before Virgil and Horace; even after Chaucer there was a Spenser, a Harrington, a Fairfax, before Waller and Denham were in being; and our numbers were in their nonage till these last appeared. I need say little of his parentage, life, and fortunes: they are to be found at large in all the editions of his works. He was employed abroad, and favoured by Edward the Third, Richard the Second, and Henry the Fourth, and was poet, as I suppose, to all three of them. In Richard's time, I doubt, he was a little dipt in the rebellion of the commons, and being brother-in-law to John of Gaunt, it was no wonder if he followed the fortunes of that family, and was well with Henry the Fourth when he had deposed his predecessor. Neither is it to be admired that Henry, who was a wise as well as a valiant prince, who claimed by succession, and was sensible that his title was not sound, but was rightfully in Mortimer, who had married the heir of York; it was not to be admired, I say, if that great politician should be pleased to have the greatest wit of those times in his interests, and to be the trumpet of his praises.

Augustus had given him the example, by the advice of Maecenas, who recommended Virgil and Horace to him, whose praises helped to make him popular while he was alive, and after his death have made him precious to posterity. As for the religion of our poet, he seems to have some little bias towards the opinions of Wickliff, after John of Gaunt his patron; somewhat of which appears in the tale of Piers Plowman: yet I cannot blame him for inveighing so sharply against the vices of the clergy in his age; their pride, their ambition, their pomp, their avarice, their worldly interest deserved the lashes which he gave them, both in that and in most of his Canterbury tales: neither has his contemporary Boccace spared them.

Yet both these poets lived in much esteem with good and holy men in orders; for the scandal which is given by particular priests, reflects not on the sacred function. Chaucer's Monk, his Canon, and his Friar took not from the character of his Good Parson. A satirical poet is the check of the laymen on bad priests. We are only to take care that we involve not the innocent with the guilty in the same condemnation. The good cannot be too much honoured, nor the bad too coarsely used; for the corruption of the best becomes the worst. When a clergyman is whipped his gown is first taken off, by which the dignity of his order is secured; if he be wrongfully accused, he has his action of slander; and it is at the poet's peril if he transgress the law. But they will tell us that all kinds of satire, though never so well-deserved by particular priests, yet brings the whole order into contempt. Is, then, the peerage of England anything dishonoured when a peer suffers for his treason? If he be libelled, or any way defamed, he has his Scandalum Magnatum to punish the offender.

They who use this kind of argument seem to be conscious to themselves of somewhat which has deserved the poet's lash, and are less concerned for their public capacity than for their private; at least there is pride at the bottom of their reasoning. If the faults of men in orders are only to be judged among themselves, they are all in some sort parties; for, since they say the honour of their order is concerned in every member of it, how can we be sure that they will be impartial judges? How far I may be allowed to speak my opinion in this case I know not, but I am sure a dispute of this nature caused mischief in abundance betwixt a King of England and an Archbishop of

Canterbury, one standing up for the laws of his land, and the other for the honour (as he called it) of God's Church, which ended in the murder of the prelate, and in the whipping of his majesty from post to pillar for his penance. The learned and ingenious Dr. Drake has saved me the labour of inquiring into the esteem and reverence which the priests have had of old; and I would rather extend than diminish any part of it: yet I must needs say, that when a priest provokes me without any occasion given him, I have no reason, unless it be the charity of a Christian, to forgive him. Prior laesit is justification sufficient in the Civil Law. If I answer him in his own language, self-defence, I am sure, must be allowed me; and if I carry it farther, even to a sharp recrimination, somewhat may be indulged to human frailty.

Yet my resentment has not wrought so far, but that I have followed Chaucer in his character of a holy man, and have enlarged on that subject with some pleasure, reserving to myself the right, if I shall think fit hereafter, to describe another sort of priests, such as are more easily to be found than the good parson; such as have given the last blow to Christianity in this age, by a practice so contrary to their doctrine. But this will keep cold till another time. In the meanwhile, I take up Chaucer where I left him.

He must have been a man of a most wonderful comprehensive nature, because, as it has been truly observed of him, he has taken into the compass of his Canterbury tales the various manners and humours (as we now call them) of the whole English nation, in his age. Not a single character has escaped him. All his pilgrims are severally distinguished from each other; and not only in their inclinations, but in their very physiognomies and persons. Baptista Porta could not have described their natures better than by the marks which the poet gives them. The matter and manner of their tales, and of their telling, are so suited to their different educations, humours, and callings that each of them would be improper in any other mouth. Even the grave and serious characters are distinguished by their several sorts of gravity: their discourses are such as belong to their age, their calling, and their breeding;

such as are becoming of them, and of them only. Some of his persons are vicious, and some virtuous; some are unlearned, or (as Chaucer calls them) lewd, and some are learned. Even the ribaldry of the low characters is different: the Reeve, the Miller, and the Cook are several men, and distinguished from each other, as much as the mincing lady prioress, and the broad-speaking gap-toothed wife of Bath.

But enough of this: there is such a variety of game springing up before me, that I am distracted in my choice, and know not which to follow. 'Tis sufficient to say, according to the proverb, that here is God's plenty. We have our forefathers and great-grand-dames all before us, as they were in Chaucer's days; their general characters are still remaining in mankind, and even in England, though they are called by other names than those of Monks and Friars and Canons, and Lady Abbesses and Nuns; for mankind is ever the same, and nothing lost out of nature, though everything is altered.

May I have leave to do myself the justice (since my enemies will do me none, and are so far from granting me to be a good poet that they will not allow me so much as to be a Christian, or a moral man), may I have leave, I say, to inform my reader that I have confined my choice to such tales of Chaucer as savour nothing of immodesty? If I had desired more to please than to instruct, the Reeve, the Miller, the Shipman, the Merchant, the Summoner, and, above all, the Wife of Bath, in the prologue to her tale, would have procured me as many friends and readers as there are beaux and ladies of pleasure in the town. But I will no more offend against good manners; I am sensible, as I ought to be, of the scandal I have given by my loose writings, and make what reparation I am able by this public acknowledgment. If anything of this nature, or of profaneness, be crept into these poems, I am so far from defending it that I disown it. Totum hoc indictum volo. Chaucer makes another manner of apology for his broad speaking, and Boccace makes the like; but I will follow neither of them. Our countryman, in the end of his characters, before the Canterbury tales, thus excuses the ribaldry, which is very gross in many of his novels.

But first, I pray you of your courtesie,
That ye ne arrette it nought my villanie,
Though that I plainly speak in this matere
To tellen yon her words, and eke her chere:
Ne though I speak her wordes properly,
For this ye knowen al so well as I,
Who-so shall tell a tale after a man,
He mote rehearse as nye as ever he can
Everich a word, if it be in his charge,
All speke he never so rudely and large.
Or elles he mot telle his tale untrue.
Or feine things, or finde wordes new:
He may not spare, although he were his brother,
He mot as well say o word as another,
Christ spake himself full broad in holy writ,
And well ye wot no villany is it.
Eke Plato saith, who so that can him rede,
The wordes mote be cousin to the dede.

Yet if a man should have inquired of Boccace or of Chaucer, what need they had of introducing such characters where obscene words were proper in their mouths, but very indecent to be heard; I know not what answer they could have made; for that reason, such tale shall be left untold by me. You have here a specimen of Chaucer's language, which is so obsolete, that his sense is scarce to be understood; and you have likewise more than one example of his unequal numbers, which were mentioned before. Yet many of his verses consist of ten syllables, and the words not much behind our present English: as, for example, these two lines, in the description of the carpenter's young wife:

Wincing she was, as is a jolly colt,
Long as a mast, and upright as a bolt.

I have almost done with Chaucer, when I have answered some objections relating to my present work. I find some people are offended that I have turned these tales into modern English; because they think them unworthy of my pains, and look on Chaucer as a dry, old-fashioned wit, not worth reviving. I have often heard the late Earl of Leicester say, that

Mr. Cowley himself was of that opinion; who, having read him over at my lord's request, declared he had no taste of him. I dare not advance my opinion against the judgment of so great an author: but I think it fair, however, to leave the decision to the public. Mr. Cowley was too modest to set up for a dictator; and being shocked perhaps with his old style, never examined into the depth of his good sense.

Chaucer, I confess, is a rough diamond, and must first be polished ere he shines. I deny not, likewise, that, living in our early times he writes not always of a piece, but sometimes mingles trivial things with those of greater moment. Sometimes also, though not often, he runs riot, like Ovid, and knows not when he has said enough. But there are more great wits besides Chaucer, whose fault is their excess of conceits, and those ill sorted. An author is not to write all he can, but only all he ought. Having observed this redundancy in Chaucer (as it is an easy matter for a man of ordinary parts to find a fault in one of greater), I have not tied myself to a literal translation; but have often omitted what I judged unnecessary, or not of dignity enough to appear in the company of better thoughts. I have presumed farther, in some places, and added somewhat of my own where I thought my author was deficient, and had not given his thoughts their true lustre, for want of words in the beginning of our language.

And to this I was the more emboldened, because (if I may be permitted to say it of myself) I found I had a soul congenial to his, and that I had been conversant in the same studies. Another poet, in another age, may take the same liberty with my writings; if at least they live long enough to deserve correction. It was also necessary sometimes to restore the sense of Chaucer, which was lost or mangled in the errors of the press: let this example suffice at present; in the story of Palamon and Arcite, where the temple of Diana is described, you find these verses, in all the editions of our author:

There saw I Dane turned into a tree,
I mean not the goddess Diane,
But Venus daughter, which that hight Dane:

Which, after a little consideration, I knew was to be

reformed into this sense, that Daphne, the daughter of Peneus, was turned into a tree. I durst not make thus bold with Ovid, lest some future Milbourn should arise, and say, I varied from my author, because I understood him not. But there are other judges who think I ought not to have translated Chaucer into English, out of a quite contrary notion: they suppose there is a certain veneration due to his old language; and that it is a little less than profanation and sacrilege to alter it.

They are farther of opinion, that somewhat of his good sense will suffer in this transfusion, and much of the beauty of his thoughts will infallibly be lost, which appear with more grace in their old habit. Of this opinion was that excellent person, whom I mentioned, the late Earl of Leicester, who valued Chaucer as much as Mr. Cowley despised him. My lord dissuaded me from this attempt (for I was thinking of it some years before his death), and his authority prevailed so far with me, as to defer my undertaking while he lived, in deference to him: yet my reason was not convinced with what he urged against it. If the first end of a writer be to be understood, then as his language grows obsolete, his thoughts must grow obscure: multa renascentur quae nunc cecidere; cadentque, quae nunc sunt in honore vocabula, si volet usus, quem penes arbitrium est et jus et norma loquendi.

When an ancient word for its sound and significancy deserves to be revived, I have that reasonable veneration for antiquity, to restore it. All beyond this is superstition. Words are not like landmarks, so sacred as never to be removed; customs are changed, and even statutes are silently repealed, when the reason ceases for which they were enacted. As for the other part of the argument, that his thoughts will lose of their original beauty, by the innovation of words; in the first place, not only their beauty but their being is lost where they are no longer understood, which is the present case.

I grant that something must be lost in all transfusion, that is, in all translations; but the sense will remain, which would otherwise be lost, or at least be maimed, when it is scarce intelligible; and that but to a few. How few are there who can read Chaucer, so as to understand him perfectly! And if imperfectly, then with less profit and no pleasure. 'Tis not for the use of some old Saxon friends that I have taken these pains with him: let them neglect my version because they have no need of it. I made it for their sakes who understand sense and poetry as well as they, when that poetry and sense is put into words which they understand.

I will go farther, and dare to add, that what beauties I lose in some places, I give to others which had them not originally; but in this I may be partial to myself; let the reader judge, and I submit to his decision. Yet I think I have just occasion to complain of them, who, because they understand Chaucer, would deprive the greater part of their countrymen of the same advantage, and hoard him up, as misers do their grandam gold, only to look on it themselves, and hinder others from making use of it. In some I seriously protest, that no man ever had, or can have, a greater veneration for Chaucer, than myself. I have translated some part of his works, only that I might perpetuate his memory, or at least refresh it, amongst my countrymen.

If I have altered him anywhere for the better, I must at the same time acknowledge that I could have done nothing without him: Facile est inventis addere, is no great commendation; and I am not so vain to think I have deserved a greater. I will conclude what I have to say of him singly, with this one remark: a lady of my acquaintance, who keeps a kind of correspondence with some authors of the fair sex in France, has been informed by them that Mademoiselle de Scudery, who is as old as Sibyl, and inspired like her by the same god of poetry, is at this time translating Chaucer into modern French. From which I gather that he has been formerly translated into the old Provencal (for how she should come to understand old English I know not).

But the matter of fact being true, it makes me think that there is something in it like fatality; that, after certain periods of time, the fame and memory of great wits should be renewed, as Chaucer is both in France and England. If this be wholly chance, 'tis extraordinary, and I dare not call it more for fear of being taxed with superstition.

Boccace comes last to be considered, who, living in the same age with Chaucer, had the same genius, and followed the same studies; both writ novels, and each of them cultivated his mother tongue. But the greatest resemblance of our two modern authors being in their familiar style, and pleasing way of relating comical adventures, I may pass it over, because I have translated nothing from Boccace of that nature. In the serious part of poetry, the advantage is wholly on Chaucer's side; for though the Englishman has borrowed many tales from the Italian, yet it appears that those of Boccace were not generally of his own making, but taken from authors of former ages, and by him only modelled; so that what there was of invention in either of them may be judged equal. But Chaucer has refined on Boccace, and has mended the stories which he has borrowed in his way of telling, though prose allows more liberty of thought, and the expression is more easy when unconfined by numbers.

Our countryman carries weight, and yet wins the race at disadvantage. I desire not the reader should take my word, and therefore I will set two of their discourses on the same subject, in the same light, for every man to judge betwixt them. I translated Chaucer first, and amongst the rest pitched on the Wife of Bath's talenot daring, as I have said, to adventure on her prologue, because it is too licentious. There Chaucer introduces an old woman of mean parentage, whom a youthful knight of noble blood was forced to marry, and consequently loathed her. The crone being in bed with him on the wedding-night, and finding his aversion, endeavours to win his affection by reason, and speaks a good word for herself (as who could blame her?) in hope to mollify the sullen bridegroom.

She takes her topics from the benefits of poverty, the advantages of old age and ugliness, the vanity of youth, and the silly pride of ancestry and titles without inherent virtue, which is the true nobility. When I had closed Chaucer I returned to Ovid, and translated some more of his fables; and by this time had so far forgotten the Wife of Bath's tale that, when I took up Boccace unawares, I fell on the same argument of preferring virtue to nobility of blood, and titles, in the story of Sigismunda, which I had certainly avoided for the resemblance of the two discourses, if my memory had not failed me. Let the reader weigh them both, and if he thinks me partial to Chaucer, it is in him to right Boccace.

I prefer in our countryman, far above all his other stories, the noble poem of Palamon and Arcite, which is of the Epic kind, and perhaps not much inferior to the Ilias or the Aeneis. The story is more pleasing than either of themthe manners as perfect, the diction as poetical, the learning as deep and various, and the disposition full as artfulonly it includes a greater length of time, as taking up seven years at least; but Aristotle has left undecided the duration of the action, which yet is easily reduced into the compass of a year by a narration of what preceded the return of Palamon to Athens.

I had thought for the honour of our nation, and more particularly for his whose laurel, though unworthy, I have worn after him, that this story was of English growth and Chaucer's own; but I was undeceived by Boccace, for casually looking on the end of his seventh Giornata, I found Dioneo (under which name he shadows himself) and Fiametta (who represents his mistress the natural daughter of Robert, King of Naples), of whom these words are spoken, Dioneo e la Fiametta granpezza contarono insieme d'Arcita, e di Palamone, by which it appears that this story was written before the time of Boccace; but the name of its author being wholly lost, Chaucer is now become an original, and I question not but the poem has received many beauties by passing through his noble hands. Besides this tale, there is another of his own invention, after the manner of the Provencals, called the Flower and the Leaf, with which I was so particularly pleased, both for the invention and the moral, that I cannot hinder myself from recommending it to the reader.

As a corollary to this preface, in which I have done justice to others, I owe somewhat to myself; not that I think it worth my time to enter the lists with one Milbourn and one Blackmore, but barely to take notice that such men there are who have written scurrilously against me without any provocation. Milbourn, who is in orders, pretends amongst the rest this quarrel to me, that I have fallen foul on priesthood; if I have, I am only to ask pardon of good priests, and am afraid his part of the reparation will come to little. Let him be satisfied that he shall not be able to force himself upon me for an adversary. I contemn him too much to enter into competition with him. His own translations of Virgil have answered his criticisms on mine. If (as they say he has declared in print) he prefers the version of Ogilby to mine, the world has made him the same compliment, for it is agreed on all hands that he writes even below Ogilby. That, you will say. is not easily to be done; but what cannot Milbourn bring about? I am satisfied, however, that while he and I live together, I shall not be thought the worst poet of the age.

It looks as if I had desired him underhand to write so ill against me; but upon my honest word, I have not bribed him to do me this service, and am wholly guiltless of his pamphlet. 'Tis true, I should be glad if I could persuade him to continue his good offices, and write such another critique on anything of mine; for I find by experience he has a great stroke with the reader, when he condemns any of my poems, to make the world have a better opinion of them.

He has taken some pains with my poetry, but nobody will be persuaded to take the same with his. If I had taken to the church (as he affirms, but which was never in my thoughts), I should have had more sense, if not more grace, than to have turned myself out of my benefice by writing libels on my parishioners. But his account of my manners and my principles are of a piece with his cavils and his poetry; and so I have done with him for ever. As for the City Bard, or Knight Physician, I hear his quarrel to me is, that I was the author of Absalom and Achitophel, which he thinks was a little hard on his fanatic patrons in London.

But I will deal the more civilly with his two poems, because nothing ill is to be spoken of the dead, and therefore peace be to the Manes of his Arthurs. I will only say that it was not for this noble knight that I drew the plan of an Epic poem on King Arthur in my preface to the translation of Juvenal. The guardian angels of kingdoms were machines too ponderous for him to manage; and therefore he rejected them, as Dares did the whirlbats of Eryx, when they were thrown before him by Entellus. Yet from that preface he plainly took his hint; for he began immediately upon his story, though he had the baseness not to acknowledge his benefactor; but instead of it, to traduce me in a libel.

I shall say the less of Mr. Collier, because in many things he has taxed me justly, and I have pleaded guilty to all thoughts and expressions of mine which can be truly argued of obscenity, profaneness, or immorality, and retract them. If he be my enemy, let him triumph; if he be my friend, as I have given him no personal occasion to be otherwise, he will be glad of my repentance. It becomes me not to draw my pen in the defence of a bad cause when I have so often drawn it for a good one. Yet it were not difficult to prove that in many places he has perverted my meaning by his glosses, and interpreted my words into blasphemy and bawdry, of which they were not guiltybesides that he is too much given to horseplay in his raillery, and comes to battle like a dictator from the plough. I will not say the zeal of God's house has eaten him up, but I am sure it has devoured some part of his good manners and civility. It might also be doubted whether it were altogether zeal which prompted him to this rough manner of proceeding; perhaps it became not one of his function to rake into the rubbish of ancient and modern plays.

A divine might have employed his pains to better purpose than in the nastiness of Plautus and Aristophanes, whose examples, as they excuse not me, so it might be possibly supposed that he read them not without some pleasure. They who have written commentaries on those poets, or on Horace, Juvenal, and Martial, have explained some vices which, without their interpretation, had been unknown to modern times. Neither has he judged impartially betwixt the former age and us.

There is more bawdry in one play of Fletcher's, called the Custom of the Country, than in all ours together. Yet this has been often acted on the stage in my remembrance. Are the times so much more reformed now than they were five and twenty years ago? If they are, I congratulate the amendment of our morals. But I am not to prejudice the cause of my fellow-poets, though I abandon my own defence; they have some of them answered for themselves, and neither they nor I can think Mr. Collier so formidable an enemy that we should shun him. He has lost ground at the latter end of the day by pursuing his point too far, like the Prince of Conde at the battle of Senneffe: from immoral plays to no playsab abusu ad usum, non valet consequentia. But being a party, I am not to erect myself into a judge. As for the rest of those who have written against me, they are such scoundrels that they deserve not the least notice to be taken of them. Blackmore and Milbourn are only distinguished from the crowd by being remembered to their infamy. Demetri teque, Tigelli, Discipulorum inter jubeo plorare cathedras.

SAMUEL JOHNSON.

(1709-1784.)

Chapter 16

On the Metaphysical Poets

The criticism of the 'metaphysical poets' occurs in the Life of Cowley, published as one of the Lives of the Poets in 1780. The name 'metaphysical poetry' was first devised by Dryden, in his Essay of Dramatic Poesy. It was revived by Johnson, and is now generally accepted by historians of English literature. It is used by Johnson, as it was used by Dryden, to express the love of remote analogies, which was a mark of the poetry of Donne and those who wrote more or less after the manner of Donne. But it has a deeper meaning than was probably intended by its inventors. It is no unapt term to indicate the vein of weighty thought and brooding imagination which runs like a thread of gold through all the finer work of these poets. Johnson did no harm in calling attention to the extravagance of much of the imagery beloved by the lyric poets of the Stuart period. But it is unpardonable that he should have had no eye for the nobler and subtler qualities of their genius, and equally unpardonable that he should have drawn no distinction between three men so incomparable in degree and kind of power as Cleveland, Cowley, and Donne. Some remarks on the place of the metaphysical poets in English literature will be found in the Introduction.

Cowley, like other poets who have written with narrow views, and, instead of tracing intellectual pleasure to its natural sources in the mind of man, paid their court to temporary prejudices, has been at one time too much praised, and too much neglected at another. Wit, like all other things subject by their nature to the choice of man, has its changes and fashions, and at different times takes different forms. About the beginning of the seventeenth century appeared a race of writers that may be termed the metaphysical poets; of whom, in a criticism on the works of Cowley, it is not improper to give some account.

The metaphysical poets were men of learning, and to show their learning was their whole endeavour; but, unluckily resolving to show it in rhyme, instead of writing poetry, they only wrote verses, and very often such verses as stood the trial of the finger better than of the ear; for the modulation was so imperfect, that they were only found to be verses by counting the syllables. If the father of criticism has rightly denominated poetry, an imitative art, these writers will, without great wrong, lose their right to the name of poets; for they cannot be said to have imitated anything; they neither copied nature nor life; neither painted the forms of matter, nor represented the operations of intellect. Those, however, who deny them to be poets, allow them to be wits. Dryden confesses of himself and his contemporaries that they fall below Donne in wit, but maintains that they surpass him in poetry. If wit be well described by Pope, as being "that which has been often thought, but was never before so well expressed", they certainly never attained, nor ever sought it; for they endeavoured to be singular in their thoughts, and were careless of their diction. But Pope's account of wit is undoubtedly erroneous: he depresses it below its natural dignity, and reduces it from strength of thought to happiness of language.

If by a more noble and more adequate conception that be considered as wit which is at once natural and new, that which, though not obvious, is, upon its first production, acknowledged to be just; if it be that which he that never found it wonders how he missed; to wit of this kind the metaphysical poets have seldom risen. Their thoughts are often new, but seldom natural; they are not obvious, but neither are they just; and the reader, far from wondering that he missed them, wonders more frequently by what perverseness of industry they were ever found.

But wit, abstracted from its effects upon the hearer, may be more rigorously and philosophically considered as a kind of discordia concors; a combination of dissimilar images, or discovery of occult resemblances in things apparently unlike. Of wit, thus defined, they have more than enough. The most heterogeneous ideas are yoked by violence together; nature and art are ransacked for illustrations, comparisons, and allusions; their learning instructs, and their subtlety surprises; but the reader commonly thinks his improvement dearly bought, and, though he sometimes admires, is seldom pleased. From this account of their compositions it will be readily inferred that they were not successful in representing or moving the affections.

As they were wholly employed on something unexpected and surprising, they had no regard to that uniformity of sentiment which enables us to conceive and to excite the pains and the pleasure of other minds: they never inquired what, on any occasion, they should have said or done; but wrote rather as beholders than partakers of human nature; as Beings looking upon good and evil, impassive and at leisure; as Epicurean deities making remarks on the actions of men and the vicissitudes of life without interest and without emotion. Their courtship was void of fondness, and their lamentation of sorrow. Their wish was only to say what they hoped had never been said before. Nor was the sublime more within their reach than the pathetic; for they never attempted that comprehension and expanse of thought which at once fills the whole mind, and of which the first effect is sudden astonishment, and the second rational admiration. Sublimity is produced by aggregation, and littleness by dispersion. Great thoughts are always general, and consist in positions not limited by exceptions, and in descriptions not descending to minuteness. It is with great propriety that subtlety, which in its original import means exility of particles, is taken in its metaphorical meaning for nicety of distinction. Those writers who lay on the watch for novelty could have little hope of greatness; for great things cannot have escaped former observation.

Their attempts were always analytic; they broke every image into fragments: and could no more represent, by their slender conceits and laboured particularities, the prospects of nature or the scenes of life, than he who dissects a sunbeam with a prism can exhibit the wide effulgence of a summer noon. What they wanted, however, of the sublime, they endeavoured to supply by hyperbole; their amplification had no limits; they left not only reason but fancy behind them; and produced combinations of confused magnificence that not only could not be credited, but could not be imagined.

Yet great labour, directed by great abilities, is never wholly lost: if they frequently threw away their wit upon false conceits, they likewise sometimes struck out unexpected truth: if their conceits were far-fetched, they were often worth the carriage. To write on their plan, it was at least necessary to read and think. No man could be born a metaphysical poet, nor assume the dignity of a writer, by descriptions copied from descriptions, by imitations borrowed from imitations, by traditional imagery and hereditary similes, by readiness of rhyme and volubility of syllables. In perusing the works of this race of authors, the mind is exercised either by recollection or inquiry; either something already learned is to be retrieved, or something new is to be examined. If their greatness seldom elevates, their acuteness often surprises; if the imagination is not always gratified, at least the powers of reflection and comparison are employed; and in the mass of materials which ingenious absurdity has thrown together, genuine wit and useful knowledge may be sometimes found, buried perhaps in grossness of expression, but useful to those who know their value; and such as, when they are expanded to perspicuity and polished to elegance, may give lustre to works which have more propriety though less copiousness of sentiment.

This kind of writing, which was, I believe, borrowed from Marino and his followers, had been recommended by the example of Donne, a man of very extensive and various knowledge; and by Jonson, whose manner resembled that of Donne more in the ruggedness of his lines than in the cast of his sentiments. When their reputation was high, they had undoubtedly more imitators than time has left behind. Their immediate successors, of whom any remembrance can be said to remain, were Suckling, Waller, Denham, Cowley, Cleveland, and Milton. Denham and Waller sought another way to fame, by improving the harmony of our numbers. Milton tried the metaphysic style only in his lines upon Hobson the Carrier. Cowley adopted it, and excelled his predecessors, having as much sentiment and more music. Suckling neither improved versification, nor abounded in conceits. The fashionable style remained chiefly with Cowley; Suckling could not reach it, and Milton disdained it. Critical remarks are not easily understood without examples, and I have therefore collected instances of the modes of writing by which this species of poets, for poets they were called by themselves and their admirers, was eminently distinguished.

As the authors of this race were perhaps more desirous of being admired than understood, they sometimes drew their conceits from recesses of learning not very much frequented by common readers of poetry. Thus

Cowley on Knowledge:
The sacred tree midst the fair orchard grew;
The phoenix Truth did on it rest.
And built his perfum'd nest,
That right Porphyrian tree which did true logick shew.
Each leaf did learned notions give,
And th' apples were demonstrative:
So clear their colour and divine,
The very shade they cast did other lights outshine.
On Anacreon continuing a lover in his old age:
Love was with thy life entwin'd,
Close as heat with fire is join'd,
A powerful brand prescrib'd the date
Of thine, like Meleager's fate.
The antiperistasis of age
More enflam'd thy amorous rage.

In the following verses we have an allusion to a Rabbinical opinion concerning Manna:

Variety I ask not: give me one
To live perpetually upon.
The person Love does to us fit,

Like manna, has the taste of all in it.

Thus Donne shows his medicinal knowledge in some encomiastic verses:

In everything there naturally grows
A Balsamum to keep it fresh and new,
If't were not injur'd by extrinsique blows;
Your youth and beauty are this balm in you.
But you, of learning and religion,
And virtue and such ingredients, have made
A mithridate, whose operation
Keeps off, or cures what can be done or said.

Though the following lines of Donne, on the last night of the year, have something in them too scholastic, they are not inelegant:

This twilight of two years, not past nor next,
Some emblem is of me, or I of this,
Who, meteor-like, of stuff and form perplext,
Whose what and where, in disputation is,
If I should call me any thing, should miss.
I sum the years and me, and find me not
Debtor to th' old, nor creditor to th' new,
That cannot say, my thanks I have forgot,
Nor trust I this with hopes: and yet scarce true
This bravery is, since these times shew'd me you.
Donne.

Yet more abstruse and profound is Donne's reflection upon Man as a Microcosm:

If men be worlds, there is in every one
Something to answer in some proportion
All the world's riches: and in good men, this
Virtue, our form's form, and our soul's soul is.

Of thoughts so far-fetched as to be not only unexpected but unnatural, all their books are full.

To a Lady, who wrote Poesies for Rings.

They, who above do various circles find,
Say, like a ring th' aquator heaven does bind.
When heaven shall be adorn'd by thee,

(Which then more heaven than 't is, will be)
'T is thou must write the poesy there,
For it wanteth one as yet,
Though the sun pass through 't twice a year,
The sun, which is esteem'd the god of wit.
Cowley.

The difficulties which have been raised about identity in philosophy are by Cowley, with still more perplexity, applied to Love:

Five years ago (says story) I lov'd you,
For which you call me most inconstant now;
Pardon me, madam, you mistake the man;
For I am not the same that I was then;
No flesh is now the same't was then in me,
And that my mind is chang'd yourself may see.
The same thoughts to retain still, and intents,
Were more inconstant far; for accidents
Must of all things most strangely inconstant prove,
If from one subject they t' another move:
My members then, the father members were
From whence these take their birth, which now are here.
If then this body love what th' other did,
'T were incest, which by nature is forbid.

The love of different women is, in geographical poetry, compared to travels, through different countries:

Hast thou not found each woman's breast
(The land where thou hast travelled)
Either by savages possest,
Or wild, and uninhabited?
What joy could'st take, or what repose,
In countries so unciviliz'd as those?
Lust, the scorching dog-star, here
Rages with immoderate heat;
Whilst Pride, the rugged Northern Bear,
In others makes the cold too great.
And when these are temperate known,
The soil's all barren sand, or rocky stone.
Cowley.

A lover, burnt up by his affections, is compared to Egypt:
The fate of Egypt I sustain,
And never feel the dew of rain.
From clouds which in the head appear;
But all my too much moisture owe
To overflowings of the heart below.
Cowley.

The lover supposes his lady acquainted with the ancient laws of augury and rites of sacrifice:

And yet this death of mine, I fear,
Will ominous to her appear:
When found in every other part,
Her sacrifice is found without an heart.
For the last tempest of my death
Shall sigh out that too, with my breath.

That the chaos was harmonized, has been recited of old; but whence the different sounds arose remained for a modern to discover:

Th' ungovern'd parts no correspondence knew,
And artless war from thwarting motions grew;
Till they to number and fixt rules were brought.
Water and air he for the Tenor chose.
Earth made the Base, the Treble flame arose.
Cowley.

The tears of lovers are always of great poetical account, but Donne has extended them into worlds. If the lines are not easily understood, they may be read again:

On a round ball
A workman, that hath copies by, can lay
An Europe, Afric, and an Asia,
And quickly make that, which was nothing, all.
So doth each tear,
Which thee doth wear,
A globe, yea world, by that impression grow,
Till thy tears mixt with mine do overflow

This world, by waters sent from thee my heaven dissolved so. On reading the following lines, the reader may perhaps cry out,

"Confusion worse confounded":
Here lies a she sun, and a he moon here,
She gives the best light to his sphere,
Or each is both, and all, and so
They unto one another nothing owe.
Donne.

Who but Donne would have thought that a good man is a telescope?

Though God be our true glass, through which we see
All, since the being of all things is He,
Yet are the trunks, which do to us derive
Things, in proportion fit, by perspective
Deeds of good men; for by their living here,
Virtues, indeed remote, seem to be near.

Who would imagine it possible that in a very few lines so many remote ideas could be brought together?

Since't is my doom, Love's undershrieve,
Why this reprieve?
Why doth my She Advowson fly
Incumbency?
To sell thyself dost thou intend
By candle's end,
And hold the contrast thus in doubt,
Life's taper out?
Think but how soon the market fails,
Your sex lives faster than the males;
As if to measure age's span,
The sobre Julian were th' account of man,
Whilst you live by the fleet Gregorian.
Cleveland.

Of enormous and disgusting hyperboles, these may be examples:

By every wind, that comes this way,
Send me at least a sigh or two,
Such and so many I'll repay
As shall themselves make winds to get to you.
Cowley.

In tears I'll waste these eyes,

By Love so vainly fed;
So lust of old the Deluge punished.
Cowley.
All arm'd in brass the richest dress of war,
(A dismal glorious sight) he shone afar.
The sun himself started with sudden fright,
To see his beams return so dismal bright.
Cowley.
An universal consternation:
His bloody eyes he hurls round, his sharp paws
Tear up the ground; then runs he wild about,
Lashing his angry tail and roaring out.
Beasts creep into their dens, and tremble there;
Trees, though no wind is stirring, shake with fear;
Silence and horror fill the place around:
Echo itself dares scarce repeat the sound.
Cowley.
Their fictions were often violent and unnatural.

Of his Mistress Bathing.

The fish around her crowded, as they do
To the false light that treacherous fishers shew,
And all with as much ease might taken be,
As she at first took me:
For ne'er did light so clear
Among the waves appear,
Though every night the sun himself set there.
Cowley.
The poetical effect of a lover's name upon glass:
My name engrav'd herein
Doth contribute my firmness to this glass;
Which, ever since that charm, hath been
As hard as that which grav'd it was.
Donne.
Their conceits were sometimes slight and trifling.

On An Inconstant Woman.

He enjoys thy calmy sunshine now,

And no breath stirring hears,
In the clear heaven of thy brow,
No smallest cloud appears.
He sees thee gentle, fair and gay,
And trusts the faithless April of thy May.
Cowley.

Upon a paper written with the juice of lemon, and read by the fire:

Nothing yet in thee is seen:
But when a genial heat warms thee within,
A new-born wood of various lines there grows;
Here buds an L, and there a B,
Here sprouts a V, and there a T,
And all the flourishing letters stand in rows.
Cowley

As they sought only for novelty, they did not much inquire whether their allusions were to things high or low, elegant or gross; whether they compared the little to the great, or the great to the little.

Physick and Chirurgery for A Lover.

Gently, ah gently, madam, touch
The wound, which you yourself have made;
That pain must needs be very much,
Which makes me of your hand afraid.
Cordials of pity give me now,
For I too weak for purgings grow.
Cowley.

The World and a Clock.

Mahol, th' inferior world's fantastic face,
Through all the turns of matter's maze did trace;
Great Nature's well-set clock in pieces took;
On all the springs and smallest wheels did look
Of life and motion; and with equal art
Made up again the whole of every part.
Cowley.

A coal-pit has not often found its poet; but, that it may

not want its due honour, Cleveland has paralleled it with the sun:

The moderate value of our guiltless ore
Makes no man atheist, and no woman whore;
Yet why should hallow'd vestals' sacred shrine
Deserve more honour than a flaming mine?
These pregnant wombs of heat would fitter be
Than a few embers, for a deity.
Had he our pits, the Persian would admire
No sun, but warm's devotion at our fire:
He'd leave the trotting whipster, and prefer
Our profound Vulcan 'bove that waggoner.
For wants he heat or light? or would have store
Of both? 'tis here: and what can suns give more?
Nay, what's the sun but, in a different name,
A coal-pit rampant, or a mine on flame!
Then let this truth reciprocally run
The sun's heaven's coalery, and coals our sun.

Death, A Voyage.

No family
E'er rigg'd a soul for heaven's discovery,
With whom more venturers might boldly dare
Venture their stakes, with him in joy to share.
Donne.

Their thoughts and expressions were sometimes grossly absurd, and such as no figures or licence can reconcile to the understanding.

A Lover Neither Dead Nor Alive.

Then down I laid my head,
Down on cold earth; and for a while was dead,
And my freed soul to a strange somewhere fled:
Ah, sottish soul, said I,
When back to its cage again I saw it fly:
Fool to resume her broken chain!
And row her galley here again!
Fool, to that body to return

Where it condemn'd and destin'd is to burn!
Once dead, how can it be,
Death should a thing so pleasant seem to thee,
That thou should'st come to live it o'er again in me?
Cowley.

A LOVER'S HEART A HAND GRENADO.

Wo to her stubborn heart, if once mine come
Into the self-same room,
'T will tear and blow up all within,
Like a grenado shot into a magazin.
Then shall Love keep the ashes, and torn parts,
Of both our broken hearts:
Shall out of both one new one make;
From hers th' allay; from mine, the metal take.
Cowley.

The Poetical Propagation Of Light.

The Prince's favour is diffus'd o'er all,
From which all fortunes, names, and natures fall;
Then from those wombs of stars, the Bride's bright eyes,
At every glance a constellation flies,
And sows the court with stars, and doth prevent
In light and power, the all-ey'd firmament:
First her eye kindles other ladies' eyes,
Then from their beams their jewels' lustres rise;
And from their jewels torches do take fire,
And all is warmth, and light, and good desire.
Donne.

They were in very little care to clothe their notions with elegance of dress, and therefore miss the notice and the praise which are often gained by those who think less, but are more diligent to adorn their thoughts.

That a mistress beloved is fairer in idea than in reality is by Cowley thus expressed:

Thou in my fancy dost much higher stand,
Than woman can be plac'd by Nature's hand;
And I must needs, I'm sure, a loser be,
To change thee, as thou 'rt there, for very thee.

That prayer and labour should co-operate are thus taught by Donne:

In none but us, are such mixt engines found,
As hands of double office: for the ground
We till with them; and them to heaven we raise;
Who prayerless labours, or without this, prays,
Doth but one half, that's none.

By the same author, a common topic, the danger of procrastination, is thus illustrated:

That which I should have begun In my youth's morning, now late must be done; And I, as giddy travellers must do, Which stray or sleep all day, and having lost Light and strength, dark and tir'd must then ride post.

All that Man has to do is to live and die; the sum of humanity is comprehended by Donne in the following lines:

Think in how poor a prison thou didst lie;
After, enabled but to suck and cry.
Think, when't was grown to most, 't was a poor inn,
A province pack'd up in two yards of skin,
And that usurp'd, or threaten'd with a rage
Of sicknesses, or their true mother, age.
But think that death hath now enfranchis'd thee;
Thou hast thy expansion now, and liberty;
Think, that a rusty piece discharg'd is flown
In pieces, and the bullet is his own,
And freely flies; this to thy soul allow,
Think thy shell broke, think thy soul hatched but now.

They were sometimes indelicate and disgusting. Cowley thus apostrophizes beauty:

Thou tyrant, which leav'st no man free! Thou subtle thief, from whom nought safe can be! Thou murderer, which hast kill'd, and devil, which would'st damn me.

Thus he addresses his mistress:

Thou who, in many a propriety,
So truly art the sun to me.
Add one more likeness, which I'm sure you can,
And let me and my sun beget a man.

Thus he represents the meditations of a lover:

Though in thy thoughts scarce any tracts have been
So much as of original sin,
Such charms thy beauty wears as might
Desires in dying confest saints excite.
Thou with strange adultery
Dost in each breast a brothel keep;
Awake, all men do lust for thee,
And some enjoy thee when they sleep.
The true taste of tears:
Hither with crystal vials, lovers, come,
And take my tears, which are Love's wine,
And try your mistress' tears at home;
For all are false, that taste not just like mine.
Donne.
This is yet more indelicate:
As the sweet sweat of roses in a still
As that which from chaf'd musk-cat's pores doth trill,
As th' almighty balm of th' early East,
Such are the sweet drops of my mistress' breast.
And on her neck her skin such lustre sets,
They seem no sweat-drops, but pearl coronets:
Rank sweaty froth thy mistress' brow defiles.
Donne.

Their expressions sometimes raise horror, when they intend perhaps to be pathetic:

As men in hell are from diseases free,
So from all other ills am I.
Free from their known formality:
But all pains eminently lie in thee.
Cowley.

They were not always strictly curious, whether the opinions from which they drew their illustrations were true; it was enough that they were popular. Bacon remarks that some falsehoods are continued by tradition, because they supply commodious allusions.

It gave a piteous groan, and so it broke;
In vain it something would have spoke:
The love within too strong for't was,

Like poison put into a Venice-glass.
Cowley.

In forming descriptions, they looked out, not for images, but for conceits. Night has been a common subject, which poets have contended to adorn. Dryden's Night is well known; Donne's is as follows:

Thou seest me here at midnight, now all rest:
Time's dead low-water; when all minds divest
To-morrow's business, when the labourers have
Such rest in bed, that their last church-yard grave,
Subject to change, will scarce be a type of this;
Now when the client, whose last hearing is
To-morrow, sleeps; when the condemned man,
Who when he opens his eyes, must shut them then
Again by death, although sad watch he keep,
Doth practise dying by a little sleep,
Thou at this midnight seest me.

It must be, however, confessed of these writers that if they are upon common subjects often unnecessarily and unpoetically subtle, yet where scholastic speculation can be properly admitted, their copiousness and acuteness may justly be admired. What Cowley has written upon Hope shows an unequalled fertility of invention:

Hope, whose weak being ruin'd is,
Alike if it succeed, and if it miss;
Whom good or ill does equally confound,
And both the horns of Fate's dilemma wound.
Vain shadow, which dost vanish quite,
Both at full noon and perfect night!
The stars have not a possibility
Of blessing thee;
If things then from their end we happy call,
'T is hope is the most hopeless thing of all.
Hope, thou bold taster of delight,
Who, whilst thou shouldst but taste, devour'st it quite!
Thou bring'st us an estate, yet leav'st us poor,
By clogging it with legacies before!
The joys, which we entire should wed,

Come deflower'd virgins to our bed;
Good fortune without gain imported be,
Such mighty customs paid to thee:
For joy, like wine, kept close does better taste;
If it take air before, its spirits waste.

To the following comparison of a man that travels and his wife that stays at home, with a pair of compasses, it may be doubted whether absurdity or ingenuity has the better claim:

Our two souls therefore, which are one,
Though I must go, endure not yet
A breach, but an expansion,
Like gold to airy thinness beat.
If they be two, they are two so
As stiff twin-compasses are two,
Thy soul, the fixt foot, makes no show
To move, but doth, if th' other do.
And though it in the centre sit,
Yet when the other far doth roam,
It leans, and hearkens after it,
And grows erect, as that comes home.
Such wilt thou be to me, who must
Like th' other foot, obliquely run.
Thy firmness makes my circle just,
And makes me end where I begun.
Donne.

In all these examples it is apparent that whatever is improper or vicious is produced by a voluntary deviation from nature in pursuit of something new and strange, and that the writers fail to give delight by their desire of exciting admiration.

SAMUEL TAYLOR COLERIDGE.
(1772-1834)

Chapter 17

On Poetic Genius and Poetic Diction

The following passage forms Chapters xiv and xv of Coleridge's Biographia Literaria, published in 1817 It has been selected as giving a less imperfect impression of his powers as a critic than any other piece that could have been chosen The truth is that, great in talk and supreme in poetry, Coleridge was lost directly he sat down to express himself in prose His style is apt to be cumbrous, and his matter involved. We feel that the critic himself was greater than any criticism recorded either in his writings or his lectures The present extract may be defined as an attempt, and an attempt less inadequate than was common with Coleridge, to state his poetic creed, and to illustrate it by reference to his own poetry and to that of Wordsworth and of Shakespeare. In what he says of Shakespeare he is at his best.

He forgets himself, and writes with a single eye to a theme which was thoroughly worthy of his powers. In the earlier part of the piece, and indeed indirectly throughout, he has in mind Wordsworth's famous Preface to the Lyrical Ballads, which is to be found in any complete edition of Wordsworth's poems, or in his poise writings, as edited by Dr. Grosart.

During the first year that Mr. Wordsworth and I were neighbours, our conversation turned frequently on the two cardinal points of poetry, the power of exciting the sympathy of the reader by a faithful adherence to the truth of nature, and the power of giving the interest of novelty by the modifying colours of imagination. The sudden charm, which accidents of light and shade, which moonlight or sunset, diffused over a known and familiar landscape, appeared to represent the practicability of combining both. These are the poetry of nature. The thought suggested itself (to which of us I do not recollect) that a series of poems might be composed of two sorts. In the one, the incidents and agents were to be, in part at least, supernatural; and the excellence aimed at was to consist in the interesting of the affections by the dramatic truth of such emotions, as would naturally accompany such situations, supposing them real. And real in this sense they have been to every human being who, from whatever source of delusion, has at any time believed himself under supernatural agency. For the second class, subjects were to be chosen from ordinary life; the characters and incidents were to be such as will be found in every village and its vicinity where there is a meditative and feeling mind to seek after them, or to notice them when they present themselves.

In this idea originated the plan of the Lyrical Ballads; in which it was agreed that my endeavours should be directed to persons and characters supernatural, or at least romantic; yet so as to transfer from our inward nature a human interest and a semblance of truth sufficient to procure for these shadows of imagination that willing suspension of disbelief for the moment, which constitutes poetic faith. Mr. Wordsworth, on the other hand, was to propose to himself as his object, to give the charm of novelty to things of every day, and to excite a feeling analogous to the supernatural, by awakening the mind's attention from the lethargy of custom, and directing it to the loveliness and the wonders of the world before us; an inexhaustible treasure, but for which, in consequence of the film of familiarity and selfish solicitude, we have eyes, yet see not, ears that hear not, and hearts that neither feel nor understand.

With this view I wrote the Ancient Mariner, and was preparing, among other poems, the Dark Ladie, and the Christabel, in which I should have more nearly realized my ideal than I had done in my first attempt. But Mr. Wordsworth's industry had proved so much more successful, and the number of his poems so much greater, that my compositions, instead of forming a balance, appeared rather an interpolation of heterogeneous matter. Mr. Wordsworth added two or three poems written in his own character, in the impassioned, lofty, and sustained diction which is characteristic of his genius.

In this form the Lyrical Ballads were published; and were presented by him, as an experiment, whether subjects, which from their nature rejected the usual ornaments and extra-colloquial style of poems in general, might not be so managed in the language of ordinary life as to produce the pleasurable interest which it is the peculiar business of poetry to impart. To the second edition he added a preface of considerable length; in which, notwithstanding some passages of apparently a contrary import, he was understood to contend for the extension of this style to poetry of all kinds, and to reject as vicious and indefensible all phrases and forms of style that were not included in what he (unfortunately, I think, adopting an equivocal expression) called the language of real life.

From this preface, prefixed to poems in which it was impossible to deny the presence of original genius, however mistaken its direction might be deemed, arose the whole long-continued controversy. For from the conjunction of perceived power with supposed heresy I explain the inveteracy, and in some instances, I grieve to say, the acrimonious passions, with which the controversy has been conducted by the assailants.

Had Mr. Wordsworth's poems been the silly, the childish things which they were for a long time described as being; had they been really distinguished from the compositions of other poets merely by meanness of language and inanity of thought; had they indeed contained nothing more than what is found in the parodies and pretended imitations of them; they must have sunk at once, a dead weight, into the slough of oblivion, and have dragged the preface along with them.

But year after year increased the number of Mr. Wordsworth's admirers. They were found, too, not in the lower classes of the reading public, but chiefly among young men of strong sensibility and meditative minds; and their admiration (inflamed perhaps in some degree by opposition) was distinguished by its intensity, I might almost say, by its religious fervour. These facts, and the intellectual energy of the author, which was more or less consciously felt, where it was outwardly and even boisterously denied, meeting with sentiments of aversion to his opinions, and of alarm at their consequences, produced an eddy of criticism, which would of itself have borne up the poems by the violence with which it whirled them round and round.

With many parts of this preface, in the sense attributed to them, and which the words undoubtedly seem to authorize, I never concurred; but, on the contrary, objected to them as erroneous in principle, and as contradictory (in appearance at least) both to other parts of the same preface and to the author's own practice in the greater number of the poems themselves.

Mr. Wordsworth, in his recent collection, has, I find, degraded this prefatory disquisition to the end of his second volume, to be read or not at the reader's choice. But he has not, as far as I can discover, announced any change in his poetic creed. At all events, considering it as the source of a controversy, in which I have been honoured more than I deserve by the frequent conjunction of my name with his, I think it expedient to declare, once for all, in what points I coincide with his opinions, and in what points I altogether differ. But in order to render myself intelligible, I must previously, in as few words as possible, explain my ideas, first, of a poem; and secondly, of poetry itself, in kind and in essence.

The office of philosophical disquisition consists in just distinction; while it is the privilege of the philosopher to preserve himself constantly aware that distinction is not division. In order to obtain adequate notions of any truth, we must intellectually separate its distinguishable parts; and this is the technical process of philosophy. But having so done, we must then restore them in our conceptions to the unity in which they actually co-exist; and this is the result of philosophy.

A poem contains the same elements as a prose composition; the difference, therefore, must consist in a different combination of them, in consequence of a different object proposed. According to the difference of the object will be the difference of the combination. It is possible that the object may be merely to facilitate the recollection of any given facts or observations by artificial arrangement; and the composition will be a poem, merely because it is distinguished from prose by metre, or by rhyme, or by both conjointly. In this, the lowest sense, a man might attribute the name of a poem to the well-known enumeration of the days in the several months:

Thirty days hath September,
April, June, and November, &c.

And others of the same class and purpose. And as a particular pleasure is found in anticipating the recurrence of sounds and quantities, all compositions that have this charm superadded, whatever be their contents, may be entitled poems. So much for the superficial form. A difference of object and contents supplies an additional ground of distinction. The immediate purpose may be the communication of truths; either of truth absolute and demonstrable, as in works of science; or of facts experienced and recorded, as in history. Pleasure, and that of the highest and most permanent kind, may result from the attainment of the end; but it is not itself the immediate end. In other works the communication of pleasure may be the immediate purpose; and though truth, either moral or intellectual, ought to be the ultimate end, yet this will distinguish the character of the author, not the class to which the work belongs.

Blest indeed is that state of society, in which the immediate purpose would be baffled by the perversion of the proper ultimate end; in which no charm of diction or imagery could exempt the Bathyllus even of an Anacreon, or the Alexis of Virgil, from disgust and aversion! But the communication of pleasure may be the immediate object of a work not metrically composed; and that object may have been in a high degree attained, as in novels and romances. Would then the mere superaddition of metre, with or without rhyme, entitle these to the name of poems? The answer is, that nothing can permanently please which does not contain in itself the reason why it is so, and not otherwise. If metre be superadded, all other parts must be made consonant with it. They must be such as to justify the perpetual and distinct attention to each part, which an exact correspondent recurrence of accent and sound are calculated to excite. The final definition then, so deduced, may be thus worded.

A poem is that species of composition which is opposed to works of science, by proposing for its immediate object pleasure, not truth; and from all other species (having this object in common with it) it is discriminated by proposing to itself such delight from the whole as is compatible with a distinct gratification from each component part. Controversy is not seldom excited in consequence of the disputants attaching each a different meaning to the same word; and in few instances has this been more striking than in disputes concerning the present subject. If a man chooses to call every composition a poem which is rhyme, or measure, or both, I must leave his opinion uncontroverted.

The distinction is at least competent to characterize the writer's intention. If it were subjoined that the whole is likewise entertaining or affecting, as a tale, or as a series of interesting reflections, I of course admit this as another fit ingredient of a poem, and an additional merit. But if the definition sought for be that of a legitimate poem, I answer, it must be one the parts of which mutually support and explain each other; all in their proportion harmonizing with, and supporting the purpose and known influences of metrical arrangement. The philosophic critics of all ages coincide with the ultimate judgment of all countries, in equally denying the praises of a just poem, on the one hand to a series of striking lines or distichs, each of which, absorbing the whole attention of the reader to itself, disjoins it from its context, and makes it a separate whole, instead of a harmonizing part; and on the other hand, to an unsustained composition, from which the reader collects rapidly the general result unattracted by the component parts.

The reader should be carried forward, not merely or chiefly by the mechanical impulse of curiosity, or by a restless desire to arrive at the final solution; but by the pleasurable activity of mind excited by the attractions of the journey itself. Like the motion of a serpent, which the Egyptians made the emblem of intellectual power; or like the path of sound through the air, at every step he pauses and half recedes, and from the retrogressive movement collects the force which again carries him onward. Praecipitandus est liber spiritus, says Petronius Arbiter most happily. The epithet, liber, here balances the preceding verb, and it is not easy to conceive more meaning condensed in fewer words.

But if this should be admitted as a satisfactory character of a poem, we have still to seek for a definition of poetry. The writings of Plato and Bishop Taylor, and the Theoria Sacra of Burnet, furnish undeniable proofs that poetry of the highest kind may exist without metre, and even without the contradistinguishing objects of a poem. The first chapter of Isaiah (indeed a very large proportion of the whole book) is poetry in the most emphatic sense; yet it would be not less irrational than strange to assert that pleasure, and not truth, was the immediate object of the prophet. In short, whatever specific import we attach to the word poetry, there will be found involved in it, as a necessary consequence, that a poem of any length neither can be, nor ought to be, all poetry. Yet if a harmonious whole is to be produced, the remaining parts must be preserved in keeping with the poetry; and this can be no otherwise effected than by such a studied selection and artificial arrangement as will partake of one, though not a peculiar, property of poetry. And this again can be no other than the property of exciting a more continuous and equal attention than the language of prose aims at, whether colloquial or written.

My own conclusions on the nature of poetry, in the strictest use of the word, have been in part anticipated in the preceding disquisition on the fancy and imagination. What is poetry? is so nearly the same question with, what is a poet? that the answer to the one is involved in the solution of the other. For it is a distinction resulting from the poetic genius itself, which sustains and modifies the images, thoughts, and emotions of the poet's own mind. The poet, described in ideal perfection, brings the whole soul of man into activity, with the subordination of its faculties to each other, according to their relative worth and dignity. He diffuses a tone and spirit of unity that blends, and (as it were) fuses, each into each, by that synthetic and magical power to which we have exclusively appropriated the name of imagination.

This power, first put in action by the will and understanding, and retained under their irremissive, though gentle and unnoticed, control (laxis effertur habenis), reveals itself in the balance or reconciliation of opposite or discordant qualities: of sameness, with difference; of the general, with the concrete; the idea, with the image; the individual, with the representative; the sense of novelty and freshness, with old and familiar objects; a more than usual state of emotion, with more than usual order; judgment ever awake and steady self-possession, with enthusiasm and feeling profound or vehement; and while it blends and harmonizes the natural and the artificial, still subordinates art to nature, the manner to the matter, and our admiration of the poet to our sympathy with the poetry. Doubtless, as Sir John Davies observes of the soul (and his words may with slight alteration be applied, and even more appropriately, to the poetic imagination),

Doubtless this could not be, but that she turns
Bodies to spirit by sublimation strange,
As fire converts to fire the things it burns,
As we our food into our nature change.
From their gross matter she abstracts their forms,
And draws a kind of quintessence from things;
Which to her proper nature she transforms
To bear them light on her celestial wings.
Thus does she, when from individual states
She doth abstract the universal kinds;
Which then re-clothed in divers names and fates
Steal access through our senses to our minds.

Finally, good sense is the body of poetic genius, fancy its drapery, motion its life, and imagination the soul that is everywhere, and in each; and forms all into one graceful and intelligent whole. In the application of these principles to purposes of practical criticism as employed in the appraisal of works more or less imperfect, I have endeavoured to discover what the qualities in a poem are, which may be deemed promises and specific symptoms of poetic power, as distinguished from general talent determined to poetic composition by accidental motives, by an act of the will, rather than by the inspiration of a genial and productive nature. In this investigation, I could not, I thought, do better than keep before me the earliest work of the greatest genius that perhaps human nature has yet produced, our myriad-minded Shakespeare. I mean the Venus and Adonis, and the Lucrece; works which give at once strong promises of the strength, and yet obvious proofs of the immaturity, of his genius. From these I abstracted the following marks, as characteristics of original poetic genius in general.

- In the Venus and Adonis the first and obvious excellence is the perfect sweetness of the versification, its adaptation to the subject, and the power displayed in varying the march of the words without passing into a loftier and more majestic rhythm than was demanded by the thoughts, or permitted by the propriety of preserving a sense of melody predominant. The delight in richness and sweetness of sound, even to a faulty excess, if it be evidently original, and not the result of an easily imitable mechanism, I regard as a highly favourable promise in the compositions of a young man. "The man that hath not music in his soul" can indeed never be a genuine poet. Imagery (even taken from nature, much more when transplanted from books, as travels, voyages, and works of natural history), affecting incidents, just thoughts, interesting personal or domestic feelings, and with these the art of their combination or intertexture in the form of a poem, may all by incessant effort be acquired as a trade, by a man of talents and much reading, who, as I once before observed, has mistaken an intense desire of poetic reputation for a natural poetic genius; the love of the arbitrary end for a possession of the peculiar means. But the sense of musical delight, with the power of producing it, is a gift of imagination; and this, together with the power of reducing multitude into unity of effect, and modifying a series of thoughts by some one predominant thought or feeling, may be cultivated and improved, but can never be learnt. It is in these that Poeta nascitur non fit.

- A second promise of genius is the choice of subjects very remote from the private interests and circumstances of the writer himself. At least I have found that where the subject is taken immediately from the author's personal sensations and experiences, the excellence of a particular poem is but an equivocal mark, and often a fallacious pledge, of genuine poetic power. We may perhaps remember the tale of the statuary, who had acquired considerable reputation for the legs of his goddesses, though the rest of the statue accorded but indifferently with ideal beauty; till his wife, elated by her husband's praises, modestly acknowledged that she herself had been his constant model. In the Venus and Adonis this proof of poetic power exists even to excess. It is throughout as if a superior spirit, more intuitive, more intimately conscious even than the characters themselves, not only of every outward look and act, but of the flux and reflux of the mind in all its subtlest thoughts and feelings, were placing the whole before our view; himself meanwhile unparticipating in the passions, and actuated only by that pleasurable excitement which had resulted from the energetic fervour of his own spirit, in so vividly exhibiting what it had so accurately and profoundly contemplated. I think I should have conjectured from these poems that even then the great instinct which impelled the poet to the drama was secretly working in him, prompting him by a series and never-broken chain of imagery, always vivid, and because unbroken, often minute; by the highest effort of the picturesque in words, of which words are capable, higher perhaps than was ever realized by any other poet, even Dante not excepted; to provide a substitute for that visual language, that constant intervention and running comment by tone, look, and gesture, which, in his dramatic works, he was entitled to expect from the players. His Venus and Adonis seem at once the characters themselves, and the whole representation of those characters by the most consummate actors. You seem to be told nothing, but to see and hear everything. Hence it is that from the perpetual activity of attention required on the part of the reader; from the rapid flow, the quick change, and the playful nature of the thoughts and images; and, above all, from the alienation, and, if I may hazard such an expression, the utter aloofness of the poet's own feelings from those of which he is at once the painter and the analyst; that, though the very subject cannot but detract from the pleasure of a delicate mind, yet never was poem less dangerous on a moral account. Instead of doing as Ariosto, and as, still more offensively, Wieland has done; instead of degrading and deforming passion into appetite, the trials of love into the struggles of concupiscence, Shakespeare has here represented the animal impulse itself so as to preclude all sympathy with it, by dissipating the reader's notice among the thousand outward images, and now beautiful, now fanciful circumstances, which form its dresses and its scenery; or by diverting our attention from the main subject by those frequent witty or profound reflections which the poet's ever active mind has deduced from, or connected with, the imagery and the incidents. The reader is forced into too much action to sympathize with the merely passive of our nature. As little can a mind thus roused and awakened be brooded on by mean and instinct emotion, as the low, lazy mist can creep upon the surface of a lake while a strong gale is driving it onward in waves and billows.

- It has been before observed that images, however beautiful, though faithfully copied from nature, and as accurately represented in words, do not of themselves characterize the poet. They become proofs of original genius only as far as they are modified by a predominant passion; or by associated thoughts or images awakened by that passion; or when they have the effect of reducing multitude to unity, or succession to an instant; or, lastly, when a human and intellectual life is transferred to them from the poet's own spirit, Which shoots its being through earth, sea, and air. In the two following lines, for instance, there is nothing objectionable, nothing which would preclude them from forming, in their proper place, part of a descriptive poem:

Behold yon row of pines, that shorn and bow'd
Bend from the sea-blast, seen at twilight eve.

But with the small alteration of rhythm, the same words would be equally in their place in a book of topography, or in a descriptive tour. The same image will rise into a semblance of poetry if thus conveyed:

Yon row of bleak and visionary pines,
By twilight-glimpse discerned, mark! how they flee
From the fierce sea-blast, all their tresses wild
Streaming before them.

I have given this as an illustration, by no means as an instance, of that particular excellence which I had in view, and in which Shakespeare, even in his earliest as in his latest works, surpasses all other poets. It is by this that he still gives a dignity and a passion to the objects which he presents. Unaided by any previous excitement, they burst upon us at once in life and in power.

Full many a glorious morning have I seen

Flatter the mountain-tops with sovereign eye.
Sonnet 33.

Not mine own fears, nor the prophetic soul
Of the wide world dreaming on things to come,
Can yet the lease of my true love control,
Supposed as forfeit to a confined doom.
The mortal moon hath her eclipse endured,
And the sad augurs mock their own presage:
Incertainties now crown themselves assured,
And peace proclaims olives of endless age.
Now with the drops of this most balmy time
My love looks fresh: and Death to me subscribes,
Since, spite of him, I'll live in this poor rhyme,
While he insults o'er dull and speechless tribes.
And thou in this shalt find thy monument,
When tyrants' crests and tombs of brass are spent.
Sonnet 107.

As of higher worth, so doubtless still more characteristic of poetic genius does the imagery become, when it moulds and colours itself to the circumstances, passion, or character, present and foremost in the mind. For unrivalled instances of this excellence the reader's own memory will refer him to the Lear, Othello, in short, to which not of the 'great, ever living, dead man's' dramatic works? Inopem me copia fecit. How true it is to nature, he has himself finely expressed in the instance of love in Sonnet 98:

From you have I been absent in the spring,
When proud-pied April drest in all his trim
Hath put a spirit of youth in every thing,
That heavy Saturn laugh'd and leap'd with him.
Yet nor the lays of birds, nor the sweet smell
Of different flowers in odour and in hue,
Could make me any summer's story tell,
Or from their proud lap pluck them where they grew
Nor did I wonder at the lily's white,
Nor praise the deep vermilion in the rose;
They were, but sweet, but figures of delight,
Drawn after you, you pattern of all those.

Yet seem'd it winter still and, you away,
As with your shadow I with these did play!

Scarcely less sure, or if a less valuable, not less indispensable mark Gonzmou men Poihtou ostis rhma gennaion lakoi, will the imagery supply when, with more than the power of the painter, the poet gives us the liveliest image of succession with the feeling of simultaneousness!

With this he breaketh from the sweet embrace
Of those fair arms, that bound him to her breast,
And homeward through the dark laund runs apace:
Look how a bright star shooteth from the sky!
So glides he in the night from Venus' eye.
Venus and Adonis, 1. 811.

- The last character I shall mention, which would prove indeed but little, except as taken conjointly with the former; yet without which the former could scarce exist in a high degree, and (even if this were possible) would give promises only of transitory flashes and a meteoric power;its depth and energy of thought. No man was ever yet a great poet without being at the same time a profound philosopher. For poetry is the blossom and the fragrancy of all human knowledge, human thoughts, human passions, emotions, language. In Shakespeare's Poems the creative power and the intellectual energy wrestle as in a war embrace.

Each in its excess of strength seems to threaten the extinction of the other. At length, in the drama they were reconciled, and fought each with its shield before the breast of the other. Or like two rapid streams that, at their first meeting within narrow and rocky banks, mutually strive to repel each other, and intermix reluctantly and in tumult, but soon finding a wider channel and more yielding shores, blend and dilate, and flow on in one current and with one voice.

The Venus and Adonis did not perhaps allow the display of the deeper passions. But the story of Lucretia seems to favour, and even demand, their intensest workings. And yet we find in Shakespeare's management of the tale neither pathos nor any other dramatic quality. There is the same minute and faithful imagery as in the former poem, in the same vivid colours, inspirited by the same impetuous vigour of thought, and diverging and contracting with the same activity of the assimilative and of the modifying faculties; and with a yet larger display, a yet wider range of knowledge and reflection; and lastly, with the same perfect dominion, often domination, over the whole world of language.

What, then, shall we say? even this, that Shakespeare, no mere child of nature; no automaton of genius; no passive vehicle of inspiration possessed by the spirit, not possessing it; first studied patiently, meditated deeply, understood minutely, till knowledge, become habitual and intuitive, wedded itself to his habitual feelings, and at length gave birth to that stupendous power, by which he stands alone, with no equal or second in his own class; to that power which seated him on one of the two glory-smitten summits of the poetic mountain, with Milton as his compeer, not rival.

While the former darts himself forth, and passes into all the forms of human character and passion, the one Proteus of the fire and the flood; the other attracts all forms and things to himself, into the unity of his own ideal. All things and modes of action shape themselves anew in the being of Milton; while Shakespeare becomes all things, yet for ever remaining himself. O what great men hast thou not produced, England, my country! Truly, indeed, Must we be free or die, who speak the tongue, Which Shakespeare spake; the faith and morals hold, Which Milton held. In every thing we are sprung Of earth's first blood, have titles manifold. WILLIAM HAZLITT.

Bibliography

Bakhtin, Mikhail M. 1986 [1930-9, 1981]. Discourse in the novel. Trans. (1981) by Caryl Emerson and Michael Holquist. In Hazard Adams and Leroy Searle (eds.), Critical Theory Since 1965. Tallahassee: Florida State Univ. Pr. 665-78

Bathrick, David. 1992. Cultural studies. In Gibaldi, Joseph, ed., Introduction to Scholarship in Modern Languages and Literatures. New York: MLA. 320-40.

Bove, Paul A. 1990. Discourse. In Frank Lentricchia and Thomas McLaughlin (eds.), Critical terms for literary study. Chicago: Univ. of Chicago Pr. 50-65.

Cixous, Helene. 1986 [1975, 1976]. The laugh of the Medusa. Translated [1976] by Keith Cohen and Paula Cohen. In Hazard Adams and Leroy Searle (eds.), Critical Theory Since 1965. Tallahassee: Florida State Univ. Pr. 309-20.

Culler, Jonathan. 1992. Literary theory. In Gibaldi, Joseph, ed. Introduction to scholarship in modern languages and literatures. New York: MLA. 201-35.

Derrida, Jacques. 1986a [1970, 1978]. Structure, sign, and, play in the discourse of the human sciences. Translated [1970] by Alan Bass. In Hazard Adams and Leroy Searle (eds.), Critical Theory Since 1965. Tallahassee: Florida State Univ. Pr. 83-94.

Derrida, Jacques. 1986b [1967, 1977]. Of grammatology. Translated [1976] by Gayatri C. Spivak. In Hazard Adams and Leroy Searle (eds.), Critical Theory Since 1965. Tallahassee: Florida State Univ. Pr. 94-119.

Derrida, Jacques. 1986c [1970, 1978]. Differance. Translated [1970] by Alan Bass. In Hazard Adams and Leroy Searle (eds.),

Critical Theory Since 1965. Tallahassee: Florida State Univ. Pr. 120-36.

Eco, Umberto. 1990. The limits of interpretation. Bloomington:Indiana Univ. Pr.

Foucault, Michel. 1986a [1969, 1977]. What is an author? Trans. (1977) by Donald F. Bouchard and Sherry Simon. In Adams, Hazard and Leroy Searle, eds., Critical theory since 1965. Tallahassee: Florida State Univ. Pr. 137-48.

Foucault, Michel. 1986b [1970, 1971]. The discourse on language. Trans. (1971) by Rupert Swyer. In Hazard Adams and Leroy Searle (eds.), Critical Theory Since 1965. Tallahassee: Florida State Univ. Pr. 148-62.

Frye, Northrop. 1957. Anatomy of criticism. Princeton.: Princeton Univ. Pr. 186-223.

Gilbert, Sandra M. 1979. Literary Paternity. In Hazard Adams and Leroy Searle (eds.), Critical Theory Since 1965. Tallahassee: Florida State Univ. Pr. 486-96.

Greenblatt, Stephen. 1995 [1990]. Culture. In Frank Lentricchia and Thomas McLaughlin (eds.), Critical terms for literary study. Chicago: Univ. of Chicago Pr. 225-32.

Jameson, Frederic. 1981. The political unconscious: Narrative as a socially symbolic act. Ithaca: Cornell UP. 103-50

Jardine, Alice A. 1986 [1982]. Gynesis. In Hazard Adams and Leroy Searle (eds.), Critical Theory Since 1965. Tallahassee: Florida State Univ. Pr. 560-70.

Jehlen, Myra. 1990. Gender. In Frank Lentricchia and Thomas McLaughlin (eds.), Critical Terms for Literary Study. Chicago: Univ. of Chicago Pr. 263-73.

Johnson, Barbara. 1990. Writing. In Frank Lentricchia and Thomas McLaughlin (eds.), Critical terms for literary study. Chicago: Univ. of Chicago Pr. 39-49.

Kristeva, Julia. 1986 [1979, 1981]. Women's time. Translated [1981] by Alice Jardine and Harry Blake. In Hazard Adams and Leroy Searle (eds.), Critical Theory Since 1965. Tallahassee: Florida State Univ. Pr. 471-84.

Leitch, Vincent B. The discourse of history. In Deconstructive criticism: an introduction and survey. New